PUPPY CHOW

CHOW

IS BETTER THAN

PROZAC

PUPPY CHOW

IS BETTER THAN

PROZAC

The True Story of a Man
and the Dog Who Saved His Life

BRUCE GOLDSTEIN

WITH TOM AMICO

DA CAPO PRESS
A Member of the Perseus Books Group

Set in 12.5/14 point Filosofia Regular by the Perseus Books Group
Library of Congress Cataloging-in-Publication Data
Goldstein, Bruce, 1969–
Puppy chow is better than Prozac : the true story of a man and the dog who saved his life / Bruce Goldstein.
   p. cm.
  ISBN-13: 978-1-56858-384-6 (alk. paper) 1. Goldstein, Bruce, 1969–Mental health. 2. Dog owners—New York (State)—New York—Psychology.
  3. Manic-depressive persons—New York (State)—New York.
  4. Labrador retriever—Therapeutic use. I. Title.

SF422.86.G65 2008
636.752'7—dc22
[B]
                                                  2007046740

First Da Capo Press edition 2008

Published by Da Capo Press
A Member of the Perseus Books Group

This memoir is a product of the author's recollections and is thus rendered as a subjective accounting of events that occurred in his/her life. Some names and identifying characteristics have been changed to protect privacy.

Da Capo Press books are available at special discounts for bulk purchases in the United States by corporations, institutions, and other organizations. For more information, please contact the Special Markets Department at the Perseus Books Group, 2300 Chestnut Street, Suite 200, Philadelphia, PA 19103, or call (800) 255-1514, or e-mail special.markets@perseusbooks.com.

2 3 4 5 6 7 8 9

To Mom, Dad, and Sharon,
To Brooke,
And to everyone who has ever loved a dog

In memory of Craig Demeter

CONTENTS

PART TWO: MANIC'S BEST FRIEND

PART THREE: BRUCE, HEAL

ACKNOWLEDGMENTS

I never understood how it took some writers ten years to get a book published. Until mine took a little longer. *Puppy Chow Is Better Than Prozac:* 1997–2008.

There have been so many people that have helped me along my journey that I have a special place in my heart for every one of them.

First and foremost, I thank Tom Amico. He was with me as a dear friend, back when I was losing my mind and he was *really* with me ten years ago when we began writing all hours of the night—downing pot after pot of black coffee. When I brought Tom on as collaborator back in 1997, neither of us had ever written a book before. I had the story, a really rough manuscript, and a great title. Once we got together, we just started writing, and that's when the project came to life. Tom also brainstormed promotional ideas with me, as well as conducted interviews with my family, friends, and doctors in order to help me tell my story accurately. He dedicated three years of his life to the beginning of this project. We never thought it would go for another eight years. And as I kept on rewriting and refining my voice, version after version, he was always there to read and give his input when I needed him. Tom, thank you.

Next, I thank Randal Alquist, the most amazing photographer on earth, for making Ozzy shine like the furry little angel that he is. He shot the front cover and all of the other stunning black-on-black Ozzy shots throughout the book—some of the best dog photography I've ever seen in my life. Thanks man, for giving me all of your time and believing in my project.

I also thank my awesome *New York Times* photographer, Joe Fornabaio, for following us around the city, documenting a day in the life of me walking Ozzy. More like Ozzy walking me. One of my favorite shots is the one where Ozzy is dragging me down the street, smiling right into the camera. He also made me look pretty good for the inside flap shot.

I thank Keith Wallman (formerly of Avalon) for acquiring my book and getting his team behind it. I thank Shaun Dillon and Renée Sedliar, my amazing editors, at Da Capo, for sharpening the edges of my manuscript. I thank Cisca Schreefel, my project editor, for shepherding *Puppy Chow* through the publishing canals and keeping things on track. I thank my incredible publicist, Lissa Warren, and her team for building the biggest buzz around town. I thank the art department for their amazing, eye-catching book jacket, and I thank everybody else at Perseus Books and Da Capo for making my first book a great experience. I'm fortunate that I got to work with such a wonderful group of people.

And then there's Ryan Conti. The ultimate PR guy. I can't thank him enough for getting my book into the right hands. For getting my book finally published. Ryan always believed in my story and never stopped promoting it. Thank you Ryan, from me and Ozzy. We wouldn't have made it here without you.

I can't say enough about Jason Baruch, my top notch attorney/agent at Sendroff & Baruch, for sticking by me all these years. And for not charging me extra for chewing his ears off. Thanks Jason.

My loving family is a given. If they didn't give me the love and support that I needed to get through my mental meltdown, I wouldn't be here today. I wouldn't be the person that I've come to be. So I send the biggest hug out to all those I love: my incredible parents, Marilyn and Stuart Goldstein; my amazing sister, Sharon, for taking such good care of me; and then there are those whom I consider my other parents: my Aunt Zena and Uncle Joe, and my Aunt Toby and Uncle Marty. They have always been there for me as well. And I send a shout out to all of my cousins: Howie and Laurie, Beth and John. And Adam.

I can't express how much my friends mean to me. They were always there when I needed them whether they would talk to me as I cried to them at all hours of the night, or how they would sit there and listen to me read early excerpts from my book to them over and over again. A big thanks to all of them. In no particular order, I thank Gina Fortunato, Evan Silver, Jimmy McAdam, Ron Modica, James Thompson, Steven Rosen, Marcus Nelson, Craig Mannion, Tom Christmann, Lisa Garone, Jennifer Grace, Jason Gaboriau, Lexie Neonakis, and Marianne Arini, and an extra special thanks to George Chambers, aka Ozzy's Uncle, for taking such good care of Ozzy when I've gone away. Because of George, Ozzy has never spent a night in a kennel. And to Julian DeArmas, for helping me build all those black, *Puppy Chow* presentation boxes over the years. Hey man, one of them finally worked.

I also thank my dear friend, Craig Demeter, who recently passed away from cancer. Craig always advised me about my writing. To trust my own voice. To keep it unique. And most important he's the one who advised me when I wasn't sure what title to go with. He said, "Bruce, you have to go with *Puppy Chow Is Better Than Prozac.* It's so perfect." Craig will be missed by many. But I know he'll be looking down on me and Ozzy, smiling, at the book signings. Hey, Craig, if you're listening, I hope you know how much you meant to me.

I also have to thank Frank. No idea what his last name is. He was just some guy who happened to be sitting next to me in the Barnes & Noble café when I first started writing *Puppy Chow*. And for the next ten years, he'd listen to me read early excerpts. He loved my writing. He always encouraged me to keep going. To never sell out. He gave me so much confidence when I needed it most. Thanks, Frank. Wherever you are.

I thank Terry King for taking such good care of my computers, Mike Collica, of mikeynyc.com, for designing my awesome Web site. I thank Claudia Kawczynska for welcoming me into *The Bark* magazine. I thank James Patterson, Andy Behrman, and Lee Harrington for writing my first blurbs. I thank Ozzy's amazing veternarian, Dr. Daniel Giangola, of animal Health Center, for taking such great care of my little guy. And I raise my mug to all of the random coffee shops around the city that have let me camp out with my laptop and my slobbery Labrador over the years.

And where would I be without my amazing, caring, psychologist, Dr. Tamalonis. She helped me in so many ways. She helped get me stable enough to the point where I'd be able to get a dog. I saw her for over eleven years, and if I saw her today, I'd give her one great hug for the hundreds of hugs she gave me when I really needed them.

Ozzy and I will never forget the love and support from Dorothy Cavallo of Stonehaven Labradors. She's been there for us since the beginning. Till this day, I still call if I have a question, and she always says, "No problem, but you just gotta send me pictures. I love pictures." Thank you, Dorothy. We love you.

And then there's Brooke, the love of my life. My wife. I can't thank her enough for always being there for me. For supporting me. For believing in me. For loving me and Ozzy. Our lives wouldn't be the same without her. I feel blessed to have found my soul mate.

I'm sorry if I missed anybody. If I did, you know who you are. It's been eleven years. The memory starts to slip after a while.

So I just want to thank you, God, the Universe, for answering my prayers and sending down my furry little angel. Because back then, I was scared to death. I *really* had no idea how I was ever going to get better.

And Ozzy, what can I say that hasn't already been said?

I love you little guy. You gave me my life back. You taught me to love again.

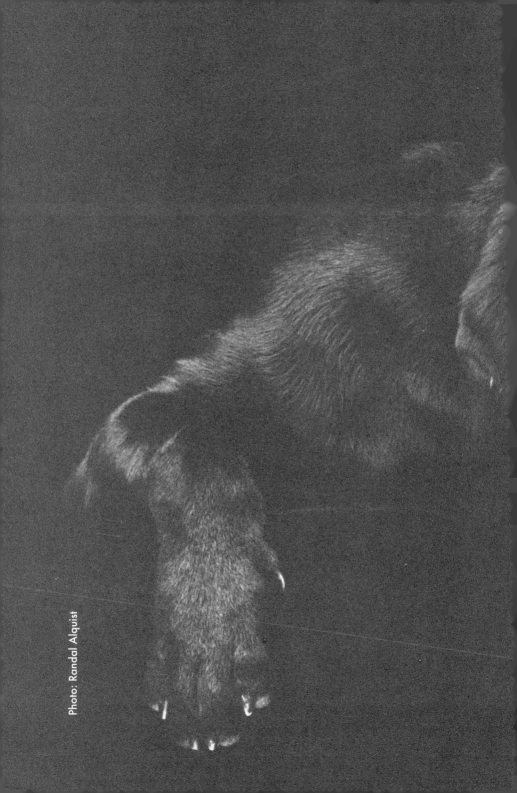

Photo: Randal Alquist

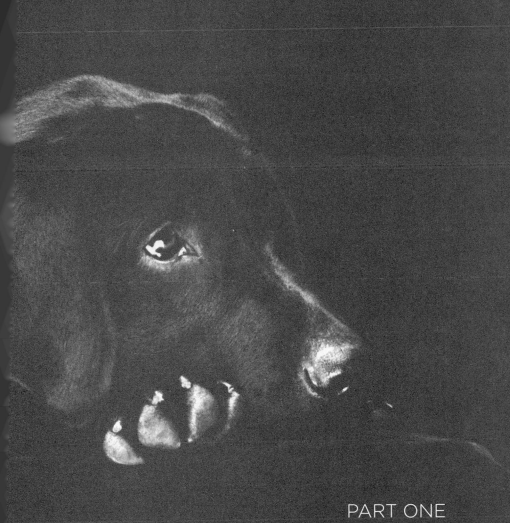

PART ONE

MOODSWING MEMOIRS

Dear God,

Please save me.
Please save me from myself.
I have become my worst enemy.
I have lost control of my world.

I am solitary confinement.
I am despair.
I am the great wallower of self-pity.
I am unpredictable terror,
I am elation.

My imagination.
My creation of hallucination.
A world of isolation.
A world of anxiety.
A world of fear.

I am unbridled creativity.
I am my prisoner of darkness.
I will never let myself leave.
I am death.

Please release me.
Release me from my chemically conceived concentration camp.
Remove my shackles to sanity.
Return me to your world.
Where I once had control.

I beg of you.
Please save my soul.
Before my dark twisted reality buries me alive.
Kill me or make me laugh.
Bring back that funny kid from fifth grade.
I am Manic Depression.

And then God sent down Ozzy.

2

1

HURRICANE BRUCE

It had been six weeks since the knives in my sink tried to kill me. Summer was here. Unfortunately, I was stuck in the dark dead of winter. My serotonin wouldn't bloom, and there was nothing that could retrieve me from the depths of depression. I was sick and tired of asking God to save my life. And I was sick and tired of Satan taking it.

Mirror, mirror on the wall, who's that sad-looking man curled up in a ball?

It was Saturday morning. I was hiding under the comforter, dreading the day ahead. My loft bed, surrounded by wooden posts, looked like a crib—or a fortress, depending. "I don't want

3

to go. I don't want to go," I said, my pleas muffled. Deep in my heart I knew I had to go. Because I had nowhere else to go. This was my last chance to live.

So I took a deep breath and gathered whatever strength I had left. I begged God to please take care of me, as I faced my worst fear and forced myself out of bed. Step by step, I crept down the ladder. Getting up was a lot more difficult without my mother coaching me from the other end of the phone. "C'mon, you can do it," she used to say. "It's time to get up. Up, up, up." Sometimes it would take an eternity. "Up, up!" She called me every morning for months before going to work, until she got hit with The Big M, menopause. Now I was on my own.

"Up, up, up," I told myself the whole eight steps down. "There's nothing to be afraid of. There's nothing to be afraid of."

When I hit bottom, all I wanted to do was climb back up. Instead, I stood there in my maroon underwear without moving for about five minutes, unable to make a decision. "The shower, the shower, not yet." The shower could be a really bad place. The black satin curtain. The tiles. The torture chamber for my negative thinking. But the shower wasn't what I was most afraid of that morning. In order to even get to the shower I had to walk past the kitchen. Charismatic cutlery. The knives weren't through with me yet.

It was always dark in my apartment, which explained my dead plant collection. The only light came from the glass terrace door in the living room, fifteen feet or so from where I was standing. I made it my short-term goal. In slow motion, I walked under my loft, past the computer table into the living room, which was the same room but with higher ceilings. There was a large empty space on the wall above the entertainment center where one of my paintings used to hang. Two demonic faces. One red, one yellow. Screaming swirls of fiery energy at each other. People were frightened of it. It had to come down.

Reaching the glass door, I peeked through the plastic Venetian blinds to see what was going on outside myself. *Oh my God.* It was darker out there than in me. The sky was black and blue. The rain, pissed-off purple. I put my face up against the cold glass like a little kid to get a closer look. Out of nowhere, the god of thunder struck. The city shook. I jumped back as a flood of light lit up the room, exposing everything.

Thinking that had to be the worst of it, I slid open the door and stepped out onto my semi-enclosed, white stucco, completely drenched terrace, my observation deck. The wind howled like a monster. I was soaked in seconds. Terrifying lightning scarred the skyline. I had to hold onto the railing with all my might, as I watched Lexington Avenue give the Hudson River a run for its money.

Not an ideal day for a drive, but I'd made up my mind. I slid the glass door shut and faced my own natural disaster. My head flooded with the people I'd hurt. The emotional blood that was shed. Odds were against me. Even I was against me. All that remained was a scared little boy in a man's body. I couldn't wait any longer for my storm to just pass. After drying myself off with an old yellow towel, I called for a ride. Allen was such a good friend. He was always there when I needed him.

"No way," he said. "Bruce, you know I would do anything for you, but let's wait till it stops raining. It's crazy out there. I'm taping up my windows as we speak. Aren't you watching the news? It's Hurricane Bertha. A nor'easter. There's flooding everywhere. People are being rescued by row boat, for God's sake. They're telling everybody to stay at home. And to certainly not drive. Unless you have a death wish."

"Yeah, but Allen, I have to go, or it'll be too late. We'll go slow."

"Bruce, are you listening to me? It's suicide out there."

It was suicide in here. The night before, after I had given up on the thought of even getting a dog, after I had basically given up on life, Dorothy, this dog breeder, had called out of nowhere. She said she had two puppies left, one of which was *special* according to her nephew, and she said this couple was coming by her house to have a second look at him. "Don't you understand I have to go. Allen, I have to go, because if I don't . . ."

"Ahh, don't start cryin'," Allen pleaded. "It's just that it's too dangerous."

"I don't care. I'm going. We'll talk later. Bye . . ."

"Wait, Bruce. Wait! This is crazy. You told me you've forgotten how to drive."

"I'll just remember. I have no choice."

"All right, give me time to get dressed. I'll be over in a little bit."

Thirty minutes later there was a *Hefty-Hefty* cinch sack at my door. Despite wearing garbage bags over his clothes, Allen was drenched. Water was spilling out onto my linoleum. "Bruce, you have no idea," was all he said.

"What, did you run here?"

"Yeah, I did. I couldn't get my mother's Mazda. So we're going to have to take your car."

Grabbing the keys, Allen went down to get the car while I finished getting dressed. Black pants. Checkerboard flannel. Yankees baseball cap. Prayer.

When I got outside, I was almost turned inside out and blown away like a three-dollar umbrella. Strapping myself into my trusty green Toyota, already named Toto, it felt like we were going white-water rafting, instead of embarking on a two-and-a-half-hour journey in the hopes of saving my soul. "You sure you want to do this?" Allen asked. I nodded, "Yes." And we were off to see some woman named Dorothy, somewhere over the gasoline-stained rainbow.

At fifteen miles per hour, we were sailing one of the only cars on the highway. "Allen, watch out for that chair!" We didn't need windshield wipers, we needed a trash compactor. Garbage cans and multicolored lawn furniture were flying everywhere.

So much water was coming down we couldn't tell which lane we were in. With a wicked sense of humor, the wind tossed us around like an empty Sprite can. We almost hit a van, then a guard rail. Dirty, menacing rain drops banged on the windshield like they wanted to come in. Salty tears blurred my vision. Then everything went foggy. The defroster stopped working. I had to wipe the glass with my sleeves.

Allen asked me to crack the window. Big mistake. "Whoa, whoa. Close it! Close it!"

"Allen, are you okay? Can you see?" I started to panic. "This really is crazy. Maybe we should pull over onto the shoulder and wait for it to stop. I'm serious. Allen, pull over!" What the hell were we doing?

Allen didn't even look over at me. Squinting through the deluge, he never took his eyes off the road for a second. "Don't worry, Bruce. I'm fine," he said, holding the steering wheel in a death grip. *God, I hope you know where you're taking us. Please, please don't let us crash.* But maybe it was Satan who was navigating. Wave after wave of unspeakable despair. I couldn't see what was in front of me. And I couldn't turn back. I had nothing to go back to. I no longer knew how to get back. I needed a miracle. Just a small one. God didn't need to part the Long Island Expressway for us. I just wanted him to put me back together again.

Then as ninety miles per hour winds tossed us from one side of the asphalt to the other, this warm feeling filled my heart. This calming presence. And I just knew no matter how bad it got, we had to get there. I had to meet this dog.

I wouldn't have thought this had anything to do with that weekend in Martha's Vineyard. When I lost my will to live.

When I lashed out at one of my closest friends. When I cried out to God to answer my prayers. To heal me. When I begged the Master of the Universe for mercy. I prayed for a miracle that day in the woods. I just didn't know for the longest time that He had heard me.

2

THE GRINCH WHO STOLE
MEMORIAL DAY WEEKEND

On a soothing backdrop of blue, under an afternoon moon, the sun was opening people up like tulips. Blades of green grass were rising up through sidewalk cracks. Squirrels and purple pigeons were playing together like school children and a Rottweiler was relieving himself on a parking meter. It was the end of May, and everybody was so happy on the corner of Lexington Avenue and East Twenty-seventh Street—the heart of Little India, New York City. Almost everybody.

Up in the sky, in a tan brick building, beyond the cabbies and clouds of curry, I leaned over the ledge of my balcony to look down upon the little Whos in my Who-the-Hell-Caresville, as they merrily loaded up the rental van for our Martha's Vineyard holiday getaway. I had an odd group of friends. We had attended the Fashion Institute of Technology together four years earlier, and most of us were in advertising. There was Charlie, the good looking preppy from Boston, sporting red pants by Ralph Lauren, and Kim Lee, his spunky girlfriend, who was a hair stylist on Broadway. David Weiss, the next Spielberg, was there with his camcorder in one hand, and Isabella's hand in the other. He was short, Jewish, cleft chin—from Long Island. She was tall, dark, Chinese, Venezuelan—from heaven. Then there was Liam McNulty, a six-foot something Irishman who loved football and Guinness and wasn't seen without his Chewbacca key chain. Liam brought along his heavy-set friend, Spencer from Texas, who brought along his friend, marijuana from Thailand. Allen Bloomberg, the up-and-coming actor, showed up with his Sheltie named Barney, who looked like a stumpy Collie named Lassie. And then there was Ricky. Michael J. Fox meets *Baywatch* in his Bahama-mama board shorts and red baseball cap. Ricky liked dancing on bars and screaming. He called me "The Big Watusie."

Instead of running downstairs to join the welcoming committee, I stepped back inside my purgatory apartment and collapsed into the mouth of my black leather couch. I just sat there in the dark, staring at my television, watching nothing but my demented reflection. My eyes were watery; my goatee was shaggy. I just sat there, I just sat there thinking. I just sat there contemplating how frightening it would be for me to leave my familiar surroundings. I was scared to be around people. I was scared to use somebody else's bathroom. And what if I started seeing that evil face in my head again? "No. No. No. I can't. I can't. That's it. I'm not going."

Twenty minutes later, a dark shadow hovered over me like a building. "Brucie, Bruce, you funky goose, are you ready?" I looked up. It was Liam McNulty. He'd showed himself in. Most of my friends had copies of my keys for moments like this.

"C'mon dude, everybody's waiting."

When I didn't answer him, he knew it was happening again. He called it my "funk." Despite my blank stare, Liam kept knocking on my door of desperation.

"C'mon, Bruce, let's go."

It was no use. I wasn't home. I was off in some kind of depression dimension.

"C'mon dude, we're gonna have a great weekend. Now snap out of it."

That was like telling a blind man to see. "Just see. It's so easy." Since this had been going on for months, my friends had learned how to deal with me. When I couldn't make up my mind, they made it up for me. Liam grabbed me and my overstuffed black duffel bag.

"C'mon Bruce, you're going."

From the moment I heard the metal door on the red van slam shut behind me, I felt like a prisoner. My stomach dropped. My face turned white. Despite the fact that I was with all of my friends, I never felt more alone in my life. When Spencer popped in his homemade tape of dope smokin' tunes and everybody started singing along, I wanted to jump out the window and go home. But it was too late. I was in for a long weekend. Everybody was. With my lithium secretly packed, our five-hour journey began. A thousand bottled-up feelings on the wall, a thousand bottled-up feelings . . .

3

MIGHTY MOUTH

Traffic was miserable on the West Side Highway. To pass the time, my friends played this celebrity name game that required a good memory, a sense of humor, and quick reflex thinking. I checked none of the above. I sat all the way in the back next to the dog to avoid them. Charlie went first. "Julia Roberts," he said. Then Kim Lee had to name a famous person beginning with "R," the first initial of the previous celebrity's last name. "Ray Charles."

Next up was David who jumped up and shouted, "Chubby Checker!" Since that name had the same two initials, the game reverted back to the previous player.

Kim Lee went again. "Cindy Brady," she said.

Back to David. "Barbara Walters," he came up with.

Isabella shouted, "Wayne Newton!"

And leave it to Liam to come up with "Nellie Olson."

Like a child in school dreading the teacher to call on him, I prayed it would never be my turn. When Spencer said, "Oliver Twist," I said, "Oh shit." They were coming around to Ricky. I was next. When he said, "Tommy Lee Jones," I said nothing. I froze. I had no response. I wished I didn't exist. I wanted to evaporate. I couldn't concentrate. I couldn't think of anything, except how I couldn't concentrate, and even if I could think of something to say, I was afraid to speak. I was afraid to say the wrong thing. I didn't trust my brain. Luckily, while everybody was getting impatient waiting for me, Allen yelled out, "Judy Blume!" What a relief. The pressure was off. I could relax a little. But just as I was catching my breath, before I could finish drying off my forehead, it was Ricky's turn again. "Chuck Mangione," he said, and I desperately needed a celebrity starting with "M." I was dead. "Bruce! Bruce! Bruce!" everybody was yelling. My ears were echo echo *echoing*. "C'mon Bruce, just name somebody!"

I felt beads of sweat drizzling down the sides of my face. "Uhhh, uhhhhh . . ." Nothing. I felt like somebody had siphoned my vocabulary. It was impossible to focus on the letter "M" when my think tank was on "E." Then out of nowhere, I felt this burst of energy shoot through me like somebody injected my veins with Jolt cola and an eight-ball of cocaine. I started breathing really heavy, and my head started shaking. There was somebody else living inside of me, and he had awakened. Every cell in my body was tingling. I couldn't sit still. I was vibrating. My mind was racing faster than my speeding heartbeat. I felt invincible. Powerful. Confident. I felt like I could do anything. And then, when nobody was expecting a response out of me, I jumped up from my sweaty seat like my spine was a spring, and I screamed out the syllables that would set me free.

"Mighty Mouse!" Here I come to save my day! "Go again, Ricky!"

"Mickey Mouse!" he screamed.

Back to me: "Mike Myers! Yeah, baby!" I was back. I was me again.

Ricky squealed, "Marilyn Monroe!"

I blurted out, "Marla Maples! Right back at you!"

Everybody was cheering, "Bruce! Bruce! Bruce!" I felt like I was on stage. Back from the grave. From the little brain that couldn't, I could do anything I damn well pleased. Allen was clapping. Isabella was elongating my name. "Go Bar-uuuuuuu-uuce!" she screamed. I was talking with my arms, rubbing my fingers through my goatee. I was howling like Al Pacino. "*Who-wahhh!*" Nonstop animation. Nothing bothered me. I had no fear. For the first time I was looking forward to Martha's Vineyard. I wanted to go deep sea fishing. Scuba diving. I wanted to fly a little plane like Snoopy vs. the Red Baron. Unfortunately, I only felt that way for twenty minutes.

Ten, nine, eight, seven, six, five, four, fear, anxiety. Soon I felt the negative chemicals fill my brain. It was like I had disappeared, and this other guy was sitting in my place. He had no personality, and he was nervous and sweating. I hated him. He was scared of everything, and he was ugly. He was worthless. He had no purpose. Just look at him. His long face pressed up against the rear window, watching the orange sun go down, wallowing in self-pity. "Oh it's you again," I said. He didn't answer me. His glassy eyes said everything.

Sniff. Sniff. Sniff. What's that smell? Barney threw up all over the place. "Uhh, Allen, your dog stinks." This joy ride was over. First stop, somewhere in Massachusetts. We spent the night in a Best Western.

4

DIARRHEA OF A SAD MAN

In the misty morning under moody skies, the nine of us plus
Barney headed for the ferry to Martha's Vineyard. New Bedford
was like a ghost town out of a *Scooby-Doo* episode. A mile off to
the west stood a motionless old Ferris wheel, a remnant of a
one-time fun park. Unamused, I waited anxiously at Billy
Wood's Wharf for our boat to float in. My four-day forecast
called for hazy days, highs, lows, and tremendous pressure
fronts. A 90 percent chance of depression for Friday, Saturday,
and Sunday, with a 10 percent chance of elation. Monday,
melancholy. And for the remainder of my life—mostly shitty.
My mood was so thick when we boarded the ferry *Schamonchi*

that I kept my distance from my friends. They had heard enough about my demons.

"Hey Allen, does your chest ever pound so hard you think you're having a heart attack?"

"Hey Charlie, did you ever see evil faces in your head? It's normal to see faces, right?"

"Hey David, do you ever get depressed? . . . No, I mean *really* depressed?"

"Bruce, that's enough. I just want to have fun this weekend," David said just before we had left. "Oh, okay." That put me in my place. Now I felt more isolated than ever. I was contagious. Instead of walking the plank, I hung my head over the rusty railing. Atlantic winds camouflaged my saltwater tears. I was lost at sea. I was lost in life. I was lost without Paige.

Long, vacant weeks had passed since we had spoken. I had needed to call her. My friends warned me about opening up the wound that had just started to heal. They said it would just make things worse, that I had to get over her. I didn't care. I didn't think it was possible to feel worse. Wrong. A couple of days earlier, I had been fantasizing about us getting together for old times' sake. I thought maybe there was a chance we'd go to Jones Beach like we used to. I broke down and made the call. Contrary to my imagination, Paige said she was on her way to dinner with some guy and that basically, I wasn't on any future menu of hers either. "I have plans to go away Memorial Day weekend, Bruce, and so should you." *And so should you.* She had plans for every weekend of the summer, she said. Her and her house in the Hamptons. Then she said, "Bruce, I'm sorry, but you have to get on with your life. I'm getting on with mine. I have to go now. Good-bye." The tears of pain I thought were gone forever opened the floodgates of my emotional dam. My one-time love, my "Snugglebutt," had butchered me as she severed our relationship. My cut was bleeding again.

Eight months. That's all we were. But Paige, *Paige* was my first love. I was twenty-five years old, and Paige Whitestone was my first real girlfriend. Before Paige, I never had a special someone. So everything we did together, I treasured. From going shoe shopping to doing the dishes. The hand-holding, the pet names, the little kisses were a whole new world to me. A simple thing like Paige calling me on the phone everyday just to say "Hi" made me so happy. I had spent so much time with Paige that my friends hardly saw me anymore. I even started dressing in her style. I traded in my big black boots for a pair of toe-baring Birkenstocks. There was no sign of Bruce anywhere. And when she left me stranded at a bitter coffee shop back in January, I didn't know how to be alone again. I had lost my independence. How the hell do you get over somebody you had spent every minute of the day thinking about? I mean, how do you just say, "Good-bye, have a nice life," to your best friend? I stopped dwelling on the past, the moment I spotted the island.

As the current pulled us in, my friends started pallin' around and laughing away. David had Isabella. Charlie had Kim Lee. Liam had Spencer. Allen had Barney. Ricky had his walkman and suntan lotion. And I had no one but the haunting voices in my head and my gurgling intestines. Who was I going to play with?

The first thing we did when we abandoned ship was rent another friggin' minivan to take us across the island to the house where we were staying. We made a quick stop at the local supermarket to get the bare essentials: Heineken, hamburgers, and Charmin. I couldn't believe my friends thought two rolls would be enough. When they weren't looking, I squeezed another four-pack into my backpack. I wasn't taking any chances.

Ever since I was nineteen, my stomach has been in turmoil. Staten Island's premium gastroenterologist, Dr. Kaplan, blamed my excessive diarrhea on a combination of stress, greasy french fries, and the milk in my Rice Krispies. "Stay away from dairy and roughage" were the doctor's orders. After months of sharp shooting pains in my gut, keeling over in public and pooping *a lot of blood*, it was time to pump pints of white barium into my rectum to get to the bottom of my bowels. A barium enema, an upper and lower GI series, and a sigmoidoscopy (use your imagination) revealed I had Crohn's disease, alias ileitis. I was one of the one in ten thousand who suffered from this disease with no known cause or cure. For two years, I tried everything to get better. Diet after diet. Anti-inflammatories: Asacol, Azulphidine, Pentasa. I took folic acid. I took a steroid called Prednisone—the best the medical industry had to offer—and I still had to be rushed—really rushed—to the operating table. I had an intestinal blockage which had punctured a hole in my ileum. Poisonous gases had been spreading throughout my body. I needed emergency surgery. *Yesterday.*

As I was going under the knife, I got really frightened. I wasn't scared of dying. I was scared of living. I was worried that the rest of my life I'd be constrained to wearing a colostomy bag—a porto-potty attached to a newly reamed rectum just above my hip. I'd be handicapped. I'd never fall in love. I'd never have a family. I'd have no friends. But as a result of my resection, thank God I only lost thirty-five pounds and two feet of my small intestines. My surgeon told me that I only had had a 30 percent chance of living, and out of that 30 percent, I had a 65 percent chance of complications. That put things into perspective. I was grateful not to be dead. The only problem was that Crohn's disease is a stubborn disease. Once you've had it, it could always come back, anytime, anyplace in your gastrointestinal tract. Inflammation from your esophagus to your anus. And it did.

My diarrhea was now worse than ever. With less intestinal footage, my finagled food processor passed things through a lot faster. It drained me of all my energy. It made my joints ache. It made my moods swing. I became irritable, angry, and nervous, and being nervous made my stomach more upset, which made me more upset, which made my stomach a complete mess. It was a vicious cycle—mental and physical. I tried everything to plug up my irritable bowels. I guzzled bottles of Pepto Bismol. I took every new pill on the market. I tried God knows how many gastroenterologists, and then I gave up on modern medicine and tried acupuncture. When needles weren't for me, I went to see Dr. Wah, a witch doctor herbalist in Chinatown. Aside from brewing ancient teas from the Orient, I tried eating the "right" foods. But there were no right foods. No dairy. No roughage. No bread. No coffee. Nothing worked until I tried Imodium A-D, a temporary Band-Aid for my inflammation, but not a cure. There was no cure. It was something I had to learn to live with. I had good days and Crohn's days. And on those days when I'd feel sorry for myself, I'd go outside and "coincidentally" run across somebody worse off than me. It's amazing how many people without legs you see when you're having a bad day.

Every day revolved around my stomach. I was constantly conscious of my colon. "If I eat this, will I make it home in time?" Wherever I went, I always scoped out the nearest bathroom. Some people brushed after every meal. I flushed. I avoided social events. I didn't want to stink any place up. I lived in fear and embarrassment. Being around women was the worst. I was able to hide it from Paige until the first night we slept together, when she insisted I take my shirt off. "Oh my God, Bruce, what happened to you?" she said.

"Oh this." I had a seven-inch scar going down my stomach, a surgery souvenir. One time a girl on the beach asked me if I had been shot there. My friends called me Scarbelly.

Paige was great about it, though. "It's okay, Brucie. Going to the bathroom is a biological function," she said. She even offered to go with me for a colonoscopy. Paige made it so much easier for me to deal with my Crohn's, and now that she had left me, me and my stomach were out of control. Flammable hemorrhoids. I lost ten pounds. God, I wished she was with me in Martha's Vineyard. It was just me and my butt-pluggin' Imodium. Luckily, before we left Manhattan, I popped enough chalky green caplets to back up the Holland Tunnel.

When everybody piled back into the van, they started jumping around like a bunch of crazy fifth graders on a class trip. "Watusie, are you psyched or what?" Ricky said as he smacked me on the back. "Oh yeah," I said. But he had no idea what I was really thinking. I was sinking. I was sinking fast. I knew I had to pull myself out of this mental quicksand or I was in trouble, so I tried tuning into the radio. Bad idea. They were blasting Dio, *"We're off to see the witch and we may never, never, never come home."*

The trees out the window looked dark and dreary. I wanted to go home so badly. And then they started in with the recreational activities. When Liam and Spencer started yakking about kayaking, I started panicking that I couldn't swim. Ironically, this was the ocean where they filmed *Jaws*, and the mechanical man-eating shark they used just happened to be named Bruce. Their excitement was doing me in. I felt like I was nine years old again, trapped on that yellow bus in my red swim trunks, off to the YMCA for swimming lessons. I was thinking about the time I got thrown into the pool. I had nothing to hold on to. I couldn't breathe. What the hell was I gonna do on this trip if I was scared to go in the water? I wasn't going horseback riding either. When Charlie said, "Who wants to go horseback riding?" my overactive imagination started overreacting again. I envisioned that I'd tear a ligament or mess up my vertebrae. The last time I rode a horse was my first and last time. His name was Random.

The more my friends' neurotransmitters got boosted, the more mine got short-circuited with fear. "Let's rent bikes! Let's go bungee jumping!" they chanted. We were getting closer and closer, I could feel it. So could Barney. He was going crazy, jumping all over the seats. I tried to focus on the good things. "Think positive," my mother would always say. "I'm gonna have a good weekend. I'm gonna have a good weekend."

"Look, there it is, 1624 Elm Street," Kim screamed when she spotted the green, two-story country house sticking out of the woods. My hands were clenching the seat as we pulled into the long, winding driveway. My face felt redder than a beefsteak tomato. All I kept thinking about was running away, heading back to New York City. My heart was beating heavy. When the van came to a complete stop, so did I. My face drooped like a weeping willow. As they started unloading the luggage, I was about to unload my feelings all over the place. When everybody started walking toward the splintery staircase, one duckling after another, I pulled David aside and told him that "it" was happening again.

"Just relax," he said

"No, David you don't understand. This is really bad."

"What's wrong? What's wrong with Bruce?" Isabella sounded concerned.

I looked severe, and it showed in their faces. That made me more worried. While we were standing by the van, before every-body noticed what was happening, Ricky walked over and said, "I'll take him." But before Ricky could grab me, I darted down the driveway. Over damp, matted leaves, through a swirl of gnats, across the muddy road, deep into the willowy woods, I felt Ricky's presence behind me like a bloodhound hot on my teary-eyed trail. I kept running and running. The only thing on my mind was where I was going and I wouldn't know where that was until I got there. I was in so much mental pain that I barely felt the branches whipping me in the face. When I realized I couldn't escape myself, I stopped dead in my tracks.

Where was I?

I was standing in a circular clearing surrounded by pine trees and large rocks. It smelled green. Off to the side was a little

stream. I was getting bit by giant mosquitoes, and there must
have been thousands of gnats hovering around me. This was the
end. I didn't know what was to come of me. Twenty-six years old.
I had accomplished nothing. Why did God send me here in the
first place if I was over at such an early age? I tilted my head back.
I looked up to the sky, and at the top of my vocal chords, I
screamed to the Master of the Universe, "Why are you torturing
me? What happened to Bruce Goldstein, and when are you giving
me back to me? I can't live like this anymore!" My cries for help
echoed throughout the ecosystem. Black birds flew out of trees.

I screamed until I got it all out of me. I needed my whole arm
to wipe away the liquid terror streaming out of my eyes. I got so
lost in my voice that when my lashes separated, I was surprised
that I was standing in the same place. Everything was blurry. My
vision on life was impaired. I was all out of breath. My chin dug
deep into my chest. My shoulders heaved up and down till I had
nothing left. I collapsed. Lying on the ground, I looked up from
falling down. "God, help me. I don't want to die. I need a miracle. Please help me. Give me a sign."

And there it was—a mere five-foot-four, 110 pounds towering
over my shriveled-up body like a Boy Scout without his manual.
He was just standing there, with his crazy blond hair tucked under his backward red baseball cap. It was Ricky. Funky shorts,
yellow tee. How the hell was he going to remove the thorn stuck
in my psyche? He had his hands in his pockets. He looked more
hopeless than me. He just stood there searching his miniature
book of life experiences till he found the right thing to say.

He took a deep breath, knelt beside me, put his arms around
me, and said, "Bruce, you know this is just temporary. You're
just going through a rough time, man. Every day gets better and
better. You'll see. You'll be okay before you know it."

"Yeah, right. That's what you always say, Rick. Not this time.
I'm so fucked-up. I'm so fucked-up. How the fuck can I be so

fucked-up in a beautiful place like this? I mean look at me, groveling for God's sake. I'm a grown man crying like a baby."

"Bruce, I know it sucks what you're going through, but remember when Nicole left me."

"Yeah."

"Well I never told anybody this, but one day I couldn't take it anymore. I hurt so much that I just had enough. I decided to walk in front of a bus and just end it. But then I said, 'What the hell am I doing?' I didn't want to die. Not like this. I could see the evening news: 'Ricky Adams splattered on Second Avenue.' It was ridiculous. So I pulled myself together. And I got better. And so will you. You just can't see that now. It takes time. You know what they say, time heals all wounds. Well, they're right."

"Yeah, Ricky, yeah. But this is different. It's more than Paige. It's more than that possessed advertising agency. It's . . . Ricky, I wasn't gonna tell you this, but the doctors were right. I am crazy. I mean I'm manic depressive, bipolar, I have a chemical imbalance like my Uncle Max. And, and, and I'm on lithium. I'm on fucking lithium."

"I know."

"What do you mean, you know?"

"Well I didn't know about the lithium part. But I knew something was going on with you. I mean, c'mon, I'm your friend. I've been around you the last few months. You weren't exactly . . . normal."

"Yeah, I know."

"When did you start taking the lithium?"

"A few weeks ago. After the Central Park thing, you know, with you know who, and the knives and what-not, so I finally said fuck this and went to see a psychiatrist."

"Good for you, Bruce. I'm proud of you."

"What for? I took their stupid drugs. I'm supposed to be better by now. Lithium is supposed to be some miracle salt. Well, look at me. Some miracle. I'm more fucked up than before. At least I used to have highs. Real highs that lasted more than five minutes. Screw this. I had enough of this shit. I'm throwing it out when we go back to the house."

"No, Bruce."

"No? Whadayah mean no?"

"I mean you can't. It'll work. Trust me, you just started taking it. You have to give it more than a few weeks. It takes time."

"How do you know? I mean, how do you fucking know?"

Ricky got real close to me. He looked me in my eyes. He got this real serious look on his face, and he almost started crying. He said, "Bruce, I know."

Ricky told me I reminded him of somebody he was real close to. He told me about the time he came home early from school and found his mother hysterical in her closet. "Bruce, she was really freaking out man, it scared the hell out of me," he said. "She was having some kind of psychotic break from reality. And all because of a mouse." She had been cleaning out the garage when suddenly this little critter ran out from underneath the car. The next thing she knew, she was eleven years old again in a cramped apartment screaming, "Get away from me!" to some- body nobody else could see. Ricky had to rush her to the mental hospital, where the doctors prescribed her some medication, and she was eventually back to herself. "Bruce, I'm not gonna lie to you, it took like five months for her to get better," he said. "But she's okay now and that's all that matters."

When Ricky finished his story, he rubbed his eyes, and he told me not to worry about anything this weekend. "Bruce, you're gonna be all right. Trust me. It just takes time. It takes time. Just stay on the lithium. Listen to your doctors. And you'll be fine."

"Yeah, but what if, what if I get scared?" I said. "What if *It* comes back again? What if *He* comes back?"

"Bruce, come here."

"What?" He had his arms wide open.

"Just come here."

He gave me a hug and his word that he'd look after me. "Bruce, I'll be there," he said. "Nobody's gonna hurt you. Don't worry. Now, I know it's hard, but just relax and try and have a good time."

"Yeah, but what about ..."

"Bruce, stop it," he said. He hesitated. "I love you ... and I'm not gonna let anything happen to you."

My eyes started running again. I gulped. "You promise?" I said.

"I swear."

"Hey Ricky, one more thing, you're not gonna tell anybody about the lithium, right?"

"What lithium?" He smiled.

"Thanks, man, I'm lucky to have you as a friend."

"Hey, Bruce, you've always been there for me."

I took out my Swiss army knife and started carving my name in a tree. *B...R....U...C...*, when I was on the *"E,"* we heard something rustling in the leaves. Ricky freaked. He was scared of snakes. "Bruce, let's get the hell outta here," he said.

We walked back from the woods, but I knew I wasn't out of them yet.

5

MOPING MANIC ON A MOPED

The Martha's Vineyard terrain was rocky, hilly, and treacherous, the turns sharp and intimidating. Renting mopeds was not my idea of a good time. The problems started with my helmet. There was something wrong with it. "Is my helmet right? Is my helmet right?" As much as they said it was fine, I still kept asking my friends if it was fine. "Bruce, it's perfect. Stop fucking with it." And then the kickstand was giving me problems, so I asked Liam.

"What's wrong with you, Bruce? What's to know? What are you—stupid?" he said. *What are you—stupid? Stupid?* echoed in my head.

Liam's wicked words threw me back to the sixth grade when I used to get picked on every day. I hadn't thought about that in years. I hadn't thought about a lot of things in years. It was only recently that the things I had blocked out were coming back to haunt me. It was like somebody pressed the negativity switch in my brain and unleashed all of my demons.

Everybody revved their engines. I was still adjusting my mirror. I was clumsy with my clutch. They left me in the dust. It only took five minutes to find out why they made us wear helmets. Up ahead, around the bend, the accident I had warned everybody about like a neurotic school mom monitor happened. Charlie wiped out around a sandy dune and banged up his arm and leg, a bleeding, cut-up mess. Quick-thinking Kim Lee turned her moped into an ambulette and drove him to the hospital, where he spent the rest of his day getting stitches. The rest of us followed the Mad Maxes of Martha's Vineyard—kickstand wizard Liam and his sidekick Spencer—across the island. We were headed to some stupid lighthouse on the Edgartown Cliffs.

Ricky zoomed passed me. Then David and Isabella, who were neck and neck. Then even Allen was in front of me. There were times I couldn't see anybody. I thought about them losing me, or crashing into a tree. I passed a possum splattered all over the street. I wondered what his family was going to think when he didn't come home that night.

The roads were winding. The sun was shining. My tears made my vision blurry. And the wind was blowing sand and bugs in my mouth. Where the hell was Ricky? He said he would be there if I needed him. But what the hell was he going to do for me anyway? What the hell was anybody going to do for me? They all meant well. My friends and family. But at the end of the day, I was still all alone. We're all alone. And when you're all alone there's nobody to stop the wicked thoughts of suicide from romantically tempting your soul.

Eventually I caught up with the hardly Harley Davidson bunch. They had stopped for lunch. Their bikes were parked on the side of the road. "Hey, Bruce, over here!" Isabella yelled. They were down by the water, sitting on the sand eating sandwiches they had gotten from somewhere. Isabella gave me a hearty hello. "Ham or turkey?" she asked.

"It doesn't matter."

Then Liam, Lord of the Kickstand, butted in. "Hey Bruce, what took you so long?" I gnawed on my Boar's Head and turned my cheek toward the ocean, ignoring him. He had no idea that I vowed to never talk to him again. When Charlie started up a game of touch football with a plastic Pepsi bottle, I said, "Screw this shit," and I took a long walk on the beach till there were no more people, just slimy green seaweed and washed-up, old army helmet–looking horseshoe crabs. It smelled dead. SWIM AT YOUR OWN RISK a sign said. Live at your own risk. What's the difference? I climbed up an abandoned lifeguard chair. And I just sat there. Brooding in my dark manner. Staring out into the ocean. The blue. The clouds. The gulls. What the hell is the point of it all? I heard barking.

There, off in the distance I saw this guy and his blond girlfriend getting all touchy, feely, playing Frisbee with their fluffy yellow dog in the sand. I put my head in my hands. I started crying again. I missed her so much. *So much.* "Paige, where are you?" Where was she now when I needed her most? I pictured Paige swimming in her plaid red bikini with some Ivy League asshole in Southampton. "Oh Cliffy, care for another game of water polo?" How could she do this to me? We were so good together despite our different upbringings.

Paige came from money. I came from mommy clipping coupons. I was a JAP—Jewish American Procrastinator—from the smallest outer borough in New York City. I was bred a few miles and a world away from Manhattan, over the Verrazano, near the largest landfill in the world. The same place big-haired Melanie Griffith in *Working Girl* schlepped from—*Stat'n Ilan.* Where everybody was Jewish or Italian. They either kept kosher or they kept quiet. Paige was a WASP—White Anal Sophisticated Preppie—first class from Savannah. Her mother was a lawyer. Her father was a dentist. My Dad sold Hush Puppies to lawyers and dentists who drove Jaguars. My Dad always said, "Don't end up working for crazy *meshuggeners.* You'll be rich one day, Bruce. And you won't have to work like a dog." I had always thought money would make me happy. Man, was I wrong.

The tide was coming in. The sun was going down. My friends were calling my name to start heading back. "Yeah, yeah, I'm coming." I wiped my eyes. I threw a rock.

Everybody had a long day so they retired early. Charlie and Kim Lee claimed their own bedroom on the main floor. So did the other lovebirds, David and Isabella. Liam and Spencer were downstairs smoking doobies, while slick Ricky was next door to them, putting on cucumber facial cream. He was sharing a room with Allen and Barney. "Allen, get that slobbering beast away from me!" he screamed. What was he complaining about? I didn't get a room. They put me down the hallway, practically in the hallway, next to the washer and dryer. My bed was a pull-out, crusty old couch with springs popping out. My night table was a water heater. It was so dusty. And there were spiderwebs everywhere. It was hard to breathe. I went upstairs to get fresh air before I attempted to sleep. I sat on the back porch in my jean shorts overlooking the lake at the foot of a hill, under the stars. A fool's full moon. I spoke to the only one who understood me, who wasn't sick of listening to me. My journal was all ears.

May 24, 1996. "Felt really, really, low today on mopeds. When it happens, it's terrible. I can't talk. My brain feels flooded. They know it happens when I get quiet. Before was so bad, it was overwhelming. I get so far away sometimes. God, I wish it would go away. Make it go away already. I can't live like this anymore. The lithium doesn't do anything but make me more depressed."

Before I went back downstairs, I took my lithium. Not because I wanted to, because it was all I could do. With my white pills in one hand, a glass of water in the other, I said my mental mantra. *"Every day in every way I'm getting better and better. Every day in every way I'm getting better and better."* I said it, but I didn't believe it.

6

ANTI-ANTIDEPRESSANTS

I never wanted to go on lithium, let alone see a therapist. "That's for weak, insecure people," I said. Therapy was Paige's world. Not mine. I had always gotten by on my own. I was just fine—I was just going through a rough time. Besides, my symptoms made perfect sense. Everybody who's unemployed gets depressed. Everybody who gets dumped feels like shit. Paige had a different opinion. Before she left me she said, "Bruce, I really think you should see someone. You have a serious condition. One minute you're running around my apartment naked, jumping up and down on the bed, laughing your head off like a crazed lunatic, the next minute you're curled up in a ball on my couch, crying hysterically. You don't see yourself like I do. You go from high to low ten times a day. You have like a multiple personality disorder or something. And quite frankly, I don't know how much longer I can listen to you talk about that evil face in your head. Bruce, you *really* sound crazy and you need to get help. From a professional. Someone who can really help you. Because I can't do it anymore. I just can't." Before Paige dumped me, I had more therapists' numbers crumpled up in my underwear drawer than I had underwear. Every time I flipped out, she slipped me another one. I never threw them out just in case one day I really needed one. Yeah right? I didn't need a therapist. I had my friends to talk to. At least I thought I did until they decided it was in everybody's best interest to drop the basket case off on somebody else's doorstep. When David wanted me to stop using his telephone number as a suicide hot-line, he gave me a real one he saw advertised on television. When Ricky could no longer dedicate his afternoons to looking for me, worrying if he was going to find me dead, bullet in the head, sprawled out on the floor of my apartment, he scribbled down his therapist's number—the one he saw after his girl-friend broke up with him. "Bruce, I really think you should see someone," he said. "There's nothing to be ashamed of. I mean, what have you got to lose?"

My stubborn ego. My control. Nobody's brainwashing me. Nobody's reprogramming me to be a psychological zombie. I don't need any outside help. "Fuck the shrinks" was my motto. They're gonna tell me about *me?* What the hell do *they* know? I've always solved my own problems. I've been in bad moods before. Going to see a doctor would mean that I had lost, that I couldn't fix myself by myself. But worse, going to see a shrink meant that maybe there was something really wrong with me, and that scared the hell out of me. I was afraid of never being the Bruce I once was. I was afraid of the doctors changing me, of them altering my personality permanently. So no matter how

Photo: Julian DeArmas

depressed I got, I fought it. I started hanging around the self-help section in Barnes & Noble. I turned to a little blue book called *You Can't Afford the Luxury of a Negative Thought.*

When that didn't help I packed twelve credit cards for my nine-day manic extravaganza. I brought my big-hearted, long-haired friend, Julian, along for the high. We took four helicopter rides over four active volcanoes on four Hawaiian Islands. It was breathtaking. We hovered through double rainbows. Amazing! We kissed waterfalls. God spoke to me. He said not to worry. "Bruce, you will be okay." And then there were the strippers we hooked up with on the beach. Tatiana had the biggest breasts in Waikiki. She was the first girl I kissed since Paige. She was the first girl I ever kissed that could pole dance to "Kung Fu Fighting." That night I regained my self-esteem.

It was a week of spontaneous luxury. Luaus in Kawaii. Mahi Mahi in Maui. Mai Tai after Mai Tai *after Mai Tai.* Whale watching and tons of sushi. But even after my eighteen-grand spending spree, I still ended up curled up in a ball, crying hysterically, contemplating the meaning of my life from my twenty-eighth-story balcony. Thank God Julian was there with me. *Thank God.* I had traveled over 4,698 miles to the most beautiful place on earth to get away from it all, but I couldn't get away from myself. When I got back to New York, I was still going up and down. It was like I had never left. I was cursed like Bobby Brady. It wasn't Aloha. It was A-lo-hi.

Despite all of the phone numbers, despite the pleas from my friends to seek help, I wasn't calling anyone. My answer was still "No." I was still determined to beat this thing alone. Until I was all alone. I had to quit my job. Paige was gone. And my friends and family could only spend so much time on the phone listening to me moan and groan. I was living in solitary confinement. At first I missed people, but after a while I was afraid of them. I hadn't felt this way since I was a little kid and I wouldn't go to Howard Finkelstein's birthday party unless my mother went with me. I spent my days hiding out in my dark apartment with my dust mite–infested palm tree. Then one day I was slouching on my couch watching daytime television, and an advertisement for depression came on: "Do you feel empty? Do you cry excessively? Have you stopped being interested in things?" I burst out in tears. I grabbed my wallet and took out my health insurance card. When I hung up, I had a ten-thirty the following morning with a Mrs. Sally Morgan.

The anticipation was killing me. After tons of paperwork, I went in.

I sat directly across from a little woman with a soup-bowl haircut. I was all jittery. I couldn't stop fidgeting with a goddamn paper clip, *paper clip, paper clip.* I would've bitten my nails, but I didn't have any left. I was way into the skin. Deep beneath the surface. When Mrs. Morgan picked up her clipboard and crossed her legs, I felt like a formaldehyde specimen. I felt vulnerable, like I was on display—some crazy kid exhibit.

"Whenever you're ready, Mr. Goldstein."

"You know I was just thinking, there's nothing wrong with me. I don't know what I'm doing here. This is all a big mistake," I said, cracking my knuckles.

"Well why don't you just let me be the judge. Tell me what's been going on lately."

"Lately." I hesitated.

"Lately." I started breathing heavy.

"Lately." My leg started shaking.

I rocked back and forth in my chair. "There's something wrong here, lady," I was thinking. It didn't make sense to tell this total stranger what was wrong with me, unless she knew me when I was right, when I was me—whenever the hell that was. So I traveled back in time, trying to locate the last period of my life when I remembered being truly happy. January 1996, 1995 . . . , when I got to 1994, the buzzer went off inside. I popped out of my chair like a cherry Pop-tart. *Action.*

"All right, you wanna know what happened? You wanna know what happened? After I graduated, I was working at one of the hottest ad agencies in the city, and it was *amazing.* They were paying me all of this money to basically hang out with my friends, watch *Beavis and Butt-Head*, and eat eel and octopus with extra wasabi every night till midnight and then and then *and then* I sent a little ad that I wrote with the words 'rear-end' in the headline to *Adweek* to get some press, but *Adweek* said I made the luxury car look cheesy, and the next thing I know, my boss Charlie's flying in on the redeye to ream me a new A-hole. They had a big meeting, they said some shit about me almost losing the agency a billion dollar

account, *blah, blah, blah,* and then Charlie said, 'Sorry Brucie, you have a great career ahead of you, but it's not gonna be
here.' Can you believe that? After all I did for that agency.
Well, whatever, I got over it when I met Paige, and she took
my mind off of advertising—I had the best summer of my
life—I was in love for the first time and Paige taught me how
to eat artichokes and I taught her how to spend a lot of money
on shrimp and lobster cocktails and we went to Vermont in
the fall to see the leaves change and it was so beautiful, they
were green and red and yellow and then we went to—"

"Mr. Goldstein, Mr. Goldstein, can you get to the point before your time runs out?"

"What? Before my time runs out. . . . What *exactly* do you
mean, before my time runs out?"

"You only get fifty minutes."

"Listen, I didn't even want to come today. The only reason
I'm here is because my time is already up." I couldn't believe
the nerve of this woman. This was what getting help was about?
She looked at me like my name was 555-66-6038. She probably
didn't care if I slit my wrists.

"Continue, Mr. Goldstein."

"Uhhhh, so where was I? I'm blank. See, I forget where was I
was. What was I saying? Brain fart. This always happens to me. . . .
Uh, uhh, oh yeah, yeah, yeah, yeah, okay I got it, so I went back to
advertising in the fall. I got hired as a freelancer making eight
hundred dollars a day at another hotshot agency. *Big* mistake. I
should've gotten outta that death trap right away—that creative
concentration camp—everything was going great until they gave
my office to a Swedish girl with blue eyes and four teeth and they
put me in this closet of an office behind the mailroom and I was
totally isolated. They gave me the crappiest assignments in the
agency. They told me specifically, 'Don't be creative Bruce. Just
get it done, Bruce,' so that's what I did. And after a while since I

wasn't using my brain, I lost all of my confidence. I had no more self-esteem, I mean, I used to be so positive and now I couldn't look anybody in the eye. I couldn't even talk right—it wasn't like me. I had no idea what was happening to me. But I figured it was because it was a new job and I didn't know anybody and I was just stressed out or something. That's all. But then one day I was walking by these big windows and it was all gray outside and it looked like it was gonna snow—but it was freakin' October and it wasn't gonna snow—and I suddenly felt low and empty and scared and I just stood there and I was like, 'What the hell am I scared of?' But later on that day the feeling faded and I was okay, so I never told anyone. I blamed it on the weather change. But then I started feeling scared every day and I cried one night and I was like, 'What the hell am I crying about?' I hadn't cried in like ten years. So I blamed all this shit on the agency. The place was cursed. It really was. Somebody actually died there."

"Really?" Mrs. Morgan said.

"Yeah really, some account guy had a heart attack at his desk. He worked himself to death writing ads for some stupid soap presentation. It's a crazy business. It's crazy. I'm serious. I dreaded going to work in the morning more than anything and the only reason I didn't quit was because they were paying me a lot of money. People would've thought *I* was the crazy one if I quit. All day long I had to keep telling myself, 'The money. The money. The money. You're doing this for the money.' And when telling myself wasn't enough, I wrote my day rate—eight hundred dollars—on my alarm clock and on my arm. I wrote it on those yellow Post-its and stuck them around the office and then I etched it on the bottom of my boot. See. See. Look. Look . . ."

I showed Mrs. Morgan the rubber sole of my combat boot. She nodded her head. "Go on, Mr. Goldstein," she said. She continued watching me like I was a black-and-white television set.

"Okay, so where was I? Oh yeah. So I was feeling scared every day and then something crazy happened. One afternoon, out of nowhere, I felt totally fine—I felt better than fine—I felt *amazing!* I was my old self again. I was funny. I had so much energy. I was kicking soccer balls around the office with my partner, Jack. One day we smashed a copier. *Bam!* It felt so good to be alive. I had been working there for months and this pretty girl Frida said she had never noticed me until that day and then just when I was normal, I had to go flip out at the friggin' dentist office across the street from where King Kong climbed the Empire State Building. I was just sitting in the waiting room, with the fancy-schmanzy pink plush carpet, reading magazines, one after another, and I was flippin' pages and flippin' pages and I was flippin' pages and then out of nowhere my heart started palpitating and then my mind started racing and I was sweating and everything and I just had to get the hell outta there so I ran downstairs and started pacing back and forth in the lobby for like twenty minutes and I didn't know what the hell was going on and then out of nowhere it stopped. I was back to normal, just like that, like you know . . . you know . . . the Incredible Hulk. I had no friggin' idea what the hell just happened to me, my shirt was soaked and all stretched out and when I went upstairs to see the dentist, the first thing Hacksaw Hannah did was take my blood pressure and I was like, 'Why are you taking my blood pressure? Why are you taking my blood pressure?' I didn't know what the hell was going on with me. I thought it was just stress again so I tried relaxing. So that night I lit a cinnamon-scented candle and rented that movie, *Angel Heart,* you know with Robert De Niro, when he plays Louis Cipher, get it? *Louis Cipher*—the devil? Lucifer."

Mrs. Morgan nodded, "Yeah, yeah I get it, go on."

"You saw it?"

"No, I didn't see it. Continue, Mr. Goldstein."

"Well, when the movie ended I couldn't stop thinking about the bloody chickens and then the *buzzzzzzzzing* started in my body, like an electric current was running through my veins, and . . . and . . . and I thought I was possessed or something but I couldn't tell anybody because they would've thought I was crazy and I knew I wasn't crazy but then I thought it was too much caffeine so I stopped drinking coffee and I switched to green tea and it still didn't go away so I started drinking red wine with dinner but alcohol just covered it up for a little while, a Band-Aid, and then it was worse than ever. I started crying everyday. I mean *everyday*—and most of the time I didn't even know why I was crying. And then there was my heart attack. I couldn't believe I was having a freakin' heart attack at twenty-five years old. My friend Allen had to rush me to the emergency room on Christmas Eve and after waiting two hours, they said there was nothing wrong with me and I screamed, 'What the hell are you talking about? Feel my chest! Feel my chest!' and the doctor said, 'Maybe it's your thyroid.' It wasn't my thyroid, whatever my thyroid was. And then I started seeing this scary face with sideburns in my head and it wouldn't go away! Like it was tattooed on my brain!"

"You saw faces, Mr. Goldstein?"

"Yeah, just one—over and over again. I tried getting away for New Year's Eve with Paige and the monster in my head followed me upstate. I flipped out and almost drove us off a cliff driving down from Mohonk Mountain House. It really scared Paige. 'Bruce, slow down you're scaring me! You're scaring me!' she screamed."

"Mr. Goldstein, tell me more about this face."

"It kind of looked like this guy I worked with. Every time I worried about a deadline, I saw his face—but it was all distorted—and all of this anxiety came with it. And even if I wasn't thinking about him, out of nowhere I would think, 'Hey I'm not thinking of the face, it's gone,' and then it was back and sometimes I would just go looking for it even though I knew it would scare me. You know like a flame on a lighter. You know it's hot but for some reason you just have to keep touching it and touching it and touching it."

Mrs. Morgan nodded her head. "Uh'um, I get it," she said. "Go on, continue."

"I tried to get rid of it. I read somewhere that if you write something down that's been bothering you and burn it, you can destroy it forever. So I drew a picture of what it looked like and then I lit it on fire over my toilet bowl. I watched it turn to ashes and I screamed for it never to bother me again. But that didn't work. There was only one thing left for me to do. So I called in sick for work and I never went back—and the face went away with it—it just kind of dissolved. But that's when Paige said she needed more space and left me and that really fucked me up— sorry, I mean messed me up—but I fell apart. She was my first love and I didn't know how to deal with it—I was so lost—I was crying constantly—and then my stupid stomach started freaking out—I have Crohn's disease. . . ."

"You have Crohn's, Mr. Goldstein?" she said. "That's god-awful."

"You're telling me? Sometimes I'm in the bathroom over eight times a day. I hate my stomach. But I've gotten used to it. It's all of this anxiety and crying all the time that's killing me. And I still can't believe that my friend David asked me if I was thinking about killing myself."

"Well Mr. Goldstein, are you thinking about killing yourself?"

"No. But the fact that he even asked me scared the shit out of me. He got me thinking, 'Well, am I going to kill myself?' I mean, I didn't think I was going to kill myself. But I didn't know what the hell I was doing anymore. I mean, I knew it was more than the agency, and more than Paige leaving me. I was like, 'What the hell is wrong with me?' But you know what the problem really is?"

"What Mr. Goldstein? Tell me. Please do."

"There isn't one."

"What?"

"You heard me. I feel fine. Never felt better. That shit's all over. I feel great today. *Hunky dory.* I feel like my old self again. Why, I don't even know what I'm doing here. This shit doesn't make any sense. What the hell am I doing here? *What the hell am I doing here?* Huh? Huh? I just came for everybody else's sake just to shut them up. There's nothing wrong with me. See? See? This is a big waste of time. Yours and mine."

Mrs. Morgan backed up and stood by the door. I was dying to know what she was going to make of my way-off-Broadway performance.

"Well, what do you think? I'm normal right? I'm just going through a rough time in my life," I said. "Speed bumps. Speed bumps. That's all they are. Right? Right? So whadayah think. Whadayah think, huh?"

It was silent for a moment.

"What do I think?" she said. "I think you should be on medicine."

"What?" I blurted out.

"I think you should be on medication, Mr. Goldstein. That's all there is to it."

"What? What the hell are you talking about? Are you out of your fucking, godforsaken mind? You don't know anything about me. You just met me. I don't need any medicine. You don't understand. I don't even know why I'm here. There's no way I need medicine. Screw that, I'm not taking drugs. Nobody's cuttin' my head open . . ."

"Mr. Goldstein, there's really no reason to raise your voice," she said.

"Who's raising their voice? This is how I talk. What? What? Next you're gonna tell me I need a speech therapist."

"You're not gonna make this easy, are you? Wait here for a second."

"Wait? Wait for what? Your electroshock treatment? Your Frankenstein lobotomy?" I paced back and forth. I read all the rainbow posters. I mushed my face up against the glass window pane like a little kid. Dozens of overlapping skyscrapers. Millions of snowflakes. The Goodyear blimp. I started laughing. Good year, right. I imagined popping it with a pin. I started talking to myselves. I needed a second opinion. "What am I doing here? I'm smarter than them. This place is a nuthouse. I'm fine. You're fine. We're fine, Bruce. They're the crazy ones," I said. "I'm outta here." I started heading for the door. Not so fast, sonny boy. Mrs. Morgan was back. And she brought along a friend.

"Bruce, this is Dr. Agnes Czeberowski," Mrs. Morgan said. Reddish hair. Smirky smile. Funky glasses. She looked like the little lady in *Poltergeist* who dispersed demons. "Bruce, she's a licensed psychologist."

"Then who the hell are you?"

"I'm a social worker. It's my job to find out where you belong."

"What?" I felt like I just wasted my breath. "What? I'm outta here. You guys are the ones who need therapy."

"Hold on. Now, hold on, Bruce," this Dr. Czeberowski lady said in a soothing voice, like a concerned relative or a fairy godmother. "And tell me what's going on here."

"Nothing's going on. I just don't belong here. That's all."

Before I could finish my sentence, Mrs. Morgan cut me off. "He's bipolar, Agnes. He's a manic-depress—"

"No! No! No! No! No!" I shot up like a bottle rocket and yelled in my defense. "No I'm not! No I'm not!" I was screaming with my hands.

But Mrs. Morgan didn't give up. She was determined for her opinion to be heard. She never raised her voice. "Agnes, he shows all signs and symptoms of classic manic depression. Extreme highs and lows, racing thoughts. He sees faces. My recommendation for this patient is immediate medication, possibly hospitalization."

"No! No! No! No! I'm not going to any hospital. What are you fuckin' kidding me!" I exploded, throwing myself between the two of them, blocking the little doctor imposter from making anymore false accusations about me.

When she said, "Agnes, look at him. He's manic right now, he's grandiose," I started jumping up and down, waving my arms high and low, left and right like I was Shaquille O'Neal playing center court. "You don't know what you are talking about! I'm not crazy! I'm not going to any insane asylum!"

Dr. Czeberowski remained silent, drawing her own conclusions. "Bruce, calm down, nobody is sending you to any hospital," she whispered like she was trying to hypnotize me. "Now, why don't you tell me what happened." I ignored the anti–social worker completely and I gave Dr. Czeberowski the Cliff Noted version of my four-month mental meltdown.

"Whoa, Bruce, you've been through quite a bit."

Mrs. Morgan butted in. "He has Crohn's disease too, Albina."

"Well that makes sense. The shortest nerve is from the brain to the stomach."

"Whatever," I said. "All of this psychological evaluation is bullshit. I already know the meaning of life, anyway. I just read Deepak Chopra's *Seven Spiritual Laws of Success*."

"I know Deepak," the redheaded, psychological-size fire hydrant said.

My eyes lit up. "You know Deepak?" I got goose bumps. Maybe this shrink's not so bad, I thought.

"Yeah, I've attended his seminars."

"Oh, yeah? Well I ran out and bought twenty-four copies of his book and gave them to all of my friends. I told them this would heal them of all their ailments."

"Okay there, Mr. Bruce. Deepak's good," she said. "Keep reading his work. But maybe you need a little bit more help than that right now."

"Screw that. I'm not taking drugs. I'm not losing my creativity."

"Bruce, calm down. I'm not asking you to. I'm not a psychiatrist. I'm a psychologist. I can't prescribe medicine," she said. "Talking things out is my thing." Then she started staring at me. "Come over here."

"Why?"

"I want to look at you. C'mon, I won't bite, Bruce."

She got real close, almost touching. She looked in my eyes. The diagnosis was in. "Oh, you're sick, Bruce. You're really *sick*. You're depressed. But I don't know if you're ready for therapy without medicine. It all works together."

I shook my head. "No, no pills."

"Bruce, let's just set up an appointment with a psychiatrist. See what she says?"

"No pills."

"All right Bruce, let me put it like this. You have to cross a bridge to get better. 'The bridge of recovery,' I'll call it. And you have two choices on how to get over it. You can either walk over like you've been doing. But the way things have been going, you may never get there. You might jump. Or you could take a helicopter and get over your depression a lot faster. You could feel better in a couple of weeks. You can start living again."

"I'm not taking Prozac. That shit's not for me. No drugs." I put my hands over my eyes. I started crying.

"Bruce, I wish you would reconsider. You don't know what you're dealing with."

"No pills. That's it. I'm sick of this. Whatever happened to positive thinking?"

"Bruce, thinking is where your problem is."

"Yeah, yeah, yeah. Well, I was just thinking—maybe I will get there faster by helicopter, but I'll be a hell of a lot stronger if I make it over by foot."

"Okay, Bruce. You made your point. No pills. Not now. But will you at least meet with me for therapy a couple times a week? C'mon, what do you say?"

I nodded.

"Good. Good. Before you leave let's make an appointment with my receptionist."

As we headed toward the door, Dr. Czeberowski looked at me. "Hey, Bruce, you know you must be blessed," she said. "God must really like you that you ended up with me. I only get the special ones."

"Yeah, Kmart specials," I smiled. "Thanks, Dr. Czeberowski."

"Call me Dr. C."

On the subway home, I wrote in my journal. *I will beat this. I will beat this. I want to live.* I sketched a bridge. Then I drew a stick figure all the way on the left. He had a long way to go. Let the healing begin.

7

TUESDAYS WITH DR. C

Her office was a rain forest. I'd never seen so many plants, and she had pictures of her pets everywhere. She had a tiger cat named Tigger, who licked people; she had a spotted fish named Spot, who liked to be petted by people; and she had a black French poodle named Marvin, who was more intelligent than most people. Sometimes she brought her furry cotherapist to work with her. One time she even let me take him for a walk with her. We held my session in the dog run in Riverside Park. It felt good playing with all the dogs.

Every week was basically the same. I'd run up there in a desperate panic—red and dripping with sweat. I'd creep into her office, curl up on the couch, and I'd read her the latest excerpts from my jangled journals. I'd start crying midsession. Within seconds, my sobbing turned to giggling. Then I'd be extremely confident. I'd tell her my latest visions. How I was going to be a famous film director and fly to Cannes and then she'd say I was manic. "What the hell are you talking about? I'm not manic. If I was manic, don't you think that I'd know I was manic and that I would tell you I was manic?"

I'd talk to her so much that I wouldn't give her a chance to talk back and I'd keep talking past my appointment till she walked me through the crowded reception area to the front door and I'd say, "But, what about . . ." She'd say, "Bruce, write it down. Save it for next time."

"But Dr. C, suppose there isn't a next time? Suppose there isn't a next time? You're not with me when it happens. Nobody is. I mean the only time I feel normal is when I'm here with you talking about it. As soon as I leave your office and I'm alone again it starts happening again. I start thinking and thinking and thinking and then just like that I'm freaking out again. I can't even have a conversation with somebody without my sub-conscious interrupting me. It stops me in the middle of a thought. I forget what I'm talking about. I go blank. And then people have no idea why I just got so quiet. 'Bruce, are you all right? Are you all right?' I just can't stop thinking about it. Please help me. I just want it to leave me alone already."

"I know you do Bruce. I know you do. And it will leave you alone soon."

"You promise?"

"Yes, Bruce. I promise."

Dr. C was a woman of her word. She tried every method to kick my depression without resorting to medicine. She tried yoga, positive thinking, and breathing techniques. She gave me a psychological tarot card reading. She even tried pushing puppies on me. Pet therapy. "Bruce, you should get a dog.

When you're ready. I mean a dog will do wonders for you. It's just a lot of responsibility."

"Yeah, maybe when I'm ready. But right now I can barely take care of myself. Let's stick to the present."

Dr. C meant well. She had good intentions, but nothing worked. Her stress management class was the worst experience yet. When it was my turn to introduce myself to the class, I felt like somebody had put a plastic bag over my head. I couldn't catch my breath. "Hi, my name is Bruce Goldstein, and I'm having a panic attack right now," I said. The class thought I was being funny. *I was not being funny.*

After a month of therapy, I showed no signs of improvement. Dr. C begged me for the last time to take medication. "Bruce, you won't get better without it. Before we can get to the root of your problems, we have to calm your chemicals down. Now come on, just take the helicopter over the bridge already."

"No, I can't," I said. "I can't."

"What do you mean you can't?"

It would have been a lot easier to take medicine if I was just depressed. But I was a living, breathing roller coaster. Every time I got high—manic—I thought I was better. Until the next time. My moods must have changed ten times a day. It was very hard for me to keep track of me. My journals looked like they were written by two totally different people. Two extremes. What a disease. I could only imagine what it was like for my friends, my family, and my shrink. They had *some* patience with me.

"Bruce, just take the medicine. You don't know what you're dealing with," Dr. C said. "You're making a very big mistake. *A very big mistake.*"

She wasn't kidding.

8

SUNDAY AFTERNOON WITH SATAN IN CENTRAL PARK

It was a sunny afternoon. I was at a street fair in Union Square with Ricky. We ate curly fries smothered in ketchup. I was having a pretty good time until he left me to go to a wedding. I watched him disappear in the distance. I stood there with my hands in my pockets. *Now what am I going to do? Now what am I going to do?* I thought. I started walking. I felt that all too familiar feeling coming on. I tried to fight it. *I tried.*

With nowhere to go, I glided in a daze across the steamy black pavement back toward my apartment. My empty apartment. Apart from everybody and everything.

Bruce, go back to your apartment and kill yourself.

Why did I just think that? I didn't want to kill myself. But the voice—my voice—in my head said it again. *"Bruce, go back to your apartment and kill yourself. Kill yourself."* I couldn't get those words off my mind. If I made any attempt to get it off my mind, it was on my mind again. *"Bruce, go back to your apartment and kill yourself. Kill yourself,"* I said.

I was crossing Twenty-third Street. I had a few more blocks to go. It followed me home.

"Bruce, kill yourself. Bruce, go upstairs to your apartment and kill yourself. Kill yourself."

I ran up three flights of stairs telling myself, "I'm not going to kill myself. I'm just going to grab my backpack, a journal, a book to read, and I'm going to Central Park where there are plenty of people."

I walked by the kitchen. The sink called me near. *"Closer, closer, closer, come here, Bruce. Kill yourself. Kill yourself."* I froze in the doorway. Two big black handled knives were sitting at the top of the pile of dirty dishes. *"C'mon Bruce. Kill yourself."* When I saw my reflection in the sharp and shiny metal, I grabbed my backpack and got the hell out of there.

"Don't worry, Bruce, we'll get you later. We'll get you later," they hissed.

I kept telling myself, "This isn't happening. This isn't happening." But it was.

I ran out of my building. I walked really fast all the way up Twenty-eighth Street toward Seventh Avenue to catch the number one train. My heart was pounding. "Only two more blocks." Pounding like it wanted to get out. "God, please let me make it." Just as I was crossing Fifth Avenue, I started getting really hot. Sweat was oozing down my sunburned face like candle wax. I smelled sulfur. Then an overwhelming dark presence surrounding me. An evil ether. I tried to run away, but it was no use. No matter how fast I went, I couldn't escape it. He was inside of me.

Demonic images flooded my brain. I saw Lucifer, the fallen angel, surrounded by flames. I saw biblical scriptures. Pictures of purgatory. Pitchforks. The end of days. My mind raced back through history. I thought of all of the evil in the world. The wars. The manslaughter. I tried thinking of something else—anything else—but I couldn't change my channel. I couldn't shut it off. Something much larger was forcing me to think these horrible things. "Get outta my head! Get outta my head!" I pleaded. I looked up in the sky for hope. But all I saw were gargoyles.

I didn't know what was happening. Where it was coming from, or how it got inside of me. Then it made perfect sense. I was a marked man. 666, the number of the beast, had always been with me. Those demonic digits were smack dab in the middle of my social security number. And now the Prince of Darkness had come to get me. Satan waited till I was weak to persuade me to join him and his pitchfork propaganda. I wasn't joining anybody. I ran across Seventh Avenue, down the stairs into the subway. I dropped my token into the turnstile, but I was too late. I watched my train pull away. I had to wait. It was hot and sticky. Rats ran across the tracks. Tourists lined up along the platform for the next train. I stood there in silence—terrified. I wanted to scream for help, but the Statue of Liberty–lovin' out-of-towners wouldn't believe me. They would've called me crazy.

I started rubbing my fingers feverishly through my goatee. Could they see what was happening to me? Sweat poured from my forehead. I looked up to the decrepit ceiling. "God, help me. I don't want to feel this way." I was a shriveled-up piece of nothing in the palm of the universe. This was my judgment day. "Please, God, send me back to my old life. I'll be forever good. I want to be on your side. Release me from these evil clutches. Set me free."

I heard a train coming. My escape. I took a deep breath. I started walking toward the platform. I looked down. My feet were on the yellow line—on the edge. I knew this could be it. Since I wasn't going to join the Prince of Darkness, I feared being tossed onto the tracks against my will. I was worried that when they found my body in a million pieces, everybody would think I had jumped. Nobody would ever think the devil made me do it. "No. No. No. God, give me strength." I turned around. I walked over to an old brown bench. I sat down and pulled out my journal. I wrote as fast as I could. Scribble scratch.

Whoever finds this must know the truth: The devil is trying to kill me. The devil is very real. I'm fighting as hard as I can. I want to live. Whoever finds this, please tell my family and friends that I love them. Mommy and Daddy and Sharon. Love. Love. Love. God. God. God. God. God, please save me. Help me fight this.

When the train rounded the bend and I felt its hot blistery breath, I dug my fingernails into the wood, and I prayed that I wouldn't be thrown to my death.

"Please, please, please leave me alone! Good is better than evil. Love will conquer all. I have too much to live for. I don't want to die. I will not take the easy way out. God. God. God. God. God. God. God. God . . ." I wrote over and over again until the train reached its screeching halt. When the doors opened, I thanked God that I wasn't under it. I pried my fingers from the bench. I walked over. I watched my step as I stepped inside. I looked down, between the cracks. Total blackness. The doors shut.

The cursed car shook back and forth. Dark tunnels. Loud noises. I wanted my ride to end. Please God. Make it stop. All I could do was hold on. Ladies and gentlemen, you are arriving in hell. Passengers please remain seated till the train comes to a complete halt. Hope you enjoy your stay. We're not responsible for any personal belongings you might leave behind in your old life. Where you're going, you won't need them anyway.

"Fifty-ninth Street, Columbus Circle next," the conductor said. I got off and ran toward Sheep's Meadow in Central Park. It was a large green area with gray skyscrapers in the background. Rollerbladers, baby carriages, beach blankets, and happy yellow dogs catching Frisbees. I heard a group of hippies singing Beatles ditties. *"All you need is love. Love is all you need."* There were cheery cherry blossoms everywhere. The scent of hot dogs and sauerkraut was in the air. A melting pot of people sunbathing like seals. My safe haven.

I walked onto the lawn. I looked around. I found a place to sit down. I tried pretending the evil presence wasn't there. I sat Indian style. I looked straight ahead. But I couldn't stop thinking of it. A new face entered my head. It was my own. Except it was red and I had grown horns. My pointy goatee didn't help. I should've shaved it off.

I tried to smile to make it go away. But in my mind's eye, it only made me appear more like a demon. I felt so frightened. I was trapped inside an invisible monster costume. I had nobody to talk to. Suddenly, I felt somebody with somebody else creeping up behind me. They slithered past me. And in an eerie sinister voice, like when you play "Stairway to Heaven" backward, they left the most disturbing message in my ear.

"IN THE NAME OF SATAN."

The hair on my neck stood up. I immediately flung open the cover of my journal. I whipped out my black pen.

"Leave me alone! Leave me alone! Leave me alone! Good is better than evil. Love. Love. Love. God, please make him leave me alone!"

I didn't know what to do with myself. I thought being around all of these people would help. But it didn't matter where I went. I was in another dimension. I was alone in this one.

I needed to do something to take my mind off of what was happening, so I took out a book from my backpack and plopped it on my lap. *The Celestine Prophecy, the Tenth Insight.* I popped it open and flipped to the middle. I zoomed in, and stared at the randomly selected page. As I read the words "animals show us the way," something amazing happened.

A ladybug flew in my book. It actually walked around the same page, on the same exact words that I was reading. "ANIMALS SHOW US THE WAY" were the words she circled with her little feet. I smiled through my terror as the orange-and-black bug danced around the black ink. Then she stopped moving and watched me. And I watched her. And after a little while, I felt safe. The satanic presence had mysteriously worn off. Instead of feeling frightened, I felt relaxed, like I had just woken up from a long nap. I looked around the park. I heard people laughing. Children were playing. The pigeons were congregating around leftover cotton candy. I watched a baby blue balloon float up in the sky. "What the hell just happened to me? And why?" It was like I was now starring in a different movie. I went from *The Shining*'s "Here's Johnny" to *Bambi*'s "Where's Thumper?" God had saved me. I watched the lady bug walk onto my finger. And when she knew I was okay, the polka-dotted little angel flew away.

I got up. I made my way out of the park. I wanted to get home before dark.

Monday morning, when I told Dr. C and her furry sidekick about my weekend from hell, she got all psychological on me. "Bruce, Bruce, Bruce," she said. "There is no such thing as the devil you describe. You created your own devil. Out of fear. Over money. Out of guilt. Over getting fired from work, that job you used to love."

"What the hell does that have to do with anything? You're so wrong. It really happened. The devil came to get me."

"Bruce, it's all in your head. You hallucinated."

"No I didn't. How do you know? You weren't there."

"Now enough is enough. Bruce, you don't have to live like this any longer. It's time for you to go on medication."

"No!"

She shook her head. She looked angry. "What do you mean, no? You really are impossible."

"Dr. C, you don't understand. I don't need medicine."

"Bruce, what are you talking about?"

"I'm okay now. God healed me. Don't you get it? The lady bug. She was a messenger. She performed some kind of insect exorcism. It was a miracle. She walked around the page. *Animals show us the way.* And I have complete faith that God will show me the way. If I'm wrong by not taking antidepressants, the Master of the Universe will tell me. Trust me." *Trust me.*

The next morning when the knives in my sink whispered, *"You thought we forgot about you, Bruce. Well we didn't. Now kill yourself."* I ran back into Dr. C's office and I surrendered. "Dr. C, I'll take anything you want to give me. Just help me, please. Make it go away." She gave me a big hug. "Bruce, I'm so proud of you," she said. "You're doing the right thing. Now sit right there. I'm going to make an appointment for you with Dr. Stanita Williams before you change your mind again. She's a great psychiatrist. Her office is just down the hall. She's nice. You'll like her, you'll see." Bring on my helicopter to sanity.

9

LIFE SUCKS. THEN YOU DIE.
OR YOU TAKE LITHIUM

My palms were sweating as I sat in the reception area. One of the fluorescent lights was flickering. I was very anxious, scared even. A psychologist was one thing but seeing a psychiatrist was a whole other level. I felt like only crazy people in the movies, psychopathic killers, went to psychiatrists. I dreaded being alone with her. What was she going to do to me? As I was biting the skin on my fingers, as my eyes were twitching, the receptionist said, "Mr. Goldstein, Dr. Williams is ready to see you now."

When I walked in, she was anything but what I had expected. She was a fairly large black woman wearing an abstract painting.

She had a bright warm smile like a talk show host. In the calmest of calm, she said, "Hello, Mr. Goldstein. Please, please sit down. So what brings you here today?" Here we go again. Dr. Williams listened and took notes while I told her everything from Paige to Satan.

"So, Dr. Williams, what do you make of all this?"

"Well, Mr. Goldstein, I believe you are manic depressive. You have all of the symptoms. From the grandiosity that got you fired to your depressions. Mr. Goldstein, you suffer from mood swings. You're a textbook case. Bipolar is the newer name for it. But after this last episode in Central Park, you were beyond manic. You were hallucinating. What happened to you is what we call psychotic."

Psychotic. I had finally hit the big time.

"So what happens next?" I asked her.

"I think you need some medicine. I'm going to write you a prescription for . . ."

Before she could say the word, I said it to myself.

"Lithium."

And so the day had come. I was gonna take lithium, just like my uncle Max.

The first time I ever set eyes on him I was ten. It was right after I laid eyes on his candy-apple-red Sting Ray Corvette. It was like seeing Santa Claus leave your rooftop. Except Santa Claus never shook my hand and left a crispy fifty in it. Uncle Max went through cars like I went through punch balls. He turned me on to my first shrimp cocktail.

They called Maxie "The Big Cheese," and not just because he weighed three hundred and twenty-five pounds. He was one of the biggest cheese importers in America. Gouda from Holland, Stilton from England, Tallegio from Italy—you name it. If you could spread it on your cracker, chances are it was from him. If he wasn't wheeling and dealing two-hundred-pound cheese wheels in Switzerland, he was taking off in the middle of the day to fly a plane. When he felt like watching a sunset, he bought front row seats—an eighty-foot yacht. If he had the sudden urge to play tennis, he'd hail the Concorde to London.

Back when I was in school, I used to run around joking to my friends, "I'm manic, I'm manic like my Uncle Max (not having an idea at the time that I was *really* like him). Look at me, going really, really fast, able to accomplish a million things in a single bound," but I never said I'm depressed, I'm depressed like Uncle Max. I'd never seen the dark side of his illness until that Father's Day in June of 1992, when my Aunt Zoé asked me to pick up his son, Andrew, from his mother's house in Jersey, to bring him to Long Island.

When we arrived at his house, Max was nowhere in sight. Then I saw somebody that looked kind of like Max except he was wearing red pajamas, doing kiddy jigsaw puzzles, and drooling all over himself. Max had transformed into a three-hundred-pound, three-year-old baby. When he walked into the kitchen and patted me on the head in slow motion, he said, "You're a good boy, Bruce, thanks for bringing Andy." Those were the only words Max spoke to me that day. "Hey what happened to the big guy?" I stood there in confusion. It didn't make any sense to me. Max used to be so strong. Larger than life. He even convinced me he was the messiah one time. Now, my Aunt Zoé was helping him get dressed every morning. He forgot how to put on his shirt. Back then, no matter how hard I tried, I couldn't understand what happened to him. But now, eight years later, as my very own psychiatrist handed me my very own prescription, I understood. It just happens. It was a chemical imbalance. It was the cards God had dealt us. Live or die with it.

As Dr. Williams handed me my prescription, I asked her, "How come you're not putting me on Prozac like the rest of America?"

"Prozac is an antidepressant, that's just for depression," she said. "Lithium is a mood stabilizer that helps with manic depression. And you, Mr. Goldstein, being manic depressive don't just get low, you also have highs—manic highs—and as you know they can be even more dangerous than your depressions. Look at what happened to you this weekend. You have unpredictable mood swings—racing thoughts—hallucinations. We need to level you out. We need to get you back in control of your mind. And lithium will do that. It's the most effective mood stabilizer on the market. It will help balance your chemicals out and get you back to normal as soon as possible. Quite frankly, Mr. Goldstein, you'll stop seeing the devil."

"Okay, okay I'll try it. But, but, what about side effects? Will there be any side effects?"

"There might be, Mr. Goldstein, but it's more important that you be on it."

"What about my creativity? Will lithium take away my creativity?"

"It shouldn't, Mr. Goldstein."

"And how long will it take to work?"

"Just start it tonight. Give it some time. Call me in a few days. Let me know how you're doing."

"But, but, but . . . I heard this stuff can be fatal."

"Well, not exactly—only if you take a lot of it. Don't worry, Mr. Goldstein, we're starting you off with a low dosage, and we'll carefully monitor your lithium by taking regular blood tests."

"Blood tests? What?"

"Yes. It's the only way for us to find your therapeutic level."

Even holding the prescription in my hand, I was still trying to talk my way out of it, all the way out of her office. I was still worried about never being myself again. That it would take the Bruce out of Bruce. Dr. C must've heard me babbling because she ran out of her office and grabbed me in the reception area.

"Don't worry, Bruce. It will put the Bruce *back in* Bruce," she said. "You'll be all right now, you're boarding your helicopter over the bridge. It's over. It's all over. You made it. And you're in good company too. Winston Churchill, Ernest Hemingway, Vincent Van Gogh, Poe, they were all manic depressives—just like you. The only difference is that we're going to be able to save you. They didn't have the kind of treatments we have today. You're a very lucky young man." She gave me a big hug and sent me on my way.

When I went to my pharmacy, I felt like the bearded pharmacist was watching me like I was a psychopath. I imagined him thinking, "That guy's crazy. Don't take your eyes off of him for a second." I'd been filling prescriptions for years for my stomach disease, and I had never felt this embarrassed. I felt like everybody knew. "All done, Mr. Goldstein." It bothered me that he knew my name, that he knew where I lived. It bothered me even more when he said, "Have a nice day."

And so I started taking lithium. And then the lithium started taking me. It was heavy stuff. Side effects beyond belief. Excessive sweating. Dry mouth. Retardation. Extremely frequent urination. The miracle salt was draining me. And now it was four weeks later in Martha's Vineyard, and aside from the occasional high, I was more depressed than ever. Somebody put me out of my misery. Please.

10

THE BLACK DOG

"Bruce, get the hell up! We're goin' fishin'!" my friends yelled. What, the mopeds weren't enough for them? Besides the fact that Saturday was supposed to be a day of cartoons and breakfast in bed, I had a lot of trouble getting out of bed. It was more like pulling myself out of a chemically imbalanced coffin. My head was heavy, my subconscious—a sandbag. My body was in a deep sleep— "a lithium coma," I called it. Any attempt to wiggle myself back to reality triggered an invasion of negative vibrations throughout my entire nervous system. Electric-chair–like tremors shot from my twitching toes, through my thighs, up my spine, causing my cerebrum to quiver from side to side, mixing my chemicals together like bipolar pigments in a paint can. I didn't know what day it was. I didn't know where I was. My shirt was soaking wet. My vision was blurry. My eyes were red and crusty. I needed more than a cup of coffee to get my motor running.

The waves were choppy. The sky was gray. It looked like rain was coming. A lot of rain. We went on one of those "we-give-you-the-poles-and-bait" charter boat arrangements. The kind that has an old fish stick commercial sea cap'n in a yellow slicker, who's always missing a few teeth. This was my first time deep sea fishing. When I heard somebody say "sharks" and "30,000 feet deep," I said, "Where the hell are the life jackets?" The only thing good about my deep sea fishing experience with my friends was that the original plan was to go swimming. Thank God the water was freezing.

We were out there for hours. The only thing I was catching was wave after wave of despair. Charlie was using the same bait as me and he caught three nice-size blue fish. Even David and Isabella were reeling them in. Isabella said, "Oh, my God, Bruce, I got something! I got something! Look!" She had her arms wrapped around David. I was happy for them but it made me sad. I missed holding somebody's hand.

I cast out one last time before we headed back. Nothing. The seagulls circled overhead. The current helped pull us in. We docked ship. Before we left the marina, Captain Ahab said, "You mates hungry? 'Cuz no trip to the Vinyahd is complete without a meal at The Black Dog. Yah jus gottah try tha clam chowdah. R'rrr. R'rrr." Our next stop was Vineyard Haven Harbor.

I wasn't looking forward to going anyplace called The Black Dog. I had a bad feeling. That was what the great Winston Churchill named his dark periods of depression. I read that it had haunted him for years. Every time he made history, he would crash, his mood would swing. He'd end up curled up in some corner crying. The prime minister may have destroyed thousands of Nazis and kamikazes, but he was never victorious over his mental illness. It brought him down. All the way down, boy. I prayed that wasn't what was in store for me.

As we approached The Black Dog Tavern, my heart stopped. I was immediately drawn in by The Black Dog's logo on the sign post. Holy shit, so that's where that shirt's from. I had seen them everywhere for as far back as I could remember. Everyone wore one. From college interns to Bill Clinton. From hot models to my dry cleaner. Even little rich kids in strollers wore them.

I didn't know what it was, but I had always been attracted to that Black Dog icon. I never had a black dog as a kid. I never had any dogs. I had tadpoles and a painted turtle named Herman. I fed him Hebrew National hot dogs in the bathtub.

As for me and my friends, we had a pretty waitress who fed us jalapeno shrimp quesadillas at a long wooden table in a pine-paneled room. There was maritime memorabilia everywhere. Anchors, old photos, harpoons. The specials were written with red-and-yellow chalk on a blackboard that was leaning on an ancient easel. Isabella got the caramelized scallops. David ordered the baked striped bass with braised fennel because they didn't have baked ziti on the menu. I had the pan-seared codfish with lobster sauce. My compliments to the Imodium. After everybody finished eating, we made a stop at The Black Dog souvenir shop, where we were attacked by the sales racks.

Black dogs galore. There were thousands of them. That logo was everything. Hats and T-shirts. Towels and mugs. While my friends were oohing and ahhing at doggie keychains and pencil holders, I spotted a real black dog drooling in the corner. Old Zeek was watchin' the store. He was about eighty pounds or so. He was having the time of his life sticking his head in a bowl of water. He had a sloppy red tongue, big ears that drooped on the floor, and he was smiling at me. I couldn't stop staring at him. I sat down next to him and pet him on his head. I said, "So they call you Zeek, huh?" He looked at me. His tired eyes said, "You miss her, don't you?"

Paige loved dogs more than anything. First of all, she named my green Toyota "Toto." The woman of my dreams said hello to every happy-go-lucky golden retriever from Riverside Park to Little Italy, whether they were walking on a leash or tied to a parking meter, while I just stood there. And if she saw a puppy, *fugettaboutit*. She turned into a five-year-old schoolgirl. She jumped up and down and screeched like a crazy bird. "Look at the pup-peeeeee! Look at the pup-peeeeee!" She didn't care who was watching. Then she rubbed them on their bellies. "I got the spot. I got the spot," she would say. I would have bought her a dog of her own if they didn't make her break out in hives so I did the next best thing. I went up to FAO Schwarz on Fifth Avenue and bought her a stuffed one. He was brown with big ears and he was fluffy. Paige was as happy as Goofy. She named the little rascal Boomer and said, "I'm gonna love'm and hug'm and squeeze'm and I will punish him when he is bad." But when that cold day in January came, when Paige said, "I need more space," she gave him back to me in a brown paper bag. "You need him more than me, Brucie. Here, you take him."

I snuggled with the stuffed mongrel, I'll admit it. There were many nights I cried myself to sleep with him. But Boomer reminded me too much of the woman I needed, so I had to get rid of him. I didn't have the heart to throw him down the incinerator so I shoved him under my bed.

I couldn't live without Paige so we tried to be friends. *We tried.* We saw each other on weekends. She took me shoe shopping. We went jogging around the Reservoir in Central Park. We checked out museums. Then one day we were walking past a pet store on

Seventy-second Street and Paige's eyes popped opened up like Styrofoam golf balls. She said, "Oh my God, Bruce, we have to go in." She started humming, *"How much is that puppy in the window?"* Eleven hundred smackers they wanted for him. "For a dog?" I thought. "That's highway robbery." Paige informed me he was a chocolate Labrador retriever, seven weeks old, around eight pounds. "Awe, so—oh cute," she said. He had paws the size of miniature Ping-Pong paddles. She asked the manager if she could see him. "I just got him in yesterday from a local breeder," he said. Paige picked him up, she put his head against her chest. She started talking to him like she was gonna breast-feed him. "Oh, look at you. You're such a cutie. A booga-booga-boo. A booga-booga-boo," she said. I just stood there with my hands in my pockets until Paige said, "Here Bruce, you hold him."

"Nah, it's all right. I don't want to drop him," I told her as I moseyed on over to the bird section. Sticking my fingers in the parakeet cage was more my thing. Polly want a finger? Polly want a finger? "Ouch, you bit me." That beaky buzzard belonged in the fish section with a black-and-red letter sign that read BEWARE OF PIRANHA.

Paige snuck up behind me. She put the puppy's face in front of her face and started talking like she was a puppy puppet ventriloquist.

"C'mon Brucie, hold me, hold me, it's easy, it's easy. I won't bite you . . . *please.*"

"*A-choo,*" Paige sneezed.

"Nah, I'm sorry, Mr. Puppy. I don't know what to do with you."

"C'mon, Bruce, I'm starting to break out, just take him for a second."

"All right. Give him to me." I couldn't believe how soft his fur was. His ears were like velvet. And he was cute, I gave her that much. But he was squirming like a pig. Porky was nibbling my fingers. "Ouch those things are sharp. You little . . ."

"Hee, hee, hee," she laughed. "He's teething. Don't worry, Bruce. He can't hurt you. He's only a baby."

"Yeah right. Hey Paige, I think he wants to make pee-pee or something else. Take him, take him away from me." As I was trying to give him back to Paige, the li'l lover started licking my face.

"He's giving you kisses! He's giving you kisses! He likes you!"

"He's not giving me kisses. He's licking the goat cheese out of my goatee."

"Bruce, he really likes you."

"Get outta here."

"He wants to go home with you. Why don't you adopt him?"

"What are you crazy, Paige? How the hell could I take care of a puppy when I can hardly take care of myself. Besides it's impossible to have a dog in New York City. I live in a studio apartment."

"Bruce, I think you need a pet. Yeah, you guys would be great together. He'll be your best friend. You'll always have company. And it's spring. Puppy season. You could go for long walks and when the weather gets warmer you could take him swimming. Look at his paws. They're webbed. He's gonna love swimming! Bruce, I really think you should do it. I would if I wasn't allergic to him. C'mon, Brucie, you could call him . . . Hershey."

"No way, Paige. I'm not calling him Hershey and I'm not getting him. I don't want to ruin his life or mine. Here take him," I said. When I gave the bunny-sized puppy back to Paige, she waved his clumsy paw at me. "Bye-bye, Brucie."

Who knows what would've happened if I got a dog that day? Maybe I'd still have my Paige? Maybe she would've spent Memorial Day weekend with me instead of hobnobbing in the

Hamptons with The Great Gatsby? Maybe I should've just stopped day dreaming? "Hello . . . Anybody home?" She wasn't just allergic to the puppy.

Before my friends and I left The Black Dog, I grabbed myself one of those T-shirts. There was something really cool about it. I just had to have one.

11

BARNEY AND THE BASEMENT

It was our last night on the island. So everybody was resting up for the big barbecue. Everybody except Ricky. "Tick!" he screamed. "Get it off me! Get if off me!" While everybody was out fishing earlier that day, Barney had caught himself five ticks in the weeds. He gave one of them to Ricky. Luckily, they weren't in too deep. Allen was able to remove them before anybody got Lyme disease. "Oh, Barney, I'm sorry. I didn't want to hurt you, puppy." Ricky wasn't as considerate. "Get your fucking dog out of here, Allen," he insisted. Nobody else wanted ticks either so Barney was banned to the basement. Barney was a good sport. Allen gave him a chew toy and he was happy.

A few hours later, when Spencer, the fat man in the red bandanna, served up his famous dry-rubbed chicken and ribs, everybody's bellies were happy. A few screwdrivers later, when we played the Jackson Five, Ricky was really *really* happy. He jumped up on the couch in his white slacks and started dancing like Michael Jackson. "A, B, C, it's easy as one, two, three. Go Ricky! Go Ricky!" Isabella screamed. Then Izzie started kickin' it with her curvy hips and sexy lips. Who brought Jennifer Lopez? Her little man, David, put down his video camera, and the next thing I knew they were doing some kind of robot dance together. "Where's Liam and Spencer-Baby?" They were at the kitchen table, rolling doobies, puffin' the cheeba. When they passed it to me, I said, "I don't think that's a good idea." Drinking those Heinekens wasn't a good idea either, but it was too late. I was putting my left foot in and my right foot out, I was doing the hokey-pokey, I was shaking it all about. "Bruce, Bruce, Bruce. Get in here, Watusie." I jumped in the middle of the group and started break-dancing to the Fat Boys. When they played House of Pain everybody jumped up, jumped up and got down. Lamps were shaking. About an hour later when I was bouncing off the ceiling, everybody else was deflated. I wanted to go out. I was elated. "Hey Ricky, let's go out!" I screamed. "Let's go out man!" I was throwing couch pillows all around while he was lying on the ground, out of breath. "Bruce, only if you carry me," he said. I couldn't believe it. It wasn't even midnight and the weekend was over. When Allen mentioned Monopoly and El-lio's pizza, it was really over. Everybody had the munchies. "Bruce, you in or what?"

I shook the dice. "Come on baby, Brucie needs a new pair of shoes." Snake eyes. Collect two hundred bucks and pass go. "Here we go, yo." Once the game started I was on a roll. I bought everything I landed on. I put up green houses and red hotels like I was Donald Trump. Boardwalk was mine. You land on me, you die. I was wheeling and dealing until I spent all of my orange and purple cash flow. When I landed on Ricky, I owed him big-time. "Bruce, I want my money." I had to mortgage my properties. Then as my empire was crumbling before my eyes, David popped up, zipped up his sweatshirt, put on his hood, and started squirtin' away with his space age water pistol. The game was over. He pointed his super-soaker at his first victim in the kitchen. In his Tony Montana accent he said, "Hey Ricky, say hello to my little fren'."

"You idiot, this is linen!" Ricky dove for another gun and shot back at David. "David, you thinkin' what I'm thinkin'?" Ricky asked. "Yep." The two Long Island gangstas ganged up on me like a couple of wild fire hydrants. "No, no!" I screamed. I tried running away. I threw houses and hotels at them. "You're not going nowhere, Goldstein!" Ricky said. "Goldstein!" he screamed. "You're dead!"

They sprayed me into a sponge. I yelled, "Enough, enough. I'm serious. I'm not feeling well again." I told them to stop. I said, "Get outta here. Go bother Liam." But they didn't stop. They didn't care that I was waterlogged. I was flapping my arms. I was kicking my feet. I was screaming, "I gotta go to the bathroom! I gotta go to the bathroom! Just stop it already!" I thought I was gonna go right there. Thank God for Allen. When he entered the perimeter, they started messing with him. While they were giving him a wedgie, I sneaked away. David saw me. "Hey Bruce, where do you think you're going?" I didn't answer him. I went downstairs to my doorless dungeon.

The lock on the bathroom door was broken. I prayed nobody would barge in. I ran the hot water so nobody would hear anything. White smoky steam. I felt it happening again. I looked at myself in the foggy mirror. Only there was no sign of *me* anywhere. My face was red—my eyebrows squeezed together—I started to cry. Mirror, mirror, on the wall, who is that sad man hunched over in a bawl?

I started shaking. My teeth chattered. "I can't go through this anymore." I put my hands on both sides of my head. I squeezed my scalp as hard as I could. I tilted my neck back. I looked up at the ceiling. The duck-patterned wallpapered walls were closing in on me. I felt myself shrinking. I got smaller and smaller. I started thinking about how pissed off I was at Ricky and David for fucking with me, especially Ricky. He lied to me. He betrayed me. He said he was going to be there for me. "If only I could turn myself off for a second." I wanted to just stop thinking. Somebody press *Pause* already.

When I sat down on the porcelain throne, I heard my friends laughing through the ceiling. I lit more matches and ran the water louder. My heart was pounding like a war drum. My *seat* felt colder. I put my fingers over my face like chains—knuckles like bolts. I let my head bend forward. "No. Just one more night Bruce and you get to go home." *Flush.* "I hate my stomach." After I brushed my teeth, I stripped down to a pair of boxer-briefs. I couldn't wait to hide in my sleep. I climbed into bed. Just as I started drifting, I heard mischievous whispering. It was coming from down the hallway.

"*Shhh,* Ricky, be quiet or you'll wake him."

"Now what?" I thought.

Out of the corner of my eye, I watched Ricky tiptoe toward my bed. He was holding something behind his back. My first instinct was to yell "Leave me alone" but then I had another idea. I just lay there quietly. I watched him as he watched me. *Here piggy, piggy, piggy.*

First, he crawled onto my bed in slow motion. Next he crept over my body like a spider, being extra careful not to wake me. Then the moment he was about to squirt something at my face, I jumped up like a screaming catapult and swung my forearm out from under the covers like a baseball bat. I swatted him with an opened fist. I scared the living daylights out of him.

"Ow! You hit me! I can't believe you hit me!" he screamed, holding his cheek. "You're a *cr-cr-crazy* asshole! What the hell are you doing?" He grabbed the nearest thing to throw at me—a book or something. Whatever it was he nailed me in the head.

"That's it! That's it!" I said running in my red underwear after him. "You're dead!" He sped down the corridor like a little rabbit. He ran into one of the bedrooms with the rest of them and slammed the door. I huffed and I puffed and I said, "Let me in!" When that didn't work, I threw all of my weight up against the door and I busted it open. I had knocked it off its hinges. *Where'd they go? H'mmm, the closet.* "Now, I got you." When I slid open the closet door I found David and Isabella trembling under a raincoat. They were holding each other closer than they ever did on a date. Isabella was shaking. "Bruce, Bruce, stop, stop. It's me. It's me Izzie."

"I had nothing to do with this," David said, holding a water gun in his hand.

Ricky was next to them holding a broom stick. He was swinging it in my direction. I backed up. "Get that crazy person away from me! He's fucking crazy!"

"Don't call me crazy! I'm not crazy!" I bellowed. "Goddamn it! I'm not crazy!" I leaned my head back. I howled at the ceiling. "I didn't do anything! You started with me! You started with me!" Then I banged my head against the wall like a sledge hammer. I put a dent in the sheet rock. "I thought you were my friend. I thought you were my friend. You said you would look after me this weekend and you lied to me. You lied. Ahh, the hell with this. The hell with everybody." I turned around. I walked out of the room, down the hallway, back to my solitary confinement. I crawled into bed. I lay on my stomach. I smushed pillows against my face. Suffocating. I started crying. "They don't understand. They don't understand me."

The house got quiet. Nobody came in to say good night like I was some monster on an island. Then I heard footsteps. Oh, great. . . . Little footsteps. They were getting closer. I thought maybe Ricky was coming to say he was sorry. He had little feet. Or maybe he was gonna shoot me with a BB gun. I made the effort to extend my head to see where the pitter-patter was coming from. It wasn't Ricky. And they weren't feet. They were paws. It was Barney. The little Lassie looked up at me like I was a scared kitty in a tree. Then he jumped up on the bed and started licking me. He didn't care about my outburst. And I didn't care about his ticks. He made himself comfortable. He nudged his warm body up against mine. So I pet him. "Barney, you're a good boy." He opened up his mouth real wide. He sighed. He looked at me with his wise eyes. "Hey Bruce, I know you didn't mean to hurt Ricky. They don't understand you have a mental condition. It's not you fault. *It's not your fault.* Now get some rest. Things will be better in the morning. I promise."

"Thanks, Barney. You're the only one who gets it."

I pulled the cover over both of us. I pet his white and brown fur. Then for the first time in my life I kissed *a dog* on his head. And I finally understood what Allen meant when he said, "Bruce, sometimes I feel like Barney's my only friend."

At 11:15 A.M., Memorial Day, Kim Lee scrambled some eggs while everybody else scrambled around the house to get ready. Nobody said a word about the night before. So I just grabbed my bulky duffel bag and headed out the door.

I learned a lot that weekend. Memorial Day wasn't about getting drunk and stoned. It was a day set apart to honor the dead of war. I wished my war were over. Every day was a constant struggle, and I was tired of fighting. Me against me. I had nothing to look forward to when we went back to New York, nobody to look forward to. With everybody passed out in the van and Barney sleeping on my lap, I opened up my journal and wrote from my heart. "*Dear God, I wish there was something else I could do with my life. I don't want to return to advertising. Maybe I'll write a book. About what? I have no idea. . . . Maybe I'll get a dog. "*

A part of me died that weekend in the woods of Martha's Vineyard. But at 11:57 the morning we left, a very special puppy was born in Bohemia, Long Island. I just wouldn't know that until six weeks later.

12

MOM, I DON'T WANT TO GO TO LIFE TODAY

It was Tuesday morning—the day after Memorial Day. It was every morning. I was curled up under my comforter, crying like a baby. I dreaded going back to work more than anything. (I was freelancing at another ad agency.) It was hard enough for me to get up and take a shower. The phone rang. God bless my mother. "Bruce, just get up. I promise everything will be okay," she said. "C'mon, Bruce, you had a nice long weekend. You got to be with your friends, and now you have to go to work today. You can do it. C'mon, Bruce, up, up, up. You have to fight it."
  "I can't."

"C'mon, Bruce, you have to force yourself to get up. Listen, I have to get to work. Your father's waiting. I don't want to call you later and find you home."

"All right, I'm going."

One hour later, I watched the phone ring. When I heard my mother's voice on the answering machine, "Oh, Bruce, oh good, you're not home. I'll talk to you tonight," I felt guilty. I picked it up and said, "Hello."

"Bruce, what are you still doing home?"

"I dunno."

"Bruce, I'm gonna count to ten. One, two, three, four, five, six, are you still lying there?"

"Yeah."

"Well get up. C'mon, Bruce, you can do it. Force yourself."

"Ma . . . I can't. You don't understand."

"Yes you can. C'mon, we'll do it together. Bruce, hold on a second," she said. "I have a customer."

I could hear some guy with a scruffy voice buying cigarettes and a scratch-off lottery ticket in the background. My eyes got watery. I got a lump in my throat. I was amazed at my mom, working so hard in CVS, standing on her feet all day long, dealing with the public in a red apron. I used to think only famous people who made tons of money were amazing. These days, I was amazed at anybody who got up out of bed and went to work in the morning. It took real guts to earn a living.

"All right, Bruce, I'm back," my mother said. "Time to get up."

As much as I didn't want to get up, I didn't want to think about what could happen if I spent another day by myself—I didn't want to think. Thinking was dangerous, so I listened to my mother. "All right. I'm up," I said. "I'm up." I pushed the covers off me, but I held the phone close to my ear. "Don't worry, Bruce, I'm not going anywhere."

When I was a little kid, like most kids I wanted nothing to do with my parents in the shopping mall. "Ma, get outta here. You're embarrassing me," I said. I never would have thought that twenty-something years later, I'd actually need her to hold my hand. I talked to my mother all the way down the six wooden stairs.

"Ma, I'm scared."

"Bruce, you'll feel better once you get there," she said. "You know you will. You always do. Just do what you gotta do and come home. I love you, now go take a shower." She hung up.

"The shower, the shower, not yet."

I just plopped down on my couch and put on *Good Day New York*. There was nothing good about it. "I want to be normal. I want to be normal," I said. I grabbed my head and started shaking it vigorously back and forth like I was actually going to knock something back into place. That technique didn't do anything. I just felt nauseous. I moaned. I slid my body to the other side of the couch like a slug, and I grabbed for my journal hanging over the edge of my paper-covered coffee table. It was the red one, a spiral, the one I bought when I forgot how to talk, when I first went hermit. It had a black-and-white photo of a tree on the cover. My life would have been so much easier as a tree. Bark didn't have to think. I grabbed a pencil. Yellow. Number 2. I looked at the sharp point. I started thinking. "No. No. No. I'm gonna be okay." I was saved by the lead. I wrote myself back to safety. *"Things will get better. Things will get better. Things will get better. Don't worry, Bruce. Just take a shower and leave the house. Just get the hell out of here. The day will fall into place. I'll pat myself on the back tonight. Please God, take care of me today."*

The bathroom was filthy. I just didn't have the strength or a reason to clean it. It was an obstacle course of dirty towels and armpit-stained T-shirts. It looked more like a garage—and did I need a new toothbrush. It looked like I used it on my feet. There was a beat-up Gillette on the counter. By the time I got through using it, there was bloody stubble in the sink. The toilet was not ready for any lady visitors by any means, and the shower was flip-flop material—mystery green. But the most gruesome part of taking a shower was what I couldn't see. My thought patterns. My negative thinking echoed off the tiles. "I can't do this and I can't do that. No, I'm not going. Leave me alone." I would just stand there with my arms folded. I couldn't move. I was para- lyzed standing up. Self-inflicted torture. I was trapped in a rec- tangular white-walled world of mildew, caged by a black shower curtain from Bed Bath & Beyond. As steamy water stung the back of my neck, worry surfaced at my pores. I worried about everything in there. My mother always said, "When worry en- ters your mind, push it out." Or she'd say, "Bruce, I want you to remove the word 'worry' from your vocabulary." I couldn't. I used the word "worry" in too many of my sentences. When the cold metal knob in the shower cut my finger, I worried about getting an infection. I worried about getting the cold lever in the shower fixed. I worried why I didn't want to talk to anyone. I worried about my checkbook, if it was balanced. I worried that I was chemically imbalanced. I worried that I had no sex drive, that I couldn't masturbate. I worried about my inflamed intes- tines twenty-four hours a day. What the hell could I eat? And what about colon cancer? I worried that I needed a colonoscopy. When I found a fatty growth under my tricep, I thought I had skin cancer. I worried that I would never laugh again. I worried that I would never be me again—that kid who blew up a papier- mâché volcano with baking soda and vinegar and flooded the classroom in the fifth grade. I worried about being committed to a mental hospital. Worst of all, I worried that I worried about things that I shouldn't be worrying about and that made me feel guilty, and feeling guilty was worse than worrying.

When I made it out of the shower, I wrapped myself in a towel like a mummy. A dead man walking. The key to getting through the morning was to keep moving. If I didn't get dressed im- mediately, I was in trouble. I'd sit down and start thinking. It didn't matter what. Or where. As far as I was concerned every chair in my apartment was an electric chair. I used to dress to impress. Now I was too depressed to dress. But since the fore-skinned forefathers of society decided that the birthday suit was too taboo, I had to worry about what I was going to wear. Adam and Eve had it much easier with their fig-leaf fashion. There were days I would just sit in my underwear. One sock on, one sock half on. One leg in, one leg out of my pants. My pants were another problem all together. I owned about twenty pairs of black jeans, but they were of no use to me. They weren't black enough. They'd fade after one washing. And if they weren't *black* black, back to the Gap I went. Then there was lacing up my boots. "Why is this so damned difficult?" Why was everything so difficult? I was drained. Mentally. Emotionally. Physically. I had no energy. I had no spirit. No self-esteem. I had lost all of my confidence. Thank God, my first day back from the Vine-yard, I had an appointment with Dr. C. I took the R train up to Fifty-seventh Street.

13

SAY NO TO DRUGS

When I walked into Dr. C's office, I kicked off my shoes and lay down on her couch. I didn't say a word. "So tell me Bruce, how was your weekend? Did you meet anyone interesting? Did you get laid?" she asked. I shook my head from side to side. I put my hands over my eyes.

"Ahh, Bruce. I'm sorry. What happened? What's going on, huh kid?"

It took me a few minutes before I could speak. I took a deep breath, wiped my eyes, and said, "You wanna know what's happening? You have no idea. I feel worse than ever and I'm still having panic attacks and I'm sweating like a pig and this lithium isn't doing shit and I knew I shouldn't have taken it and it's screwing up my stomach. It's more screwed up than it usually is, and I can't do this anymore! I just can't. I'm taking myself off of this fucking medicine."

"Bruce, we tried it your way for months without lithium and remember what happened? Bruce, you saw the devil. You *must* take your lithium if you want to get better. And you *have* to be more patient. I told you it takes a while to kick in. You've only been on it for a month."

"I don't care. It's all bullshit."

"Bullshit, huh?"

The little woman stopped talking to me. She stood up on a chair. Marvin started barking. He was scared. "Don't worry baby. Mommy's right here." She took down this big red book. It was the size of a phone book. She dropped it in my lap. She pointed. "Here, see for yourself. How many times do I have to tell you you're a textbook case manic depressive." She showed me the list of symptoms. She read them off. "One: *Racing thoughts.* Two: *Grandiosity.* Three: *Hallucinations.* You want me to keep going? Bruce, you're as manic as they come. I knew it back in January, and I know it now. Bruce, you are bipolar. And you need to be on medicine. How can I get it through to you. You need to keep taking the lithium."

"Oh no I don't. Lithium just makes me more depressed. At least before I used to have my highs. Now I feel nothing. I'm numb. I have no sex drive whatsoever. And the days never end. I just stare and stare at the second hand—I pray for it to go faster. But it doesn't. I want to be high again. I *want* to be *manic.* I want to be myself again. I'm taking myself off this shit."

"Bruce, that's not a good idea," she said. "Listen, you have to trust me. You have to give it time. I've dealt with many patients like you. If you go off your medicine, it's going to get worse, and then it will be harder to stop it."

"But..."

"Bruce, would you just shut up a minute. God, you're impossible. Let me finish. *You just started taking it.* You must have patience. You have to find your lithium level before we can get to the root of your problems. It's the only way we can tell what's going on inside of you."

"You have no idea what's going on inside of me! Nobody does! I'm a walking torture chamber!"

"Now, Bruce, calm down. When are you seeing Dr. Williams?"

"Uh, I dunno. Next week or something."

"I'll call her and see if she can see you tomorrow. She'll adjust your lithium. Just sit there and let me call her."

"Yeah, yeah, yeah."

When I told Dr. Williams everything that had been going on with me, she nodded her head a bunch of times and said, "I'll tell you what I'm gonna do, Mr. Goldstein . . ." She raised me from 1,200 mg up to 1,600 mg of lithium. But all that did was add more side effects to the list. Basically, the side effects were the only effects. My thoughts were jumbled. I couldn't think straight. But even if I did happen to think of a sentence to say, different words would come out as if somebody else was saying them. But words hardly mattered because now I was *sl-sl-slurrring*. I wasn't on lithium. I was on *slithium*. It was so embarrassing. I had an overwhelming case of cotton mouth. A dried fruit-lip lisp. I sounded retarded, like I had a speech impediment. My pale pink, white-speckled tongue stuck to my gums like it was trapped in a jar of peanut butter. Drinking a lot of water quenched that problem, but that just fed into another one. Lithium made me pee excessively. My bladder didn't give much warning either. "I gotta go now!" was how fast it let me know about it. Between lithium and my inflamed intestines, I practically lived in the bathroom. I had a lot of close calls. One night I didn't make it. I peed in my pants outside my apartment building. Enough was enough already. Add crazy back acne and night sweats to the list. Increasing lithium was clearly not the answer. After about a week of special effects, when the stubborn depression still didn't lift, Dr. Williams cautiously prescribed me an antidepressant to work with the lithium. "But we have to be careful Mr. Goldstein, antidepressants work differently when it comes to manic depressives," she said. "Too much serotonin to your brain could trigger mania, Mr. Goldstein, and then you'd be back right where you started again."

The first antidepressant she prescribed was Prozac. The little green-and-cream-colored pill that helped thousands of depressed people get better. It didn't do anything for me except make me nauseous and kill what little sex drive I had left. Next up was Paxil. It sounded like a breakfast cereal. I took it for a week or so but Brucie didn't like it. It messed up my stomach. *Next.* Bring in the Zoloft. I took Zoloft for a week or so, à la lithium. The results were in: still miserable. I had lost all hope. I was convinced I was going to be stuck in this mentally ill abyss for the rest of my existence. Dr. Williams begged to differ. She was committed to finding me the perfect psychopharmacological combo meal that would put an end to my never-ending mentalmorphosis.

"Hang in there Mr. Goldstein, *hang in there*," she said.

"Yeah, whatever."

To me, medicine was clearly not the answer. I was more depressed than before I started taking it. I didn't care that lithium "the miracle salt" helped save the lives of celebrities. It wasn't helping me. It was sucking the last remains of life out of me. I was so tempted to throw it away. But I didn't. Not this time. I kept taking my medicine like a good manic.

14

WORKING YOURSELF TO DEATH

The mornings were tough. Once my mother convinced me to leave
the house, I would stop in the middle of Madison Square Park. I'd
stare at the trees behind the iron pronged fences. One day this
overwhelming sadness came over me. I collapsed on a park bench
amidst the pigeons and squirrels. As tears ran down my face, I had
an epiphany. That this feeling I was experiencing must have been
what Edgar Allan Poe, Virginia Wolfe, Van Gogh, and the rest of
the mentally ill artists referred to as Melancholy. I smiled through
the beauty of misery. I felt like at least they understood me.

When I managed to get to work, I kept a very low profile. I
talked to whomever I had to talk to, and then I tucked myself back

in my cocoon where I would reflect on how my butterfly had gone into hibernation that gray day back in October when my system shut down. When I began my mental meltdown. The sign in my head read DO NOT DISTURB—MISERY IN PROGRESS. On the bright side, I had a window. Unfortunately, there was no bright side. It faced bricks. Thick gray mortar. And all day long, I just sat there.

Brick by brick. Thick gray mortar. These are my headquarters. Day by day. Hour by hour. I used to be happy. Now I rot and I sour. Blacker and blacker. Tick-tock and tick-tock. I had nobody to talk to in my lonely cell block. And I just sat there. *I just sat there. I just sat there.* Thinking. I just sat there. Buzzing. I just sat there. Biting. Gnawing on delicate skin. The salty flesh beneath the surface of where my hedged fingernails begin. I just sat there. Spitting red ripped bloody scalped skinnings. And I just sat there. Pick, pick, picking them out of my teeth. I just sat there. Thinking. Buzzing. Biting. I just sat there. Away from everybody. Alone. I just sat there. Slipping and slipping away from myself. I just sat there. Slipping and slipping away from myself. Talking. To nobody. But myself. Thinking and talking to nobody but myself. Waiting for nobody. Anybody. Somebody. Somebody please answer me. Somebody. Anybody. Nobody. Nobody was home. And I just sat there. Thinking and talking to nobody but myself. I just sat there. Deeper and deeper and deeper I sunk. I just sat there. Full of sorrow. No hope for tomorrow. A worthless slug. I just sat there. Waiting. The same old tapes that played in my head. And I just sat there. "I'll never be high again. I'll never be high again." And I just sat there. Staring and staring. Brick by brick. The silence . . . The silence . . . was making me sick. The eerie sound thickened. Under my skin. I just sat there. Picking the hair on my chinny, chin, chin. I just sat there. *I just sat there.* Until somebody banged on my door. "Bruce, you in there?"

"Uh, uh, uhhh." I wiped the sweat from my head. "Who is it?" I said.

The door opened. It was my boss, Marty Birnbaum. "Hey, Bruce, can I come in? I want to talk to you about something."

"Sure."

I prayed I was getting fired. I stood next to the garbage pail and waited to be released from my duty. Instead, the long-legged legend of an adman in the long navy blue sports jacket said, "Hey Bruce, you know that shoe campaign you did? Well, the client loved it and they wanna start shootin' right away. Since you're the art director on it, I want you to supervise it." *Supervise it.* As he was speaking, I felt beads of sweat on my head getting larger and larger, and his voice was fading in and out like I kept getting dunked into a barrel of water. "Bruce, we'd love for you to stay here the whole summer." *The whole summer.* The man was guaranteeing me $800 a day, five days a week, for three months; he was talking forty-eight grand for practically doing nothing, just a bunch of print ads for some shoe company, and all I could say was "Uhhhh . . . uhhhhhh." It was hard to listen to him when the voice in my head was speaking louder than his: *"Marty, as soon as you stop talking, I'm grabbing my backpack and you'll never see me again."*

"So, Bruce, what's it gonna be. You wanna do it?" he said.

"Uhhh," I told him. "I have to think about it."

"Okay—just let me know by the end of the week," he said and walked out.

I grabbed my shit and ran out of the building as quickly as I could. I headed downtown, and I kept running until I wound up in Washington Square Park. I sat in the circle with the freaks and the derelicts. I looked around. They didn't work. They didn't have any stress. Not all of them had shoes either. But some grunge dude in a red-and-black ripped-up flannel had a boom box that was playing Nirvana. The song "Lithium" came on. I laughed a little. "They're playing my song." Of course, Cobain blew his brains out with a shotgun when he couldn't take it anymore.

Dr. C must have sensed something was wrong because that night she called me at my apartment. We had this psychic-psychopath connection. "Bruce, I have a 10:30 available tomorrow morning and I want to see you," she said.

"Uhh, I don't know. What's the point anymore? It's hopeless."

"Bruce, we'll talk about it. I'll see you tomorrow. Now don't disappoint me."

I disappointed her. I should've never gone to see her that morning. I barged in on her like a bipolar bulldozer. "Enough is enough. This sucks and lithium sucks and therapy's a waste. C'mon, what the hell do we do here every week? I'm more fucked up now than when I first met you. What the hell are you doing for me? Huh? Huh? Huh?"

"Bruce, calm down, it takes time."

"Fuck time! I wanna be better now!"

Dr. C didn't say anything. She gave me the silent treatment. She turned her back on me and started flipping through a bunch of books, jotting things down. And when she was ready, she turned around. "Here," she said in a very cold voice.

"What's this?" My face froze. I got a lump in my throat. They were suicide hotlines.

"Oh, Doc, no. I don't need these. You got it all wrong. Really, Dr. C, I'm not that sick."

"I'm sorry, Bruce, but *yes you are.* I can't help you any longer. I'm sorry."

"But, but . . ."

"But nothing, Bruce. I'm sorry. I have another patient waiting. Time's up."

"What do you mean, time's up? You're just gonna drop me like that. We've been through so much together."

"Bruce, if you feel I haven't done anything, than maybe somebody else can help you."

"Nobody can help me! Nobody!" I stormed out of there.

Later that night, my sister Sharon called to wish me a Happy Birthday. *Was she kidding?*

"Sharon, I can't take it anymore! I can't live like this anymore! I'm sick of being depressed!"

"Bruce, Bruce, you're going to be okay."

"No! Don't lie to me! I'm never gonna get better! It's over!" I flung a chair across my apartment. I broke a mirror. "It's over!"

"What are you doing over there? You're scaring me." Sharon broke down. She couldn't hold her tears back any longer. She told me she was going to take the ferry into the city that second. "Bruce, Bruce, you're scaring me. I'm coming to take care of you."

"Sharon, no. It's late and it's dangerous. Mommy won't let you."

"I won't tell her. I'll sneak out."

"Sharon, no. Don't do it."

"Bruce, I love you."

What did she have to say that for? Now, I couldn't kill myself even if I wanted to.

"I don't want you to hurt yourself."

"Sharon, I love you, too," I said. "But you don't have to worry about me. I'm not going to kill myself. I just want it all to go away. I just want to be me again."

"You will be, Bruce, soon. I'm getting dressed as I'm talkin' to you. I'll be in the city in an hour and a half."

"Sharon. No. You don't have to."

"Yes, I do."

"Sharon, no! I'm just really scared, that's all. I don't want to go to work tomorrow. I can't go back there. I hate it there, Sharon. I hate being scared."

"So don't."

"What do you mean, *don't*."

"Don't go back there. Bruce, you're freelance. Take some time off. You quit your last job when you were depressed."

"Yeah, but what about the money?"

"Who cares about the money. I'll loan you money."

"You don't have any money."

"I got some. Take it. Bruce, I don't care. Your health is more important than stupid advertising. Listen to me. Call your boss tomorrow. Tell him something came up. You have to take some time off." The thought of not working had a calming effect on me, so I acted on it. The next morning, I called in sick—indefinitely. Sick in the head. "I have to take care of something personal," I said. And I was a free man. From the corporate world anyway. Not my head.

15

GO, DOG. GO!

I gave myself the summer to find the meaning of life—to find happiness—to find me again. I wanted to enjoy what I did. I needed a purpose. A good cause. What I really needed was a new obsession. I needed to be passionate about something. A new project. A new Paige. A new career. I didn't want to go back to advertising. If only there was something to take my mind off of me, while I was trying to redefine me. If only there was some manic magical potion to heal me. I had a few months to find some meaning to my meaningless life. On my mark, get set, go! If I could just get myself out of my bed.

That had gotten a lot more difficult now that my mother was out of commission with her menopause. And Sharon was in school. But she came to visit me whenever she could. She took me for walks down side streets to avoid people. She helped me go food shopping and did my laundry. She hid with me in dark movie theaters. I caught her crying once during *Leaving Las Vegas.* She said she was upset about Nicholas Cage killing himself with alcohol, but I didn't believe her. It must have been tough for her to see her big brother—who she had always looked up to—scared to go up to the counter and buy a cookie in a café. Sharon made me feel safe, but then she had to go home. Everybody always did. No matter how much they loved me and I loved them, everybody had their own lives to live. You could only depend on people so much.

I spent my days wandering. Watching people from a distance. Wondering who was happy. Maybe the hot dog guy was? Maybe I'll be homeless? Live in a box. No bills.

Sunrise. Sunset. I still didn't have any answers. This was going to be the worst summer ever. Then one day I sunk really low. I felt like calling it quits. I planned to go home and not wake up in the morning. But then I felt a sudden urge to go to Barnes & Noble, the one on Sixth Avenue. So I went. When I got there I wanted to turn around. I was terrified of dealing with the public. But something made me go in.

As I was walking to the back of the coffee shop area to go wallow in my journal, this really tall man with a greenish complexion and big boots who was walking next to me tripped over something. He dropped his transistor radio, his coffee, and his books went flying all over the place. I bent down to help him pick up his stuff. Instead of saying thank you, he didn't even look at me. He just grunted, "Ug-ugg." And he went back to his table. "That was weird," I thought.

A few minutes later, I felt a tap on my shoulder. It was that large man again. He was holding an orange book. Goliath's hand was bigger than my foot. "Ug-ugg," he grunted again. The whole café was staring at us. "Take it," some woman whispered. So I took the children's book from the gentle giant. "Thank you," I said.

"Ug-ugg," and he split.

When I brought the orange book closer to my face to get a better look, my eyes almost popped out of my head. My whole body started vibrating. I got chills.

"Oh my God! Oh my God!" I couldn't believe what I saw.

"Oh my God! Oh my God!" There was a dog on the cover.

"Oh my God! Oh my God!" I couldn't believe what it was called: *Go, Dog. Go!*

In a split second it all made complete sense to me. The answer to all of my problems had been there all along. Get a dog! Since that day Paige took me into that pet store to find a puppy to love to replace my love for her. "Holy shit!" Since Martha's Vineyard, when Barney talked to me when nobody else would. There was my attraction toward my Black Dog T-shirt. I just had to have it. I looked down. I was wearing it. Oh my God! Oh my God! There was Dr. C and the way her poodle, Marvin, always looked at me. And there was that day with Satan in Central Park when the ladybug flew in my book and circled the words *Animals show us the way!* Those were the words that would set me free. "Go, Dog. Go!" That was the message. Loud and clear. And it came straight from my Master himself. It was written in code. It was biblical. It was the answer I had been waiting for. It couldn't have been more obvious. The book might have been called *Go, Dog. Go!* But the truth was right there. "God Dog. God!" The message was Go get dog. And for the first time in my life I knew exactly what I had to do. I bought the book, and ran the hell out of the bookstore like a rabid Jack Nicholson terrier.

"I'm getting a dog! I'm getting a dog!" If I didn't tell some-body the good news fast my head was going to explode. So I called up everybody I knew starting with Allen.

"Allen! Allen! I'm getting a dog! I'm getting a dog! I'm finally gonna do it! What do you think? What do you think?"

"Bruce, that's amazing. I can't believe it. You're gonna love having a dog, you'll see. Oh this is so exciting. Wait till I tell Barney."

"Ricky! Ricky! I'm getting a dog! I'm getting a dog! What do you think? What do you think?"

"Whoa, Bruce. That's a lot of responsibility. Are you sure you're up to that? Are you sure you can make that kind of com-mitment? Bruce, having a dog is like having a kid."

"Yeah, I know it's gonna be tough, but I'll be able to handle to it."

"Well good for you, because I wouldn't be able to do it."

I called up my friend Gina. She had just rescued a cute pit bull boxer-mix puppy from a crack house. "Gina! Gina! I'm getting a dog! I'm getting a dog! What do you think? What do you think?"

"Wow, Bruce. That's amazing! You haven't sounded this good in such a long time. I'm so psyched for you. I can't wait to meet him. And neither can my little Sezie girl."

After I called all my friends, I called up my shrinks. Dr. Williams, my medicine woman, was all for it and so was Winston, her one-hundred-and-twenty-pound Akita. "Well Mr. Goldstein, I think getting a dog is a terrific idea. Animals are great therapy." I hesitated calling Dr. C. The last time we spoke was when I stormed out of her office. I hoped she still liked me.

"Dr. C! Dr. C! I'm getting a dog! I'm getting a dog! What do you think? What do you think?"

"Bruce, slow down. Are you okay? Did you throw away your pills? You sound a little manic. You're not manic, are you?"

"No, I'm not manic. I'm getting a dog."

"Bruce, are you sure that's a good idea? Last time I saw you, you weren't doing too well."

"But you suggested I get a dog a few months ago."

"Yeah, I did, but are you sure this is the right time, Bruce? Having a dog is a lot of work. It's a lot of responsibility."

"Yeah, I know. I know. But I'm fine now. I'm better than fine. I feel amazing! I haven't felt this alive in such a long time."

"That's what I'm afraid of. We don't need any manic episodes now. But if you feel you're ready to get a dog, well all right then. Just keep me posted, okay? Call me anytime you want. I'm always here."

"I will. I will. But I won't have to. I'm better now. Thanks, Dr. C. I gotta go!"

I saved my mother for last. Good thing.

"You're what? No way, Bruce. You're not getting a dog. Now stop talking crazy talk. A dog's not for you. You have to be home to walk him and feed him. You're never home. And dogs are messy and expensive. Bruce, don't even discuss this with me. I have to make your father supper."

"But Mom, it's my life. I'm getting a dog. I'm getting a puppy. C'mon, it's the only thing that makes me happy."

"Get fish. Get goldfish if you feel the need for a pet. Your cousin Howie has goldfish. But don't you dare get a dog. You'll be sorry. Bruce, I don't want to find out that you—"

"Ma, I gotta go. You're stressing me out. I'm getting a dog."

"Bruce, don't do it. I'm warning you."

"I'm hanging up now."

"Bruce, I'm serious."

"Bye, love ya." Click. She'd come around eventually.

I spent the rest of the afternoon singing. "I'm getting a dog! I'm getting a dog! I'm getting a dog. Yippee!" I just had no idea what kind I wanted. So I hit the streets of New York to go dog watching. It became my pet project. From now on every day was dog day afternoon.

16

IN SEARCH OF THE PERFECT PUPPY

I had lived in the city for two years, and I had never noticed how much barking there was before. I felt like a little kid, and the Big Apple was my giant canine candy store. Uptown, downtown, East Side, and West, everywhere I wandered there were so many different kinds to choose from. There were big ones and small ones. Fat ones and tall ones. And I didn't know the names of half of them. Oh, the sweet smells of Lassie, Old Yeller, and Benji filled the air. There were white ones and black ones. Stuck-up looking ones and happy-go-lucky looking ones. I saw a Rin Tin Tin look-alike in Times Square. I saw a St. Bernard eating sausage and peppers at a street fair. I saw droolers. I saw spots. I saw a fu-fu poodle with a really bad haircut. I saw way too many dogs wearing red bandannas tied around their necks. I saw a horny dog humping some guy's leg in the Farmers Market. There were bulldogs and boxers. I saw a Springer spaniel frolicking about. I watched a Basset hound dragging his ears on the ground. I spotted a Dalmatian jumping up and down. I saw the cutest German shepherd with his pink tongue hanging out. I saw dogs playing fetch in the dog runs. I saw an unhappy dog owner deal with his dog having the runs. I saw a miniature Doberman pinscher. I saw a hairy husky. I saw a yuppie walking a pretentious lookin' puppy. I saw dogs that were so muscular they looked like they worked out. I saw fat dogs that looked like they spent the day lying on the couch. I saw leg lifters. Sidewalk lickers. Butt sniffers. There were golden retrievers. Dogs that looked like beavers. One afternoon I sat on the grass and watched a gray dog in Sheep's Meadow catch a Frisbee like a skinny wide receiver. I saw a yellow dog wearing the tackiest red-and-plaid vest. The dog had an embarrassed look on his face that said, "Don't blame me, my owner did this." And whoever said pit bulls were vicious didn't see Schnookie give some lady a big sloppy kiss.

Then to my surprise, I had never realized until I opened up my puppy possibility eyes nice and wide, that dogs weren't just walking the streets. They were hanging out on the inside. Bopping in Barney's. Browsing at Bloomingdale's. Lounging with the locksmith. Down on all fours in sassy shoe stores. But of all the dogs I saw, nothing amazed me more than when I watched a seeing-eye dog lead a woman into the subway. I just stood there on Sixty-third Street. How the hell did the dog know what train to take?

After days of fire hydrant shopping, I was so frustrated. I still didn't know what dog was right for me. So I ran like a maniac down Park Avenue and I stormed the doors of the Barnes &

Noble Superstore on Seventeenth Street. I ran right up the escalator, jumped off on the second floor, and ran straight for the doggie section, where I grabbed every canine book that I could carry. Then I ran back up the escalator, and I went up, and I jumped off on the next floor and I ran past my old psychology section, my old self-help section, and I headed straight for the caffeine section. I ordered the usual—a large black coffee—and I headed straight for the *sugar, sugar, sugar* section. I plopped down my books, and I took over one of those big tables. I spread out my dog literature all over the place, and I started flipping pages and flipping pages from "A" to Yorkie. Large and glossy hound dogs, Irish setters, and cocker spaniels flashed before me. But they just weren't doing it for me. So I just kept on flipping pages. I flew through *The Ultimate Dog Book*, saying "No, no, no." I didn't want a sheep dog, or a Pomeranian, or a wire-haired pointing Griffon. "That's it." Over my second large black coffee, I made a decision. "I'm getting a black one!" I'm getting a black one. I just couldn't see myself with any other color. Just like I couldn't see myself in a brown leather jacket. Leave the brown dogs, the Rhodesian ridgebacks, for the brunettes. I had a simple philosophy. Guys with black hair looked good in black. I wanted the Black Dog on my T-shirt. But I had no idea what breed he was. So I kept on flipping pages and flipping pages stopping at all the black doggie possibilities.

Rottweilers were cool but they had brown patches. Newfoundlands were too massive. Pugs were too tiny. They looked like miniature ET's. A Doberman pinscher looked like a skinny Rottie. Schipperkes were too wolfy. Bouvier des Flandres, too hard to pronounce and too curly. A Great Dane, too Andre the Giant. And I kept flipping pages and flipping pages and flipping pages and flipping pages until my heart skipped a beat when I finally found him. On page 58.

My barking black stallion. His coat was jet black, not a hint of another color anywhere on him. He had the muscular body of a bull. The thighs of a quarterback. Webbed feet. A tail like an otter. A big block head, like an anvil. And he was smiling at me. My angel was a centerfold. He was beautiful and proud and happy and cool. He looked intelligent. A champion. He was a black Labrador retriever. And he was perfect, until I read the fine print. It said that males weighed approximately eighty pounds when they were fully grown. "Shit." He was too big for my apartment. I needed a backyard for my new best friend to run around and chase squirrels. But then I read in one of my books that as long as I took him outside and gave him plenty of exercise, he'd be fine. He'd be perfectly healthy. Dogs were like humans. If I didn't go out, I'd have a bubble butt the size of a beanbag, too. "Cool! I'm getting a Lab!" This was too good to be true. "I'm getting a black dog!" I started vibrating again. "I want him! I want him!" I pointed at my photogenic friend.

The more I read about Labrador retrievers, the more I wanted one. Labs were the most popular dog in America. They had everything going for them. Not only were they good looking, but they were so smart that they used them as seeing-eye dogs and for drug sniffing. As far as grooming was concerned, there was nothing to be concerned about. Labs were short haired, and they only shed twice a year. And since they had such a great temperament—gentle and friendly—they were great with children for when I got better and had a family. And last but not least, Labs were very loyal lovable beasts, always eager to please, so I wouldn't have to worry about making a commitment and then getting my heart broken. Unless of course the furry flatleaver left me like Paige did. One day he'd just decide to run away with some Upper West Side poodle named Fifi.

I was so excited my eyes were popping out of my face. I couldn't sit still. I could hardly wait. I kept getting up and down and up and down, and I started to walk around my table in circles like a bloodhound trapped in a fish tank, mumbling, talking to myself, flipping through Labrador retriever books one after another, oohing and ahhing. "Ah look at the puppy!" I wanted to tell the whole damn bookstore how happy I was. But why tell when you can show. I started salivating like the manic mammal that I was. "I want one! I want one! I want one!" And I wanted a new one. Not a used one. I wanted a new one. Not a misused one. I wanted a puppy. I wanted to raise him myself. I wanted to teach my new dog new tricks. There was plenty of time for him to grow into the black dog on my T-shirt. I couldn't handle an old dog set in his ways. A dog with problems. Ailments. Bad habits. I had too many problems of my own. I wanted to be the first to influence him. I wanted to always be there for him. I wanted to hug him and nurture him and watch him grow. I just knew I was going to give my puppy a very good home. And I was definitely getting a male one. I just felt more comfortable with a boy dog. A woman was a completely different animal.

Getting a dog was going to be an amazing experience. I had so much to learn. I hadn't felt interested in anything like this since I first got into advertising. Since I fell in love with Paige. I hadn't felt this naive either. I knew nothing about women before Paige. So no matter how many dog books I read, I knew I wouldn't truly understand canines until I raised one. Until I loved one. But at this moment in time I could only think of dogs on the psychological level of a nursery rhyme: "See Spot fetch. See Spot run." It was impossible for me to imagine loving an animal. After losing Paige, after losing myself, it was difficult for me to imagine loving anything again. But before I could even think about loving a puppy, I would have to find a real one.

The one. *Well, what the hell am I still sitting here for*, I thought. So I jumped up out of my seat, and I ran down the escalator and out the door. Since all the pet stores were closed, this little piggy ran all the way home. Operation Labrador would begin first thing in the morning. I was so excited I could hardly sleep. The hell with counting sheep. I stayed up all night long counting puppies.

Good morning, New York City! After I took the fastest shower in the East, I washed down my lithium and Zoloft with a half a pot of Big Kauna kona coffee from Kauai. Getting dressed was easy. Khaki shorts, my worn thin Black Dog T-shirt with the yellow armpits of course, and my freaky blue sneakers because I was going to be on my feet a lot. On my mark. Get set. Go! Go where? There had to be over one hundred pet shops in the city. And I had no idea which one of them had my dog. It didn't matter though. I was prepared to hit every doggie department store until I found him. So I ran out of my apartment with a pocketful of tokens and a mother-load of hope. The first place I went was named something like Dogs R Us. They might as well have carried giraffes because they only had a doofy Dalmatian, a loud howling husky puppy, and some neurotic dog with crazy red hair that wouldn't stop slobbering. I didn't give up. Unfortunately, the next place I went I didn't have much luck either. Mutt. Mutt. Mutt. The closest thing they had to a black pup was a greyhound mixed with God knows what. By foot, by subway, by taxi, I went to every Petland Discounts and Petco on Manhattan island. Not once did I ask how much any puppies were in any windows because money was no object. But that didn't matter anyway. Because of all the dogs I saw, not one of them resembled the one on my T-shirt. All I wanted was a black Labrador re-triever puppy, but these used pet dealers, these sharks, didn't understand me. In Chelsea, some tall, skinny guy with a Texas mustache tried to push a gray dog with bird legs on me. He said Whippet good. I said Whippet bad, "I want a black Labrador retriever, please." Downtown on Bleeker Street, some freak with a green streak in his hair tried to push some pit bull on me. "He won't bite." Yeah, right. Then if I wasn't frustrated enough, this bulky biker lady in Tribeca tried to sell me a cat. "He acts like a dog," she said.

Over the next few days of pounding the puppy pavement, nothing changed. I saw all kinds of black dogs, but there was something wrong with all of them. They were either too old and skinny or they had white splotches or maybe I was too damn picky. They just weren't my type. Whatever my type was. "Maybe I'm not supposed to get a dog," I thought. "It can't possibly take this long to find him."

Since I had been to every pet store in the city, it was time to increase my options, conquer new territory. I let my fingers do the walking. I bought every newspaper that I could carry. Then I grabbed a red magic marker by its neck, and together we circled every pet store, kennel, and shelter in the tristate area. I zoomed in on Queens and Long Island. "Dog world! The Barking Barn! Yuppie Puppy! I'm there!" There was just a little problem. I had to drive there. I had a car—that wasn't the problem. I forgot how to drive. And I was terrified to get behind the wheel. I figured I'd better call Allen.

Allen was delighted to take me. He was more excited than I was about getting a dog. "Ya hear that Barney!" he screamed into the receiver.

The first kennel we walked into smelled like a big bathroom. Wall-to-wall feces-infested cages. A canine concentration camp. All the dogs looked so sad and sickly. It was like a prison for little angels. They were barking, "Let me outta here, please."

I felt so horrible. I wanted to set them all free. But I didn't find the right one for me.

Next stop: North Shore Animal League, the mother of dog shelters. It was a very clean facility. And they had tons of dogs. I saw about fifty of them. Mostly mutts and more mutts. Nothing for me. Then Allen called me over to show me these two German shepherd pups. "Bruce, get'm. Get'm both or I will," he said. "They just got here today. They're adorable. Yeah, I know they're not Labs but wouldja just look at him, look at dat face. C'mon hurry up, before somebody else adopts them. Puppies go fast here." They were like fresh produce. A couple of cute heads of lettuce.

"Okay, okay." I stuck my fingers in the cage. They didn't bite any off. So I supposed that was a good sign. But there was just no chemistry. Part of me wanted to take one of them anyway. Who cared if he wasn't all black and he wasn't a Lab. I was so drained. "Enough already." I got so frustrated. So did Allen. "Bruce, c'mon, get one of them. They're perfect."

He was right. All of God's creatures were perfect. But these guys just weren't for me. I was still waiting for my li'l black stallion to lift me off my feet. Call me crazy. But I had fallen in love with the idea that it would be puppy love at first sight. I wouldn't even have to go looking for him. He'd point his paw my way when I least expected it. What I was really hoping for was that just when I was about to give up, just when I had my share of doggy despair, the little fella would appear out of nowhere. He might bat his eyelashes at me. He might whimper and wiggle. He might pee on me. He'd use every ounce of body language to translate, "Hey, guy with the goatee, pick me." But I kept being reminded *puppy after puppy* that finding your doggy soul mate didn't work that way. I didn't give up. I believed in doggy destiny.

And at the pinnacle of my picking-the-perfect-puppy, the more I couldn't find one the more I became obsessed in finding one.

Day after day. Shelter after shelter. Pet store after pet store. Web site after Web site, I stayed up all night. Labs.com Labs.net Labs.pet. Goddamn it. I devoured the want ads till my eyes were crusty and red.

"Labs. Must sell, 10 weeks. M/Blk, vet checked, shots."

"Lab Pups M/F Blk/yellow. Adorable. Fam. Raised."

I didn't know what a lot of the abbreviations meant, but they sounded good so I kept on calling and leaving messages. They all pretty much said the same thing. Bad timing. Either their bitch just had a litter or she wasn't due for months. Or she was in "heat." I needed the pick of the litter, any litter now. So I called nearly every breeder until I finally found some puppies in Connecticut. The only problem was they were all out of black. They just had yellow and chocolate in stock.

"Don't you want a nice chocolate one?"

"No thanks."

Everybody had nice chocolate and yellow ones. No thanks. And then I finally found a person in Roslyn that had a black one. Twelve weeks old, twenty pounds. He would've been perfect but I was set on a little guy. A really little guy. Six weeks old, approximately ten pounds to be exact. I wanted the newest puppy on the planet. I wanted to be the little guy's parent from as close to incubation as possible. I read that six and a half weeks was the youngest you could take a puppy away from his mommy. Before I could take over as his parental guardian.

I shook my head left to right. Hands in pockets. I looked at my feet. Once again I had set myself up for disappointment. I had created an imaginary larger-than-life black Lab puppy in my mind that didn't exist. Just like I created an ideal advertising world, and a fantasy, carefree unleashed love life. One let-down after another. Puppy hunting was for the birds. My moods were swinging the puppy pendulum. One day I wanted a dog. The next day I feared to be near one. My depression was defeating me. Fine with me. It was Friday night. It had been the longest week of my life. Enough was enough. I was done with this dog nonsense. I gave up. I drew my blinds shut. Then I sent myself to bed without any supper and without any reason to get up. I didn't brush my teeth, I didn't take my medicine, and I climbed up in my loft. I crushed my head in the pillow. I had nothing to live for. I had bad thoughts. Really bad thoughts.

The phone rang.

"I'm not home," I said. "And I'm never coming back." I let the machine get it.

"Hello, hello, this message is for Bruce. My name is Dorothy. I'm from Stonehaven Labradors. You called me a few days ago, about my ad in the *Daily News*. You left a message with my nephew. Sorry it took me so long to get back to you. Anyway, if you're interested I have two black Labrador puppies left, just gimme a buzz. My number is—"

Here we go again. I flew out of my bed and bounced down the stairs. But I wasn't expecting anything. I didn't believe God carried the model that I had requested. Why should she be any different? I dove for the phone anyway.

"Hello, hello. What color are they?" the puppy pessimist said.

"Oh, you are home. Well, I have two puppies left, if you're still interested."

"Yeah, yeah, I know. I know. What color are they? What color are they?"

"They're black."

So far so good. But I didn't get excited yet.

"And how old are they?" I said. I felt like I was at an auction bidding for a one of a kind porcelain puppy. Do I hear six and a half weeks? Why, yes I did.

"Six and a half weeks," she said.

"Really, really and how much do they weigh?"

"About nine to ten pounds," Dorothy said. I couldn't believe it. I couldn't believe it.

"Oh, my God. I'll take him." I said. "When can I come to get him?"

"Well, Bruce don't you want to hear a little about the two of them first? They're totally different."

"Yeah, yeah, yeah. Tell me. Should I come now?"

Dorothy took her time describing the two dogs. She said one of them was shy and quiet, but with a nice temperament. "He'll make a great pet. He'll give you so much love and affection."

Next.

"Now, the other one, he's special. My nephew William is totally crazy about. He's already named him "'Christopher.'"

"Why's he so special?"

"He has a unique personality. He's a bit more unpredictable than the other one. But they're both beautiful."

"Well, I want the special one," I said. "I'll be over in a few minutes."

It wasn't that simple.

"Well, Bruce, I have to be honest with you. There's a couple coming by tonight to look at the pups."

My heart jumped. On top of that Dorothy informed me that she lived over two-and-a-half hours away from the city, all the way out in the boonies. "Bohemia, Long Island," she said.

Wherever the hell that was. But that wasn't all of it. Some crazy storm was coming.

"Hurricane? What hurricane?" I asked.

"You're kidding, right? Where have you been?" Dorothy said. "Haven't you watched the news?"

"Not lately. It's too depressing."

"Well, Hurricane Bertha is coming tonight. She's a nor'-easter. They say she's gonna visit us around midnight. They're telling everybody in our area to just stay home. You've got to be cuckoo if you want to drive."

"Yeah, but I want that puppy. The special puppy. I've been looking all over for him. Please, you have no idea how bad I have to see him. If I can't come tonight, I'll definitely be there tomorrow morning. Please hold him. I'll be there no matter what. Please, I'll give him such a great home. I promise."

"Well, the couple didn't say which one they're interested in."

"Good, good. I'll be there tomorrow no matter what."

"I can't make any promises and I can't make you not drive, but if you do, be careful. Please. We're talkin' one-hundred-and-fifteen-mile-per-hour-winds," she said. Then she gave me directions.

"Oh thank you, Dorothy, thank you so much. I'll be there no matter what."

"I know you will, Bruce," she said. "I have no doubt."

"Yes!" The second I hung up I jumped up in the air like I was in a Toyota commercial. I screamed, "Oh what a feeling" kind of stuff and I did the "I'm getting a puppy. I'm getting a puppy!" Hora all the way around my apartment. The fact that somebody else might swipe my bundle of puppy made me want a dog more than ever. That dog. My golden goose. I had a good feeling on this one. I could feel *him* in my heart. Even though I hadn't seen him or that he might be snatched up by sun up I knew we were meant to be together. But all I could do was wait. And pray. This was doggy destiny. I looked up toward the sky through my loft bed ceiling.

"Dear God," I said. "Please save me my puppy."

17

THE WIZARD OF OZZY

We had been driving forever. Shit was blowing everywhere. The closer we got to exit 56, the more I got scared. The more I wanted to tell Allen, "Forget about it, I changed my mind, let's just turn around." I mean how the hell was I going to pull this off? The commitment. The responsibility. My mother was right. I couldn't take care of a dog when I could barely take care of myself. I mean was this puppy really going to help me anyway? Who knew if he'd even like me? I mean how could he like me when I didn't like me? I drew a sad face with my finger on the gray misty window. Then I drew a paw print. I was terrified to go through with this but what else was there? I had tried everything to get better. Therapy and all the chemical cocktails. The only alternatives left were being institutionalized or a bullet in my temple. I felt so overwhelmed. I had nobody to talk to. Allen meant well, but he couldn't possibly understand the depths of my quicksand. I made up my mind. I wasn't in any condition to take care of another life. It was bad enough if something happened to me. But God forbid something happened to the puppy. That's something I couldn't live with. So once again, the answer was, "No, I am not getting a dog." I was about to say something to Allen but before I could get the words out this feeling came over me to just shut my mouth. I felt tingles shoot throughout my body. I got goose bumps on my arms under my red and black flannel. And just like that I knew I had to keep going. That I was on the right track. That we weren't going to crash. That I had to meet this puppy.

So I wiped the sweat and rain from my brow. I told myself to breathe. And I started to calm down. For about five seconds. How the hell could I calm down? Suppose "Christopher" got adopted already. Suppose that couple came by last night that Dorothy warned me about. Suppose they gave him one look and said, "We'll take *him*. Right now."

Well I couldn't take it. *I couldn't take it.* That was my pet. My new best friend. I got this heavy feeling in my heart. I felt like he was a part of me and I hadn't even met him yet. There was no way I was aborting this mission. This mission was possible. There was no stopping us now. Allen, full speed ahead. "I'm getting a puppy. I'm getting this puppy," I said. The more I thought about him not being there, the more I wanted him. The more I needed him. The more I prayed he'd be there. "Hold on puppy. Hold on little guy. We're on our way. Daddy's coming."

"Allen, Allen, drive faster. Can't you drive faster?"

Please, God. Let him be there.

And after three hours of treading water, we finally got off at the exit ramp. "Fifty-six, that's it!" Bohemia, Long Island. Bertha—was—here. The signs were everywhere. Trees were knocked down, blocked roads. A sycamore crushed a car. Flashing lights. Fire trucks. Telephone poles were blowing back and forth like weeds in a swamp. Green leaves carpeted floors. And the rain was slowing down, of course. I rolled down the window and stuck my head out. I looked up at the peanut butter and jelly sky. The grape clouds were moving really quickly east. It seemed that Bertha, the tempest, the temptress, this wet windy beast had somewhere else to be. "Bruce, where to?" Allen asked me.

I took out the soggy, ink-running directions from my pocket and navigated. "Thataway." We made lefts and rights and read blurry signs and stopped at a couple of traffic lights. "Allen, one more block. One more block and we should be there."

"Bruce, are you ready?" he said.

"Yeah, I guess."

"'Cause there it is."

The house was a ranch. Yellow, wooden. Little House on the Prairie-ish. It was surrounded by a dirty brown fence. Rustic. There was a naked oak tree guarding the entry. A survivor of the storm. Proud that it was still standing. A rusty blue pickup truck was parked in the driveway; a green sports utility vehicle was parked on the street. And my heart was beating like a Casio drum kit. Nervous? I felt like I was going on some kind of job interview, or a blind date. Sweaty palms, armpits, bubbling intestines. But this was the moment I had been waiting for. "Here goes nothing."

When we got out of the car, I stepped in a giant puddle. But then I had a better omen. I walked through a gasoline rainbow. Red, violet, yellow. On the other side of that doorway could be my pot-bellied puppy. "Allen let's go, let's go."

We followed the brown-bricked road. We followed the sidewalk up to the front door. The whole thing was freaky. We had just driven a million miles through a hurricane in a car named *Toto* to see a woman named *Dorothy* about a magical munchkin that might rid me of my misery. And hmmm, what will I call him?

The place looked deserted. The buzzer was broken. So I knocked on the screen door. When nobody showed up, I said, "What the hell?" I wanted to beat off any potential puppy purchasers so I grabbed the handle, turned it a little. "Well, it's not locked."

"Bruce, don't you think we should wait?" cowardly Allen said. "C'mon, let's wait."

Too late. *The door is ajar.* "Allen, we're not in New York anymore."

"Hello, anybody home?"

Still no answer. So we walked into the living room. It was a normal living room: brown furniture, green shaggy rug, black-and-white pictures of dogs and people—except for the fact that there were two giant wooden sandbox looking things side by side smack-dab in the middle. They were like six feet wide and two feet high, no roof. "What the hell are those things for?" We walked closer to investigate. It still hadn't occurred to me that this was called "Breaking and entering."

"Hello, Dorothy, are you here?"

"Bruce, listen. Over there?" Allen said.

Somebody was snoring. It was coming from one of the sandboxes. We approached them slowly. One foot at a time. I bent down to look inside.

"Oh, my God."

It was an amazing sight. Precious, just precious. And there were *two* of them just like Dorothy had said. Black ones. No bigger than chubby guinea pigs. They were curled up in a corner snuggled up against each other. "We made it. We made it. That couple must've changed their mind or something." They were no doubt, the healthiest, cleanest puppies I'd ever seen in my life. *"Wow!"* was how Allen put it. They looked like pricey stuffed animals from FAO Schwartz, except they were alive. More than alive. They were radiant. Coats like black velvet. Paw pads straight off the animal assembly line. And they had this pleasant puppy smell. We had certainly come to the right dog house. I just had one little problem. How was I supposed to know which one was "the special puppy"? I wanted the special one. Well, time would tell. So I sat down Indian style alongside the crib and tried to figure it out.

Dorothy had told me on the phone that there was always one Lab in each litter that was more outgoing than the others. "He's the first one to open his eyes, the most energetic, the smartest one," she said. "Bruce, I can always tell who has the most personality. But I can't take all the credit. My little nephew is the real talent of the family." She told me that William had a knack for sniffing out the elite of the litter, who he would then christen "Christopher." He had named all the special ones Christopher from the last eight litters.

"Why Christopher?" I asked.

Well, it made perfect sense. "William's best friend was named Christopher," she said "They were the cutest kids. They did everything together. But then William and his mom moved away to live with me. Well, I don't have to tell you, William was heartbroken, and he never stopped missing Christopher. So ever since then William found a best friend in every litter. He got pretty attached to some of them. And Bruce, not to make you feel uncomfortable, but William's especially fond of the one you're coming to look at," she said. "And there is something *really special* about this one."

"Isn't William gonna be upset about somebody taking his friend again?" I said. "I don't want to do that to him."

"No, he'll be all right. He's used to it. William knows the rules. He knows he has to say good-bye when somebody wants to adopt them."

That didn't make it any easier on the potential owner. After much thought I knew I had to go. I'd cross that little kid bridge when I got there. Besides maybe he wouldn't even be there. Sure enough, when we arrived at the house he wasn't. Nobody was. It was just me and Allen and the two pups in the sandbox.

"Hi," somebody said. My heart stopped for a second.

We jumped. This freckle-faced, little boy missing more than a few teeth had come out of nowhere to greet us. He looked about six, and he was wearing some kind of OshKosh B'Gosh looking get-up. "I'm William. What's your name?"

"Uh, I'm Bruce and that's Allen."

"My Aunt Dorothy said to come say hello. She's out back feeding the goats."

Goats?

"I see you met Christopher," he giggled. "He's my best friend."

Great.

"Oh yeah? Well, which one is he?"

"That one," he pointed.

"How can you tell?" I asked. "They're both sleeping."

"Yeah, but Christopher's smiling. I'll get him."

William stepped over the little fence into the box. "Come here booger, come here." He poked the puppy in his fur ball of a butt with his finger until he woke up. Then he picked him up and put him in my face. *"Hi, I'm Christopher, woof,"* William said in a doggie voice. Before I could say, "No, don't," he had plopped the baby in my lap. He left his kid on my doorstep. He had caught me so off guard that I didn't even say "hi" back. I didn't say anything to the puppy. I mean, what do you say to a dog? I felt so uncomfortable. I clammed up. Shell shock. I could barely move a muscle. I was rigid as a marble coffee table. The dog wasn't. He walked around my lap in circles till he found the right spot. "Now what?" I was trapped. My heart was beating a mile a minute. My mind was racing. I was so scared that I couldn't even pet him. I was so overwhelmed. Then, as if I wasn't under enough pressure, Allen got so excited, which to me was the same as violent. He threw his unwanted opinion in. "Oh Bruce, you have to get this puppy! He's unbelievable! He's amazing! He's the best looking Labrador puppy I've ever seen! I mean look how clean he is and shiny!" he screamed.

"Allen, *Allen*, not now, please."

"But Bruce he's exactly what you've wanted."

"Allen, not now!" People who weren't *depressed* just didn't get it. Christopher might have been the best looking puppy on the planet, I could've just won the goddamned friggin' lottery, but that didn't mean anything while I was self-detonating. Edgy. I was very edgy. Irritable beyond reason. I kept touching my face, pulling on my hope earring. The slightest peep made me jumpy. Real and imaginary.

"Allen, back up, and stop touching me."

"But I'm not touching you, Bruce."

I couldn't breathe. "Allen please. Just gimme a second, gimme a second . . ."

"*Grrrrrrr.*"

"Oh great." Somehow with all my racket going on, the puppy had fallen asleep. He looked so peaceful nestled between my knee caps that I remained seated. I liked him when he was sleeping. When he breathed, his coat shimmered like an imported fabric from Bali.

Unfortunately, twenty minutes later, when nap time was over and I still didn't know what I was going to say to him, I was really beating myself up about it. I mean I just sat there like an idiot waiting for me to do something.

The beads of sweat on my head dropped and dropped. Nothing. He was like a girl in a movie theater, and I just couldn't put my arm around him. He wasn't even female. The puppy must've sensed I had psychological problems, that I was frightened, because after a while he took control of the situation. The mighty Muppet made a move on me.

"Whoa, whoa, what are ya doing? Where ya going?"

First he crawled up my body. Then he coiled his head up like a slinky. He looked me in the eyes. And when he had my complete attention, he kissed me. "Yuck, doggie slobber." I mean he *kissed* me. He licked the boogers in my nose and the pie crust in my eyes. Then he made the cutest little sounds *like a, like a,* like a baby wookie.

"Rrrrr-u. Warr-u."

"Now, that's a nice puppy, a nice puppy."

Then instead of asking me for my phone number, the li'l varmint bit me. They weren't love bites either. Chewbacca had razor sharp teeth. First he nipped at my fingers, then he went crazy. Like a mini-maniac. He nibbled my neck all the way down to my open-toed Birkenstocks. "Ouch, ouch, Allen stop him. Get him. Take him away."

Allen picked him up. "Bruce, are you okay? He's just playing. He's teething."

I didn't want to see fang face angry so I got up and walked away. I went to see the other puppy in the corner. The mellow, boring one. The average one. What was so special about Christopher anyway? Maybe this one's for me? Maybe not.

When I plopped down next to pup number two, I felt like a big ol' loser. He just kept on snoring. He didn't even acknowledge me. *What am I doing? What am I doing here?* I wanted to go home.

Home to what? I had nothing to go home to.

While I was sulking, Allen was having a ball with Christopher. Balls. First a mini-orange basketball, then a pink sponge ball. Christopher was tearing the hell out of it. I wouldn't want piranha boy near my balls.

"Hey, Christopher, look what I got, look what I got," Allen said.

It was an old green sock or something. "Whoopty doo." They moved onto tug-of-war.

Allen made it look so easy. He was petting him and making silly noises at him. Then he started doing this goo-goo-eyed thing and I had enough.

"What's wrong with me?" I thought. "I can do that. I can totally do that. We just got off on the wrong foot." Then I thought of my mother and my sister telling me, "You can do it Bruce. You can do it. Just get up."

"Yeah, yeah, I could do it. I will do it." So I got up off my ass, walked over to the two lovebirds. I was hoping I wouldn't have to pry him out of his hands.

"Hey, Allen, could I hold him a second?" I asked.

"Sure. Of course you can. He's all yours." he said. "Wait, I'm sorry, I didn't mean *he's all yours*. No pressure."

"It's okay. Just give him to me, please."

"Here . . . you got him. You got him. Be careful, Bruce. Don't drop him."

"Yeah, I got him." It was like playing pass the potato.

I took him in my arms and sat down on the floor with him. I just held him. One thing at a time. "That's a nice puppy," I said. "You're a good boy." I copied off Allen. But I still couldn't feel anything for him. I wanted to love him so badly. I wanted to like him, even. But my chemicals wouldn't let me. My emotions were blocked up. I was numb. No fizz. Flat Dr Pepper. The only thing I could feel was his fur. Soft as silk. So I grabbed two handfuls of Christopher and I rub-a-dub-dubbed his belly. "Yeah, that's it. That's a nice puppy. That's a nice puppy."

The more I petted him, the more comfortable I started to feel with him. The more I noticed how beautiful he was. He was a perfect piece of artwork, and if you tickled him *in just the right spot,* he wiggled. Then he giggled. Out of all the dogs I had looked at, I'd never met a puppy like him. "He really is special." I admired the creature's features one by one.

He had the *smoothest* ears like a black negligee. Ping Pong paddle–sized paws. And he had blue eyes. *Blue eyes.* What dog had blue eyes? He was the ultimate Walt Disney character. A puppy platypus. He was a baby bear with Dumbo-size ears, and he had a smile like Mickey Mouse. A smile that made me smile, something I hadn't done in a while. He was a character all right. "Rarrrr, rarrrr," was just one of his sound effects and he had so many facial expressions. His eyebrows alone wiggled every two seconds. He was more than a dog. That's for sure. He was a little person in puppy clothing. The little guy was definitely growing on me. Literally. It appeared out of nowhere. It had a pink head with two hairs sprouting out of it like antennas, and it was vibrating like a diving board. Well it wasn't a caterpillar. It was the world's smallest puppy penis. I couldn't believe it. The little devil had a little boner, and he was he smiling at me? "Now, wait a second, wait a second. Don't get any ideas mister. Put that thing away."

While he was in the mood for love, I lifted up my mini-knight in black satin's shiny earflap and whispered sweet nothings. "You wanna come home with me?"

He answered me in tongues.

"Hey, hey, that tickles." He started licking me on my feet.

"Isn't that cute?" This time he didn't use his teeth. I could feel his heartbeat.

So there I was, sitting on a rug, giggling like a little kid, enjoying myself, with the coolest puppy ever. The blackest dog in existence. At last I had finally found him. For whatever reason this black beauty wasn't adopted yet. We were meant for each other. Now, all I had to do was say, "Yes," and the two of us could go home and live happily ever after. *All I had to do was say, Yes.* But I couldn't do it. I couldn't commit. I couldn't kiss the bride yet.

I sat there twisting and squirming as premature puppy paranoia set in. "What if? What if? What if?" Once again, I couldn't make a decision. *But Allen could.*

"Take him, he's yours," he said breathing down my neck. "I never saw a puppy like him and you haven't either."

"I guess he's kinda cute."

"Bruce, he's unbelievable and you know it."

"But Allen what about if I can't get out of bed . . ." I kept making excuses.

"Allen, what about William? He's gonna be upset."

"Bruce, he'll be fine like Dorothy said."

"And Allen, what if I want to go away? What if I can't handle the responsibility?"

"Bruce, we've been through all of this."

"All right, all right. Just leave me alone. And stop talking so loud. You're scaring him. Just leave *us* alone a few minutes. I need more time with him."

Since nobody gave me a time limit, I was going to take all the time I needed. We had been in this house at least an hour and not once did this Dorothy lady come in to introduce herself. Not even a quick "hello," but I wasn't complaining. I wasn't in any mood to meet any new people. I had enough on my plate.

"So where were we, puppy?" I picked up some squeaky cat toy. Then I petted his head gently. He was the softest, most adorable thing I had ever seen.

I felt Allen breathing.

"Hey, Allen, why don't you go see if you can find Dorothy before she finds us. I don't want her to think we're robbing the place." Puppy burglars.

"Okay, Bruce."

"Now what am I gonna do about you, Squeaky-boy?"

Christopher gave me this look that said, "Well, isn't it obvious." That was easy for him to say. He didn't have to walk me four times a day and put dog food on the table.

Decisions. Decisions. "God, give me strength." The plusses and minuses of puppy parenthood lobbed back and forth in my head like center court at Wimbledon.

To puppy?

Or not to puppy?

To puppy?

Or not to puppy?

Well, what's it gonna be, Goldstein?

I got really quiet. I picked "Christopher" up above my head (I hoped he didn't pee on me) and I listened to my selves think.

"Bruce, you're making a big mistake," common sense told me. "Don't do it. You'll be sorry." On the other hand my heart had nothing to do with common sense.

"Bruce, don't listen to your mind," he whispered. "He's crazy. Chemically imbalanced, remember. Listen to me. Just do it. You have nothing to lose. Get the puppy and you'll be so happy. You'll see. Unconditional love is all you need."

I was so confused. I looked way past the ceiling to the sky. I reached up to heaven and asked God one last time, "Should I? Or shouldn't I?" And then I heard a voice. His or maybe just mine.

"Bruce, just do it. Jump and I'll catch you. You could do it. I have faith in you. You've always done things when you've put your mind to it."

But *I* hadn't been *me* in such a long time. The Almighty was referring to a different guy from a different time. This was the biggest decision I couldn't make in my life.

Sitting in silence, I starred into the puppy's eyes. I petted him gently from his ears down to his chubby, chicken-size thighs. I knew that if I left that house with that puppy, my life would change forever. For better or worse. I also knew that if I left that house without that puppy, nothing would change.

"So what's it gonna be, Goldstein?" some voice in my head said. "What's it gonna be?"

"Okay, okay." I made my decision. I put the puppy back in the sandbox. Then I ran down the hallway screaming. "Yo, Allen, I'm doing it! I'm doing it! I'm taking Christopher home with me!"

Not so fast. It was time to meet the parents. *The parent.* A full-figured woman, baggy jeans, cherry cheeks, wearing her brunette bird's nest in a pink ponytail holder stood before me. Nostrils in furry bunny slippers. I walked right into her buxom bosom. A shocking yellow T-shirt. *It's a trap.* In big black letters it read: BEWARE OF PEOPLE.

"Well Bruce, I see you made it." Dorothy smiled like a healthy mammal. Big and toothy. "Sorry to be rude, but I had to take care of my animals, a lot of mouths to feed around here. So come, come, come on in. Let's have a little chat, I already met your friend, Allen, he's a nice fella, really nice. I told him to go play with William so we can talk. So sit, sit down, so we can get started. Can I get you something to drink? Coffee? And I have coffee. Hah, hah, hah."

"Sure, black." I needed the coffee to catch up to her. *And I thought I was manic.*

After Dorothy served me some Sanka, she sat down directly across from me. She put her big hands on the table. Clasped fingers. Bitten nails. Oh what big baggy eyes she had, the kind that told war stories. World War Me's. I felt like I was in trouble and I didn't do anything. But sergeant dog lady didn't know that. I was being held for questioning. She wasn't about to just hand over a pedigree to an urban cowboy like me. One of the lights was flickering from the storm, creating the perfect ambience for her intimidation, her interrogation. Lights. No camera. Action. She gave me the third degree.

"Okay, Bruce, okay, ya ready . . ."

Ready for what? I just wanted my puppy.

"Bruce, before we begin, I want to make it very clear that these puppies are my babies and I'm *very* picky and *very* protective of who I give them to. I had some bad experiences in the past." Her voice broke up a little. Her baggy eyes got even baggier and wet. Then she kicked into storyteller. "So last winter this guy calls me up. He wants to drive out to my ranch with his daughter so she could pick out her Christmas gift, so I tell him fine, fine. One of my bitches had just had a hefty litter. 'I'm looking forward to meeting you,' I told him, et cetera, et cetera . . . So they come out here, his daughter picks out a yellow one, a real sweetheart. They look like nice people so I give him her papers and I go back to doing my dishes. It was business as usual. My only request is that they send me pictures. I love pictures of my babies. Anyway, they take the puppy home, and the puppy has a few accidents in the house, no biggie, but the mother wants to send the puppy back. Only I don't know that yet. The man thinks his wife is gonna come around. She doesn't. She takes the dog straight to the pound. The second the man found out he called me and told me what had happened. I was a little upset but I told him these things happen and he gave me the phone number to the pound so I can get my baby girl back. But when I called up, they said it was too late. *That I was too late.* The puppy was destroyed earlier that morning." A few tears ran down Dorothy's cheeks. She stopped talking.

"Are you okay?" I said.

"Yeah, yeah." She got up, got a tissue, and blew her nose like a wind instrument. "Bruce, I wanted to kill that woman. It took me a long time to get over that."

"That's crazy," I said. "I can't believe that."

"You're telling me. I'm doing this for sixteen years and not once did something like that happen to one of my girls. She was so young. She had her whole life to live, she could've made somebody else so happy. So never again, *NEVER AGAIN* will I let that happen to one of my kids." Dorothy's eyes got really red, a vein was even popping out of the side of her face just above her ear. "Listen, I'm not here to bullshit you, young man. I'm gonna be completely honest with you. Frankly, when I heard you were coming from the city, I almost told you not to bother. I don't give my dogs up to people in the city, especially a single guy, a bachelor. One time I did, and it didn't work out. Do you throw wild parties?"

"No."

"Good. Now listen, Bruce, you sounded like a nice guy on the phone, I could hear a certain desperation in your voice, so I had to give you a chance, at least meet you."

"Thank you."

"So how can I be so sure that you're going to give my boy a good home?"

I didn't know. That was a tricky question. I hadn't a single clue what I was getting myself into. I didn't know if I was putting my foot in my mouth but I just told her the truth. The edited truth. How I had just been through the worst part of my life. How I fell in love for the first time. How I fell apart for the first time. I told her about how everybody told me a puppy would help me feel better. I told her how I had quit my job, "I took off the summer," and now that I had all of this time off, "This is just the perfect time for me to raise a puppy, that's it Dorothy. That's my story." And I was sticking to it as best as I could. She was nodding her head. "Uh'hmm. Uh'hmm." So I kept my motor running. "Dorothy, I promise I'm going to give Christopher all the love and the attention that he needs."

"But what happens in September?" She asked. "Who's gonna take care of him when you go back to work? And what kind of work do you do, anyway?"

"Advertising."

"That's a very demanding field. It's dog-eat-dog. You're never gonna be home."

"Oh yes I will." I told her that come fall, when Christopher was house trained and emotionally stable—when I was emotionally stable—I was going back to work. Freelance. I would be able to work from home. This way Christopher would never be left alone. "There's also a dog run in the park near my apartment," I told her. "He'll have plenty of friends to play with."

While I was putting on my dog and puppy show, the phone rang. When Dorothy excused herself, I didn't. I eavesdropped. She had one of those old skin-tone phones with the long curly wires. "Yeah . . . yeah . . . yeah." Dorothy said to the receiver. "Oh yeah, I'm always here. Just show yourself in."

"Oh shit."

It was that couple who was supposed to have shown up the night before. It got really quiet. I got really worried. Until I heard Dorothy say, "Well, it should be a lot easier to choose which one's right for you. There's—only—one—black—one—left."

There's only one left, echoed in my head. "Yes!" I smelled puppy victory. I couldn't believe this was happening. I felt an intense sense of joy. I couldn't believe I was going to bring home my very own furry little boy. When she hung up the phone she said, "All right Bruce, you can stop sweating. You and Christopher are meant for each other."

"Really, really. How do you know?"

"How do you think I know? I was watching you guys connecting from the kitchen."

"Yeah, he was connecting with my ears."

Before Dorothy made it official, she made it very clear that God forbid something should happen, and I couldn't keep the dog anymore, I'd contact her first. "My dogs are not going to be put to sleep. Never. Bruce, I'm sure you're gonna take great care of him but if you can't keep him for whatever reason, *whatever reason*, call me, I'll be available the rest of his life. I'll find him a new home. Do you understand?"

"Yes, ma'am."

Dorothy shuffled through some paperwork. I paid her $650. Chump change for a major life alteration. Then she handed over the puppy's birth certificate and pedigree. Within seconds, I knew more about his family tree than my own roots. He had thirty champion dogs in his line, a great, great, great grandma named Ballyduff Marketeer. And just like that I was a new daddy. A doggy daddy.

"It's a boy. Nine pounds, five ounces." Milkbones for everyone.

I asked Dorothy if it was okay for Allen to come in. "Sure, but we're not finished yet."

"We're not?"

"Bruce, you have a pen handy. I want you to take some stuff down . . ."

Allen sat next to me, like my secretary. I wanted him to act as my ears, just in case I missed something. Dorothy read off a laundry list of doggy supplies I'd needed to buy. I was fine until manic momma bear kicked into overdrive. She shot off her mouth at me like a machine gun. I had nowhere to run. She told me everything I ever needed to know about raising a dog but didn't know to ask, nor did I want to ask, in about twenty seconds, no in-between breaths. Fire: She went on and on about how many times I should feed him a day, and how many times I would have to change his water a day, and how many hours he needs to sleep a day, and how many times I should take him out a day. I was on puppy overload. I was way overwhelmed. Dorothy almost gave me another heart attack when she said, "Are you getting all of this down?" Hell no. I had hoped Allen was. He nodded to me. "I got it Bruce, don't you worry."

I was very fortunate to have Allen, the volunteer dog veteran, as a friend to help me get started. My puppy and I were even luckier for Allen to have Barney as a dog. Christopher was inheriting all of Barney's pretail wagg'n, puppy paraphernalia. His paw-me-downs: his old food bowls, his old chew toys, his old leash, his old collar, his once-bitten bagel rawhide bones, and his crate. My puppy was getting everything except Barney's old yellow rain slicker. He could keep that. My puppy wouldn't be getting into that. It was like making a boy wear an Easter bonnet.

"Well, Bruce, that's about it," Dorothy said. Then she handed me a doggy bag full of pamphlets.

"Thank you so much." I hugged her.

Then Allen hugged her. Then Allen hugged me. Now all I had to do was pick up my pup from the sandbox and I'd be home free. But he wasn't there. "Where is he?"

"There." Allen pointed.

"Oh great."

William was standing in a corner, leaning up against a wood-panel wall, holding Christopher close to his little five-year-old body. "This is gonna be really tough." I said to Allen.

"You can do it Bruce, he'll understand."

It didn't look that way. The only thing they seemed to understand was each other. Hand signs and eyebrow stuff. They were talking about something. They had their own secret language. I approached them slowly. "How the hell am I gonna take this little boy's puppy?" I got down on my knees and stuck my ugly mug in their conversation.

"Hi guys, what are you doing?"

"Talking about you," he said. William lifted up the puppy's ear and whispered a few more syllables. Talk about heartbreaking. It was like taking canine candy from a baby. I felt horrible taking the little guy away from the other little guy. I was about to tell Allen, "There's no way I'm going through with this," but

William wasn't telling Christopher to stay, he was saying, "Good-bye." He kissed his little pal on the head. "Bye monkey," he said. Then he handed him to me. "Take care of the man, Christopher," he said to him. "He's your new master. But I'll always be your friend." God, this kid was tough. But I could tell he was holding back his emotions. I felt awful. I saw Dorothy and Allen watching from the distance, nodding to me, "It's okay, just take him."

I took Christopher, but William wasn't through yet. He looked me in my eyes with his green eyes and handed me some saliva-soaked piece of red ripped-up rubber. "This is his favorite toy," he said. "And remember, remember, never give him old socks because then he'll always eat your good ones."

"Okay, William. I won't."

"And one more thing, make sure you take good care of him, Mr. Bruce."

Mr. Bruce. He was killing me.

"I promise. I will."

After I gave my word to a five-year-old, I cupped Christopher in my arm like I just intercepted a furry Nerf football and I was headed for the door.

"Mm-M'mmm. Mm-M'mmm."

Now what? It came from upstairs.

I walked a few feet closer to the front door, and it was staring right at me. She was staring right at me. There, fenced off behind the banister on the stairs was the mother of all black Labs. Christopher's mom, Stonehaven's Cassiopeia, was the size of a cow. And she looked so sad. Her eyes were all red. She knew it was happening again. I couldn't even look at her. Christopher was the sixth to be taken from her litter. I just stood there as Christopher twisted and squirmed in my arms, whimpering his last words to his mother. His mama bear. The woman who gave birth to him. He kicked his little legs and waved his paws. I wondered if he knew he was never going to see her again. "Just keep walking, keep walking," Dorothy whispered. "Cassie's okay. She'll be okay." I kept walking, but I was worried that ninety pounds of dark meat was going to hop over the gate and have me for a liver treat. "And where's daddy?" Fortunately, I didn't have to worry about Christopher's poppa bear. He wasn't on the premises. Dorothy told me he was a stud dog. Christopher was created by a male prostitute.

When I finally made it to the door, after a good four hours of doggy drama, I said "thank you" to Dorothy for all of her help.

"Now Bruce, don't be shy. Call if you have any questions," she said. She had no idea who she was dealing with. "And don't forget to send me pictures. I love pictures."

"I will Dorothy. I will."

When I walked down the driveway with this strange creature in my hands, it hadn't really hit me yet. Who I had just got myself involved with. As we walked closer to the car, the little rascal started squealing like a rambunctious piglet who wanted to fly. He got crazy again and I felt frightened. Hurricane Bertha might've been finished wreaking havoc. But Hurricane Christopher was about to begin. I couldn't hold onto him anymore. I didn't want to. Allen went to go sit in the driver's seat and I said, "Wha, wha, whadayah doing?"

"Bruce, I always drive."

"Uh, uh, I want to, I want to drive back to the city."

"Are you sure you're all right? Are you feeling okay? You haven't driven in months."

"Yeah, yeah, yeah, I'm fine. Don't worry."

I wasn't fine. But I felt more relaxed operating a machine that I had dealt with once before. A puppy needed a different manual—a mommy mammal manual. I wasn't comfortable with him. I didn't know how to hold him. It was gonna take practice. I didn't know how to do anything with him. So I made Allen the

designated puppy holder. I felt so sad and stupid that I didn't
know how to talk to my own animal. But Dr. Allen Doo-little
told me it was normal for me to feel this way. He said it would
take me a while to get used to him.

The same applied for the puppy getting used to me. Allen
explained to me that everything was new to the puppy. New
smells. New emotions. My apartment was going to feel like a
strange hotel. The puppy had just gotten used to Dorothy's dog
and goat house. He had just gotten used to being called
Christopher. And along came a five-foot-eleven man with a
New York accent, a receding hairline, a goatee, a pirate earring,
and a chemical imbalance, together with his puppy-napping
companion, to take him away in this green metal jalopy. Who
wouldn't be frightened? I couldn't blame the little guy for being anxious. If somebody just took me away from my mother,
I'd be upset too.

As we drove away from the house, I prayed that I had just
done the right thing. That I hadn't made a mistake that I
couldn't escape. I also prayed that I still knew how to drive
stick shift. With one eye on the road and one eye on my puppy,
I drove home like a scared new daddy. I didn't know who was
more nervous. Me or him. While I was grinding my gears he
was teething all over the seats, barking and wheezing like a
baby hyena.

After an hour or so on the highway, he seemed to have used
up all of his nervous energy and he passed out under Allen's
seat. Quiet time. I looked over at him. "Ahh, he's not that bad."
He looked so cute breathing. "Uh, look at my baby."

"Bruce, watch out for the van!" Allen screamed, grabbing the
wheel from me.

"I see it! I see it!" I didn't see it. All I saw was a future of
uncertainty and the face of a furry angel that was sent down to
rescue me. Well, he sure had his work cut out for him.

The closer we got to the city the better I started feeling about my decision. When the Empire State Building sprouted in the distance like a giant milk bone, I felt like the force was with me. When we drove through the Midtown Tunnel, the secret passage to the concrete jungle, I started feeling all tingly. I actually felt kind of happy, proud even, like a brand-new puppy poppa. Like I actually gave birth to the little fella myself. I couldn't stop looking at him. I couldn't wait to start my new life. *Our* new life together. At every traffic light, I couldn't stop myself from reaching over to pet him. *Look at those cheeks.* He was irresistible. I couldn't wait to get home and play with him. My new toy. My barking baby boy.

I lucked out and got a spot in front of my building. After I parallel parked, I took the puppy from Allen. "This is your new home now," I said, then I kissed him on his head. He looked up at me with his baby blues and smiled.

This could be the start of a beautiful friendship.

Photo: Randal Alquist

PART TWO

MANIC'S BEST FRIEND

18

DOGGY D-DAY. JULY 13, 1996

I was so excited to start my new life. The puppy was excited too. The second his paws touched pavement, Christopher christened Lexington Avenue. He started peeing right in front of my building, on the red brick walkway, under the green awning. But something was wrong. He didn't lift his leg. He squatted instead. I couldn't believe it. My boy peed with the toilet seat down. "Allen, what's he doing? He's peeing on his feet. Tell him to stop. Bad dog. Bad dog."

"Bruce, calm down, it's okay. There's nothing wrong with him," Allen said. "Barney didn't lift his leg until he was two years old. He has to watch other dogs before he catches on."

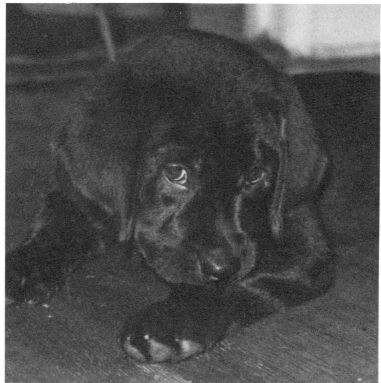

Photo: Bruce Goldstein

"Oh, okay." I bent down and picked up *Christina*. "C'mon, girl, it's time to call it a night."

Allen called it a night too. "Bruce, call me later if you have any questions, all right."

"Thanks, Allen, but I think I'll be okay tonight. I've had enough excitement for one day."

The puppy didn't.

As soon as we went upstairs, Christopher christened my apartment. I didn't even take the keys out of my door and the little pisha was using my oriental rug from Ikea as a welcome mat. He marked his territory. It was our apartment now.

I had his "room" all ready for him. I didn't paint any little duckies or cows on the walls like new parents were supposed to do. There wasn't any room for anything except the puppy. Perhaps a little pillow or a bone. It was only two feet high and two and a half feet long. Premium plastic. The color tan. And it had a little window with little silver bars that also served as his front door. It looked like a barbaric bassinet or a puppy penitentiary. An East Village–size apartment. It was tough to look at, but according to what I had read, this cramped crate thing was actually home sweet home for a new pup. Before dogs were domesticated by man, they were den animals. In the olden days, dogs were wolves who found shelter and safety curling up in caves. It was their personal space. That's why dogs loved curling up under dining room tables. And puppies were a lot like people. They liked to keep their dens clean. They didn't poop where they ate. So if I didn't want my puppy to poop where I ate, and if I didn't want him to eat my leather couch while I was sleeping, the crate was a splendid idea. This way my puppy would sleep in peace, knowing nobody could bother him in his little walk-in studio apartment on Lexington Avenue. And this way I could have peace of mind knowing that when I woke up the next morning my house would be in one piece.

After I showed the puppy his room, I didn't know what to do. Do I feed him? Do I play with him? I was anxious, overwhelmed, overtired, and I felt a dose of depression coming on, so I figured it was best to go to sleep and start fresh in the morning. "Is that okay with you, pupparoo?"

He yawned.

Well I guess that meant yes. So I tucked my special little guy in, and I started to get ready for bed. I *started* to get ready—that's it. I brushed my teeth. I took my lithium. My Zoloft. Then something stopped me. "Aruuu-uuu."

Responsibility.

"Okay, puppy, okay."

It didn't matter that I was pooped, it didn't matter that it was late. Duty called, and now I had to take my puppy out to make.

I wasn't looking forward to the potty training part of being a parent. I had dreaded it so much that I almost didn't get a dog because of it. But it was part of the job. The labor of unconditional love. And now came the moment of poop.

First I put on his little red collar that I got from Allen, then I attached his leash. After I armed myself with little plastic baggies I proceeded to the elevator to deal with my first doggie diaper disaster. Good grief.

There were two ways to go about my dog's business: To paper train or to poop-in-public train. Paper training sounded messy. Not to mention, I didn't want my puppy to mistake my Sunday *Times* for a wee-wee pad. Considering he'd have to go outside to use the bathroom eventually, I figured why not get him pooping in public right away. It seemed like a much faster, more effective way. It would also teach my boy the fundamentals of sociology. He wouldn't just be comfortable around me. He wouldn't be shy. He'd grow up to be a social butterfly in the most funky, yet fashionable, neurotic city in the world. Aside from the embarrassment, the only negative part of public puppy-pooping was that it could be fatal. There was a deadly doggy disease out there called parvo that killed innocent puppies almost instantly. Excessive diarrhea and vomiting. That's how my friend Bob Faskowitz lost his puppy, Mozart. A puppy wasn't totally safe until he had all of his shots, until he was four months old. But on the contrary, Dorothy said it was okay. The Dogmother herself had told me that it was all right to take him outside as long as I kept him away from other dogs and their feces. She said to carry him to the proper elimination area, the puppy bathroom, which would be the front of my building. After the puppy did his thing, she said to pick him up immediately. But she never told me how to pick up the poop. She never gave me a demonstration. God help me. Thank God the first time I took my puppy to potty by myself, he only did one thing. Number one. Lucky me.

It was a beautiful night. Stars were shining. It was hard to believe that there had been a hurricane earlier that day. It was even harder to believe that I had a dog. But the proof was in the puppy. He peed on my toes and I knew I wasn't dreaming. I wasn't in the mood to go back upstairs yet so I picked up my puppy and I leaned against the front of my building like I was on somebody's stoop. It felt weird just standing there. I was used to always being on the move. As I stood there cradling the critter in my arms, I was hoping this wasn't one of my manic irrational decisions that I'd regret for the rest of my life. I couldn't just throw him in the closet and forget about him like my other impulse items. He wasn't a Swedish door knocker. He wasn't a stuffed frog. He was a living, breathing creature. He was my responsibility. I had committed to caring for his black fur coat for life. His life. My life. Our life. We were going to live happily ever after together. There was just one problem: Dogs weren't allowed in my building.

According to my lease, article 10, section 16: NO DOGS OR ANIMALS OR LARGE BIRDS ARE ALLOWED TO BE KEPT IN AN APARTMENT BY ANYONE.

"Oh yeah." Between all of my mongrel mania, the mushy madness, I must have blocked it out. Besides it wasn't fair anyway. I'd seen a few old-timer dogs snooping around the building. It must've been a new rule. Considering I wasn't planning on sending him back—not yet anyway—I figured if anybody bothered me I'd play stupid. Besides, maybe nobody would notice him? Nobody ever said anything about my majestic palm tree or the smoke signals that I was sending across the entire city from the Hebrew National hot dogs that I wasn't supposed to be grilling on my terrace either. And size was definitely on my side, for now anyway—my puppy wasn't much bigger than a twelve pack of kosher franks. It would take two years till he would be fully grown—a fully grown gorilla. Until then he would be my little secret. Being that I didn't want to draw any attention to myself, I held my Mini Joe Young close to my chest. "Don't worry puppy. Nobody's evicting you," I whispered as I rubbed his furry head. "Nobody's gonna even notice you."

"Hay, look at the little puppay! He's such a cutay!" Nobody except Fran Drescher's voice double.

Out of nowhere, this red-lipsticked woman with untamed, long brown branches of hair approached me. Only she didn't approach me. She didn't even notice me. She just stuck her arm out to pet my puppy. She didn't even ask. She just started tickling his jelly belly like he was the Pillsbury dog boy.

"Rarr, warr-ruuuuu," my puppy said.

Despite the fact that the little guy seemed to be enjoying himself, I had never seen this kind of behavior before in a lady. I had never seen her and her hair around these here parts either. Maybe she had just moved in the building? Maybe not.

"Hay, I didn't know you were allowed to have a dawg in da building? They told me I couldn't have a dawg. What's his name?" she asked.

Good question. "He doesn't have one yet."

Picking a name was a very important thing. Christopher was wrong. It wasn't strong. My dog's name had to reflect his personality. It had to mean something. My dog was an extension of me. The two of us would be stuck wearing it for the rest of our lives. I had to really think about it. I had to sleep on it. *We* had to sleep on it.

"C'mon puppy, it's past your bedtime."

"Night puppay." Frannie got one more grab in. "See you tomorrow."

You will?

When we approached my apartment door, I carried him through the threshold like we just got married at some kind of holy pet store. I wanted him to feel at home in my home, not some cheap dog motel, so I put some treats on a blanket and then I tucked him in his crate. Before I tiptoed away, I whispered in one of his big floppy ears, "Good night, boy." Then I closed the latch very quietly on his little metal door and I walked away backward. Step by step, watching him, wondering about him, worrying about him—this new addition to my apartment and to my life. Before I climbed my wooden staircase to my crib in the sky, I froze. I had this maternal urge to check on the boy one last time.

"Oh, what am I worried about. He's fine." He was too new on this planet to have a care in the world. I checked on him anyway.

"Ahhh, look at him." He was already sleeping like a baby, curled up like a little piglet, snoring loud like somebody's grumpy grandfather. It felt nice to have company for a change. It had been months since I'd spent the night with Paige. I missed that warm tingly feeling of just knowing that somebody was there. "Night, little guy," I said and I headed upstairs.

I fluffed up my pillows. I pulled my black duvet up to my chin. I was drifting. For approximately four seconds.

"M'm, M'mmm."

"What the hell was that?" It wasn't my radio alarm clock. It wasn't Snoop Doggy Dog.

"M'm, M'mmm." I panicked. "Don't worry, little guy. I'm coming. I'm coming." I was too tired to think so I acted on animal anxiety instinct.

I popped up from a mininap like a half-baked Pop Tart, I banged my head on the ceiling like a jack-in-the-box, and I flew downstairs like the Road Runner. *Beep! Beep!* My baby needed me. The closer I got to him, his whining turned to screaming.

"A-woo-oooooo!" he howled. "A-woo-oooooo!"

When I got to the scene of the puppy, he seemed okay. He was just screaming his furry little head off. I guessed he was just a little unhappy about his new living arrangements. He had his face up against the bars of his crate like a prisoner in solitary confinement. Thank God he wasn't hurt. He was just homesick, and he wanted the first Greyhound back to Bohemia. I had remembered reading that when a wolf pup was separated from his pack, he would become highly emotional. So freaking out was totally normal. He was just frightened of his new dog house, his new crate, life in the Big Apple, and me. That's all. He must've been yearning to reunite with his brothers and sisters out on the Island. I didn't have to be a puppy interpreter to realize he was saying, "Where the hell is everybody? Where the hell is that loud breeder lady? Where the hell's my dog-mama? And who took the goats?" I felt terrible for the poor furry fella. He was just crying for his mommy. I could relate to how he had felt. I cried for my mommy when I was five years old when she left me alone with that scary old lady babysitter with the mustache. Not to mention I cried for my mommy when I was twenty-six years old, and I felt like the world left me alone with that chemically imbalanced curse.

"A-woo-oooooo!" he kept going and going. I wanted to let him out so badly but I knew that was a no-no. Everybody had warned me if he cried at night: "Do not let him out. No matter what," they said. "Or else you'll be doomed to a lifetime of constant barking and whining until he get what he wants." He'd get used to Bruce service. He'd think that whenever he cried, I'd come running to kiss his pushy puppy tushy.

He'd be the dog who cried woof. I'd be forever at his bark and call. There was no way I was going to let all of that puppy power go to his big head. My heart, however, had different feelings on the subject. The more noise he made, the more I wanted to cuddle, the more I wanted to bring him up to my cozy bed and give him a good night kiss. But I remembered what everybody said. "You should make the puppy sleep somewhere else instead or else you'll be making a mistake." A big and hairy wet slobbery mistake. One day that little puppy wouldn't be so little and my bed wouldn't be my bed anymore. He would steal all of my covers. He would steal the hearts of my lovers. And I'd be the one stuck sleeping in the crate. I'd be in the dog house. But at least I'd be sleeping. "A-woo-oooooo!" It was two o'clock in the friggin' morning.

In only a few hours I could see that raising a puppy was not going to be easy. I should have read the fine print before I agreed to anything—before I signed my name on the bottom of his pedigree. I was *so* tired. But now I had to be the man that my puppy needed me to be. His new mommy. I had to convince my dog that I was a dog. The alpha dog. The king of the studio apartment jungle. The leader of our pack. I had to stoop down to his level to communicate. So I put my funny, unfamiliar, furry, goateed face up to his little bars like King Kong did when he stuck his gargantuan nosy nostrils up against the little windows of the Empire State Building, and I spoke to him in the same high pitched squeaky, humiliating voice that Paige had taught me: baby talk. The language of love. Here goes nothing. I released all of my inhibitions. "Hey, puppy-upppy-upppy. Everything is going to be all right ya li'l booga. I'm here to take care of you. This is your new home now. Now calm down baby, calm down."

It was no use. He got worse. He threw a temper tantrum and started squealing like a pig. "Eeek-eek-eek!" I used to throw temper tantrums when I was a kid. My mother used to say to me, "Bruce, if you don't be quiet I'm gonna put a muzzle on you." I would've loved to put a muzzle on my monster. Not to punish him. Just to quiet him down a bit.

"Eeek-eek-eek!"

"Hush puppy." I could only imagine what the neighbors were thinking.

"Eeek-eek-eek!" he squealed. "Eeek-eek-eek!" *Now lemme outta here! Goddamn it!*
"I'm sorry puppy but I can't," I told him. "You're just gonna have to get used to it in there."
Oh yeah? He wasn't taking "no" for an answer. Since I wasn't obeying his commands, the panic stricken puppy took matters into his own paws. He tried busting out. He tried. When he slammed his bare, baby bear body up against the plastic walls he bounced back like he was a nine-and-a-half-pound furry racquet ball. I felt so badly for him. The little piggy kept huffing and puffing, but he couldn't blow his own dog house down.
By three o'clock in the morning, I felt like I was going to fall down. I kept telling myself, "It has to get easier than this, it just has to." If the helpless yelper didn't stop yapping soon, I didn't know what I was going to do. If he was a human baby, I would have just burped him or changed his diaper. Maybe not the diaper part. But he wasn't human. He was a broken record. "A-woo-woo-woo! A-woo-woo-woo!" If only he came with a volume button, I would've just pressed mute.
It was hopeless. The puppy was relentless. He had no respect for his elders. There was only one thing for me to do. I stood up on my hind legs, I took a deep breath, and I let him have it. I barked back at the bassineted blabbermouth with a vengeance.
"Shut up! Shut the hell up, puppy! Shut the hell up!"
There, I did it. I blew off all of my steam. Unfortunately, yelling didn't do a damned thing except make the domesticated beast talk back to me. The more I yelled at him, "Shut up and go to sleep!" the more he yelled at me, "A-woo-oooooo! A-woo-oooooo!" C'mon, old man, is that all you got. C'mon, give it to me. We went back and forth for eternity. Then out of nowhere there was silence. He had finally run out of energy and was fast asleep. Aside for my rapidly speeding heartbeat I didn't hear a peep. I was so excited to catch some Z's that I quickly and very,

very quietly climbed back upstairs to my tree house and got all comfortable under my forest green sheets. "Good night, puppy," I whispered. Big mistake.

"A-woo-woo-woooooo! A-woo-woo-woooooo!" The beast was awake.

"Oh God, give me a break."

I told myself, "I'm not getting up. I'm not getting up. I'm gonna ignore him and he'll eventually go back to sleep." Yeah right. This whole puppy idea was so wrong. If I'd wanted to be kept up all night, I would have gotten a pet owl. Who, who, who the hell did he think he was? Benji? And who, who, who the hell did I think I was, thinking I could handle this kind of thing. I couldn't take it anymore. I couldn't take how many times I said I couldn't take it anymore. Then as if things couldn't get any worse, he started screaming like a damsel in distress. "Awoo-weee-wooo-weeeeee!" He sounded so helpless. He wasn't the only one. I couldn't think straight. I was sweating to death. "God give me strength."

"Awoo-weee-wooo-weeeeee!"

"Oh please, puppy, shut up!"

"Awoo-weee-wooo-weeeeee!"

"That's it! That's it!" I looked down from the wooden bars of my loft at my little puppy behind bars. I was gonna really let him have it. But then I saw the whites of his puppy eyes in the dark—he was terrified—and the only thing I let him have was compassion. I had a change of heart. I stopped thinking about myself and my beauty sleep that I wasn't getting, and I focused what little energy I had left on making my houseguest feel welcome. I couldn't believe how selfish I had been. The poor thing was shaking like a bunny rabbit held captive in a wolf's den. None of this noise was his fault. He disobeyed me because he didn't understand me and he was scared of me. Not out of disrespect. At that moment I knew if this was going to work that I had to have a lot of patience with my pet.

Patience, now there's a new word in my vocabulary. There weren't any short cuts. Raising a puppy was going to take a lot of time and energy. I had a lot of hard work ahead of me. Starting immediately.

"I'm coming puppy. I'm coming." I couldn't watch him suffer anymore. I felt so guilty. I was the one who locked him up and now I didn't care what anybody said. I was the one who was going to set him free. I ran back downstairs.

The second I put my hand on the latch to release the frightened little boy, he mysteriously stopped howling. I didn't ask any questions. Divine doggie intervention. I just backed up slowly and went back upstairs.

I went under the covers. I closed my eyes. I counted sheep. And once again the puppy started strummin' his vocal chords. "Awoo-woo-woo! Awoo-woo-woo!"

It was the *longest* night of my life. I had gone up and down my ladder more times than an obsessive compulsive false-alarm fireman. No matter how hard I tried, I couldn't put out a paranoid puppy. I couldn't put myself out of misery. By the time the puppy fell asleep, it was like five o'clock in the morning. By that time I was so out of my sleep, I had given up on falling asleep. I spent the remainder of the night—about forty-three minutes—twisting and turning, wide awake, stomach churning, tears running down my face, blocking out the shards of light creeping through my blinds like a bipolar vampire. I was now ruminating over how I had made the biggest mistake of my life.

The second the sun came up, my pet "roo-roo-roo" rooster got up. The last thing I wanted to do was get up, but the puppy didn't come with a snooze button. Who was I kidding? How the hell was I gonna pull this off? Not everybody's cut out to be a mother. My biggest fear playing momma bear was that I worried about doing everything right. I worried if I was going to feed him right. I worried if I was going to walk him right. I worried if I was going to talk to him right. I worried if I was going to hold him right. I worried if

I was going to hold him too tight. And what if I dropped him? What if I hurt him? What if I broke him? What if I was too rough on him? I didn't want to traumatize him. God, how I wished this was all a dream. I tried playing dead. But the little voice inside my head reminded me what Dorothy had said. "The first thing you're supposed to do when the puppy gets up is take him out." Easy for her to say. She was in freakin' Kansas. All I wanted to do was back out. The thought of taking the dog out was overwhelming. Leashes and collars and having to see people. I just wanted to be left alone. But that puppy kept moaning and groaning. "Aroo-roo-roo! Aroo-roo-roo!" *Come down and walk me already! I have to pee!*

I had to pee too. My bladder felt like it was going to burst. And my inflamed intestines sounded like I was about to hatch hostile aliens. But I kept telling myself that from now on it didn't matter how I felt. The puppy came first. Not my spastic colon. Gone were the days of thinking about me. It didn't matter that I felt anxious and stressed. That I looked like a mess. That my face felt like a dried-out sponge—dead as a punched-in sandbag with two glassy eyes the color of bloody skies in Arizona, surrounded by bags that were so thick that they looked like I was related to an elderly elephant. It didn't matter that I felt physically weak. Or that lithium had dried out my mouth so badly I could barely speak, or that my throat was scratchy and sore from screaming. I had to forget about me. I had to do my duty. I had to take the dog out so he could pee. Or worse. So he could inadvertently help me. It didn't matter if I was angry. It didn't matter if I kept cursing my head off because somehow all of this mammal madness was supposed to help me. "How the hell is this going to help. How? How? How?" I laid in bed and screamed. "How the hell are you going to help me you, you, you puppy! You don't even have a name." Before I could find out, I had to get the hell up out of bed, go downstairs and release the little loudmouth monster from his crate.

19

TOUR OF DOODY

I slowly approached his den. I opened the latch and swung open the gate. Unfortunately, the puppy couldn't wait. Before I could grab him his bladder spoke. He took off and squirmed his way through my arms, under my legs, and ran straight to my oriental Ikea area rug. "No, puppy! No!" Too late. He had already made his mark. He had peed me a personalized puddle. Before he watered the rest of my home furnishings and used my TV as a fire hydrant, I had to take him outside. But first I had to catch him. The little nosy body ran around my whole apartment, sinking his razor sharp teeth into everything in sight, including my toes. I finally caught Piranha Boy in a corner eating one of my remote controls. "C'mon, puppy, I gotcha. Now let's go." After I adjusted his red canvas collar, I hooked him up to his black leash. As for me, I wore the same smelly clothes. Crinkly gray shorts and the same yellow armpit Black Dog T-shirt that I had slept in. After I slipped my teeth-marked toes into my teeth-marked Birkenstocks, I grabbed the proper accessories. I shoved a handful of doggy treats into my front pockets, and I shoved a handful of doggy doody bags into my back pockets. Then we were on our way.

As I went to lock the front door, I put the puppy down for one second. When I went to pick him up he had already picked himself up and left. "Wait puppy, wait!" When I finally caught up to him, I was too late. He had already decided that the blue carpet in my hallway would look better yellow. When I screamed, "No, puppy! Make outside! Noooooo! Make outside!" he just kept on peeing, smiling at me, as if to say, "Yes, daddy, make inside."

I felt so overwhelmed. I didn't know what to do first. Do I clean up the pee before my neighbors yell at me or do I take him out before he does any more damage? "I don't know. I don't know. I don't know." I just stood there like a rock watching a dog, *my dog*, urinating. My pet watering the carpet. I couldn't make a decision. I just wanted to go back to my apartment. Go back to bed. Call in sick to life like I usually did. But this was different. So I pulled myself together as best as I could. I wiped the tears from my eyes, and I carried him downstairs to finish his business in the appropriate elimination area—the front of my building. How appropriate that would be for my neighbors was another story.

When I stepped outside at 6:30 A.M., the streets were deserted. I got lucky. It was Sunday morning. Everybody was either still sleeping or out in the Hamptons. The only people awake were wired taxi drivers, the occasional red-jumpsuited jogger, and the fishnet stocking high-heeled hookers who were working hard for their money in front of the Korean deli. So rather than waste any time, I placed the puppy in the pooping perimeter so he could do his thing, and we could get out of there without anybody seeing us deface public property. The puppy had a different agenda. He was just taking his time, sniffin' every inch of the sidewalk. Every—inch—of—the—sidewalk.

"C'mon, puppy. What the hell are you doing? Go already," I whispered. "Please, please, before somebody see us."

Ten *very long* minutes later he still hadn't done anything. Then it hit me. I realized why he hadn't gone yet. This was the first time his tushy touched cement. He was a country dog and his ass preferred grass. He was adjusting to a new surface. When he finally figured out that the sidewalk was his new toilet, he got into a squatting position like a European and got ready for business. He put his weight on his front legs and he stuck his butt out. Then he let nature take its course. Now came the hard part. My part. After he gave a poop, I had to be a good New Yorker and not pollute. The time had come for me to lose my virginity to picking up dog doody. I was a nervous wreck. Giant beads of sweat dripped off my face onto the sidewalk like little water balloons. I stood in front of my building holding the puppy in my left hand (a handicap: it gave me only one hand to work with) waiting for the perfect moment until nobody was around. When the coast was clear, I got down in a crouching position, I stretched out my fingers, I put on a one-size-fits-all D'Agostino plastic bag on my hand like an inside-out baseball glove, and I hesitated. "Not yet. Not yet." I took a deep breath. I looked both ways before I barfed then I moved in for the kill. I grabbed it. *Squish*. While I was holding my puppy and my pungent pouch, I had to carefully flip the bag inside out (one handed) like a clothes-pinned nose magician. Now you see puppy crap. Now you don't. But I still smelled it. I smelled it all the way to the corner until I tossed it into the rusty metal trash can. "Now that wasn't that bad," I thought. I didn't get any poop on my hand and not one person saw me. I made a clean getaway. Now it was my turn to make. Lithium didn't show any mercy—it made me pee like an automatic fire hydrant—so I took the puppy and raced back into my building. I had a *slight* delay. Just as I was approaching my entryway, a heavy-set lady, midfifties, reddish hair à la Kathy Bates, walking a gray, mini–French toy poodle with pom-poms for a haircut, was coming out of the building next to mine. I had to get off the sidewalk, and fast. The puppy was in danger. He didn't have all of his shots yet. Strict orders from Dorothy: "Keep him away from other dogs or he could really get sick—even die." So I hugged the puppy close to my chest and made a run for it. But before I could swing open the glass door under the awning and score a touchdown, she blocked me like a linebacker. "Look Gibsey, there's a new baby in the neighborhood," she said wedging me up against the brick wall like I was a plug and she was a refrigerator. "Now go be a good boy and say hello to him."

"Uh miss, miss," I said. "I'm sorry but he doesn't have all of his shots yet. He can't say hello to your dog yet." She wasn't listening. Neither was Gibsey. He was jumping up and down like he was on a pogo stick trying to sniff my puppy's crotch. "Down boy. Get off of me, Gibsey. Wibsey. Whatever your name is. I'm sorry ma'am, he can't play with your dog until he gets the rest of his shots."

"That's a good boy. Mommy wammy loves her liddle Gibsey, wibsey, ibsey."

I couldn't believe this woman. The more I told her to stop the more she encouraged her French humping bean to keep jumping through the cracks of my arms to sniff my puppy's crack. Not to mention what he was doing to me in the process. He was doin' the humpty hump to my leg, and I was wearing shorts. But at least the puppy was safe. That was about to change. When the woman realized her perfect panting poodle was having a hard time making my dog's acquaintance, she picked him up and shoved him—pow!—right in my dog's kisser. I couldn't believe it. "Kiss him, Gibsey, kiss him," she said. "Lick your new friend."

"No don't lick him, Gibsey," I said *shoo, shoo-ing* the poodle away.

"Hey, hey, hey, lady, get your damn dog off of me," I wanted to say. I was really frightened for my dog's well-being. That's all I needed was for him to catch something. *Sure,* her dog looked clean, but how did I know how many other butts her dog sniffed in his day? Then just when I thought I'd heard everything, she invited us over to her apartment for "Play Day."

What in God's name was Play Day?

"We can do it at my place," she said. "I have a lot of space."

I imagined the worst case scenario. This giant gorgeous gal chasing me around her luxury beanstalk in her purple pumps like I was the puppy.

"Oh yeah. Yeah, we must do that sometime," I told her. Whatever the hell *that* was.

"Great, I look forward to it. I live next door in 'Eighty-eight,' apartment 8B. Are you gonna remember, 8B as in bubbly, or should I write it down?"

"No I got it. 8B. Bubbly, I'll remember." *Remember to run like hell the next time I see you and your horny poodle.*

As soon as my puppy was out of harm's way, my urinal tract instantly remembered it was about to have a water main break so I thought of corks and dams, and I ran the puppy up three flights of stairs.

I put the puppy on the floor for one second so I could get my keys out to open the door. It was one second too much. He took off. "No!" Toucan Sam followed his nose and his bladder back to the same exact spot he had peed before in the hallway. "No!

Not again," I screamed, running after him praying my pee didn't drip down my leg, hoping I didn't accidentally mark my territory over his. Without a second to spare, I was able to grab him and make it to my bathroom. I didn't trust the puppy by himself so I took him in there with me. I didn't trust him on my white, fringed bath mat either, so I held him.

Standing there with my puppy in one hand and my Willy Wonka in the other I wondered if I was ever going to have a moment to myself again. My reflection in the mirror didn't look too promising. My eyes were all crusty and bloodshot, and one of my pupils looked bigger than the other. My face was greasy from all the sweating. I'd looked better. But the dog didn't seem to care. He was licking my facial hair.

20

FEEDING TIME AT MY ZOO

What a morning. More like two mornings. I had been up for like twenty-something hours, and I couldn't think straight. I desperately needed coffee. But it didn't matter what I needed. The puppy needed to eat. And he had to eat healthy. So before I could actually feed him, I had to read about feeding him. Prior to my puppy's arrival, I had read an article that said I had to make sure I fed my puppy "puppy food," not "dog food," because puppy food had all of the vitamins and nutrients that dog food didn't have. But just when I thought I was ahead of the game, after I had digested all of that information, Dorothy, the dog lady, gave me another article to read: "Why Puppy Food Is

Worse than Dog Food for a Large Breed Puppy." Dorothy explained to me that traditional puppy food would make him grow too fast. So before I'd be able to say puppy and the bean stalk, he'd sprout into Andre the Giant—only his little bones wouldn't. They wouldn't be able to support the rest of his body. The rest was self-explanatory. Dorothy suggested I feed my puppy this new large-breed puppy chow that had just come out on the market. She gave me a sample blue-and-white striped bag to start off with, and she said I had to be very careful weaning him off his old puppy food onto his new food or else he'd get sick to his little pot belly. "Use a measuring cup," she told me.

"Uh, okay." Thank God Allen jotted down her specific instructions.

Feeding him was like a science experiment. First, I filled up his bowl with one-part old-baby kibble. Second, I had to slowly mix it in with a little new premium puppy kibble. Then I had to mix in one cup of hot water so the crunchy bits got soft and puffy so he wouldn't choke on anything hard and chunky. I topped off his meal by sprinkling on baby rice powder so he didn't get diarrhea from his change in diet. Then I mixed it all together. I let it sit for ten minutes. Breakfast was served. "Come here puppy, get it while it's hot."

While the puppy was pigging out, I filled up his other bowl to the brim, the one Allen gave me, with something cold so he could wash it all down—Poland Spring water. It didn't take too long for me to understand why Dorothy told me to buy a non-tip bowl. He didn't drink the water, he took a bath in it. He splashed it around like a child throwing spaghetti at the walls. A lot of spaghetti. "Make sure you get the largest stainless steel one they made—four quarts," she said. When I asked her why I should get a bowl that was four times the size of my puppy's head, she said, "Don't worry, Bruce, he'll grow into it."

Grow into what? A grizzly bear. What the hell did I get myself into? Having a dog that huge? How was I going to control him—a hundred pounds of moose—when I couldn't even control him when he was the size of a guinea pig? No idea. I tried not to think about it. That was easy considering I had over a hundred and one other Dalmatian-type things to think about. The first day of owning a puppy was a lot like the first day of school. I had to buy all of my supplies in one day for the whole year. Dorothy had made me a list, and I checked it a hell of a lot more than twice. The puppy was like a new toy. Batteries and all the other necessary accessories to raise him properly were sold separately. He needed a lot of accessories. Aside from food and bowls and liver treats, she said that little Santa Jaws would be teething for the next three months so I should buy him plenty of chewing toys so he didn't chew on my expensive toys, like my couch. So after the puppy finished eating I was going shopping.

Instant panic shot through me. Negative electricity. Bad vibrations. "I don't want to go shopping," I thought. "I don't want to talk to anybody." I didn't want anybody to talk to me. And suppose I got the wrong stuff? Suppose I slur at the counter? Too many thoughts at once.

Usually, if I was feeling off I wouldn't leave my apartment unless I really, really needed something like toilet paper and that was after I used up every tissue and paper towel in the house. And if I did convince myself to leave, I would just creep to the non-English-speaking Korean deli on the corner, praying that nobody would see me. I had to shop somewhere I felt safe, where I knew where everything was. The thought of shopping at a place out of the ordinary was terrifying. Especially this morning. I was exhausted. I was running on no sleep. I had the runs like nobody's business. I just wanted to lock myself in the bathroom or go back to bed but that just wasn't happening, not when there was a little mouth that needed to be fed. So no matter how frightened and insecure I was it was my responsibility to take care of my barking little booger. To get him whatever he needed. So I pulled myself together, I took a deep breath, and I called in a few of my very valuable friends—Visa, Mastercard, and American Express—to accompany me on my journey to Petland Discounts.

Stop right there! Before I go any further. Life wasn't that simple anymore. Even if I was going shopping for the dog, I couldn't just run out of my door whenever I felt the urge to go a store. I had to make sure the puppy was going to be okay when I was gone. I couldn't just toss him in his cage like he was dead weight and say, "See ya." I had to be all nice about it. I couldn't stand up and I couldn't shout. I had to get down on all fours to get on his level to make him feel comfortable. I had to place the puppy gently inside and fluff his pillow. It was a whole process. Everything was a whole process with me. And nobody ever told me I'd need voice lessons to talk to him. I had to raise my voice to an octave so high-pitched I sounded sweet like Little Bo Peep so he would feel safe and warm. It couldn't feel like I was punishing him, or scolding him in any way. Then it would feel like a dungeon to him, and he'd never want to go back in there again. Then for certain I'd never sleep again.

After I tucked him in like a good Mother Goose, I recited a spontaneous rock-a-bye-puppy nursery rhyme and I twinkle-toed backward till I was out of sight. I wasn't even allowed to say good-bye to him or he would probably start whining and crying, and I couldn't go through that again. I left the television set on the animal channel so he'd hear voices and think I was still there. Then I snuck out. "Good boy, little guy," I whispered in my own head. When I closed the door I heard him snoring. I still couldn't believe I had a dog.

21

HOW MUCH IS THAT PIG EAR IN THE WINDOW?

Parakeets and lizards and goldfish, oh my. And there were rats to feed snakes. Painted turtles. A barrel of dehydrated pointy pig ears. Pig ears? And they had Habitrail. Wall-to-wall toys. Treats for girl dogs. Big bones for big boys. There was every kind of pet toy imaginable. I felt so out of place when I got there, the branch on Third Avenue. When that stupid bell rang when I walked in, I was a goner. Everybody knew they had a new customer—a fresh fish—all eyes were on me. Manic depressive in aisle seven. But I had to keep reminding myself, "This isn't about me, it's about him. Keep walking, keep walking. Don't pay them any attention. Nobody's watching me. It's all in my head." So I grabbed a red plastic basket and went down my list. *Eukanuba, milk bones, etc. . . . Let's do this.* I stuck my neck out like a giraffe and started grabbing shit. First I got him a twenty-pound bag of food, then a black retractable leash that extended fifteen feet. I grabbed him a four-quart stainless steel non-tip monster-size water bowl and a four-quart stainless steel non-tip monster-size food bowl. I got him a new black leather collar and a canister of freeze-dried liver treats. And then there was all that personal puppy hygiene. Chewable multivitamins, check. Goldcaps brand vitamin E to keep his coat soft and shiny, check. A thermometer, check. And dental doggy care. I thought Dorothy was pushing this puppy thing a bit too far when she told me to brush his teeth. But I obeyed her command anyway. I got him his own doggy toothbrush and doggy toothpaste, and I would've never guessed dogs flossed. I didn't even floss. So I got him an extra long teething rope so that he could play tug-of-war and at the same time be cleaning his gums with it. Then it was bath time. I bought him tearless shampoo and scented soap and a brush and a comb for his silky black coat. I bought him ear cleaner to get the water out, and I bought him doggy nail clippers so he didn't destroy my couch. Shopping for the little rascal was a real workout. I was so stressed out. I was grabbing this and that and that and this. I was dripping wet, and I was running out of hands to carry stuff with and I was far from done. I was juggling all different-sized boxes and bags and chewsticks and rawhide treats. I was running up and down the aisles picking up whatever I could carry, fumbling about like a headless wild turkey. Then, while I was in hot pursuit of these stinky little vittles, something strange yet entertaining happened to me. I found myself singing jingles. Happy catchy ones like, *"Kibbles and Bits. Kibbles and Bits, I'm gonna get me some Kibbles and Bits"* and *"Bacon, bacon, bacon. I wanna gonna get me some bacon, bacon, bacon."* And as the dog commercials from my childhood barked

in my brain, I wasn't frightened or overwhelmed anymore. I felt
at home in this place. I was in pet lover's paradise.

Suddenly, bright starburst logos drew my attention. Yellow
tubs of kitty litter and eight-legged rainbow-stuffed toy octo-
puses lit up my life. I was waving my arms. My blood was
pumping ginseng. If it wasn't for the lithium making my mouth
as dry as a guy who ate a bowl of moths for breakfast, I would've
been salivating. I circled the store in awe and took it all in.
There was so much to choose from. But why choose? When you
can buy everything. Who cares if it's not on the list? Once I
started picking things up, I couldn't stop. I wouldn't stop. Why
should I stop? I was on automatic manic pilot again. And it felt
good. And at least it was for a good cause. Not me. *Him.* Considering that I didn't know what toys my little babushka would
groove on, I spoiled him rotten. I ran around, pounding my
dirty toes like a wild buffalo, picking up everything. I gave him
options. I wanted him to have all the things I never had growing up. So I grabbed him a yellow rubber cat, a trusty fire hydrant, a latex mailman, and a pointy purple porcupine after I
test-squeezed him. I just couldn't stand still. I had to keep
moving. And every time I went to pay at the register, I told the
cashier, "I'm sorry, could you wait a sec, I have to get one more
thing." One of everything. I got him a knuckle-shaped nylon
Nylabone and a carrot-flavored Nylabone. I got him a box of
milk bones. I got him a red rubber Kong and a soft and mushy
tree frog. I got him his very own Daffy Duck. And when it came
to choosing balls to buy him, I bought him all of them. I bought
him a yellow high bouncing hard rubber ball, an orange latex
basketball, a brown latex football, a white latex baseball, and a
mini-soccer ball. I was having such a ball being a pet shop boy
that I had lost track of time. I had forgotten that I had a special
little someone waiting for me back at my apartment. Then I
saw a pug in the store, trying to shoplift a cookie from the floor,

it finally dawned on me. *Oh. My God. The puppy needs me!* So I paid my tab and lugged home all of my shopping bags.

I had read that people in the United States spent over $20 billion a year on their pets. I had made my contribution to the national puppy-parent debt in one morning. I just hoped my puppy didn't make any stinky contributions to my apartment.

"Hold on, little guy," I thought. "Daddy's coming."

22

LOVE STINKS

As soon as I got out of the elevator, I heard him screeching. Not good. He sounded like somebody was hurting him, so I ran as fast I possibly could to rescue him. "I'm coming, puppy! I'm coming!" I yelled. When I entered the apartment, I smelled what he was screaming about. When I approached his crate I saw what he was screaming about. It wasn't pretty. Neither was the puppy. He had gone to the bathroom in the middle of his crate and he had gotten more than some on him. Poor little guy. He looked so frightened. He was jumping up and down, running all around his little house, banging his booty up against the walls trying to get away from it like the boogie man was trying to get him. And it was all my fault. The place reeked of poor parenting. I felt horrible. I felt guilty. I let the little guy down. How did I let such a thing happen?

"Hey wait a second, I thought dogs weren't supposed to poop where they ate?" I must have been gone a *really* long time.

"I'm sorry, puppy. I'm so sorry." It was heartbreaking. I could only imagine what was going on inside his head. I wanted to tell him not to be afraid. I wanted to tell him not to be ashamed like my mother told me when I had that accident in the first grade, when I ruined my burgundy plaid pants and the mean kids called me Sqooshy Tushy. She said, "Don't worry, it's our secret," and she gave me a bath. I wanted to tell him everything was going to be okay, instead I just stood there. Dreading the inevitable. That it was my turn to get poop on my hands. I had to get over being scared, being grossed out. I had to just get over myself. "Bruce, grow the hell up." I had to stop thinking about it and just do it. Help clean him up. So I got a roll of paper towels and got down to business.

I crouched down. I opened the latch on the crate. When I stuck my arms in there to grab him he acted like he didn't want to be saved. "Come here, come here," I whispered. "Don't be scared." He was kicking his little arms and legs and nipping at my fingers. "Calm down, calm down, puppy." He tried to make a run for it, but I managed to contain him long enough to wipe off the excess excrement that was on his fur. I wrapped him up in a few sheets of Bounty and carried him and his dirty bottom to the bathroom.

I tested the water to make sure it wasn't too hot for him, and when the temperature was just right, I put him in the tub under the spout to give him a good rinsing. I should've taken my shirt off. I should've taken all of my clothes off and got right in there with him, because as soon as the water touched him he went berserk and started squirming. I got drenched trying to keep him still. I thought Labradors were water dogs. Apparently not all of them. As the puppy was crying his head off, I tried to reason with him. "It's okay, puppy. It's okay. This will only take a few minutes." He didn't have a few minutes. While I was lathering him up with a few healthy caps full of the equivalent of Pantene for pups, he was trying to scale the walls of the tub.

"A-woo-woo-woo!"

"Oh no you don't. Hold still."

I washed him behind his ears. I washed in between his toes. I washed his stomach. And I even washed his butt—the labor of love. When I lifted up his tail, I thought about what a friend of mine, Craig Demeter, had told me before I got him. "Bruce, don't do it. Raising a dog isn't all fun. I've had to clean Hank's anal glands." His anal glands? Yuck.

After I survived that one, I was almost done. I just had to shower him off to make sure all of the soap was out of his skin so he didn't get any irritations or dandruff. Full blast was an understatement. My bathroom was now a carwash. Water, soap, and black hair sprayed everywhere. The walls, the tile floor, the soggy toilet paper holder. It looked like a storm passed through there. Hurricane Christopher was here.

When I returned the water knobs to their off positions, I looked down at the puppy. As overtired and delirious and wet as I was I couldn't help but laugh. It was hard to believe that that little thing caused such a big mess. And that was just the appetizer. When I went to grab a towel from behind the door and told him to "stay," he thought I said, "Go run around my apartment like a soaking wet sea lion." My head had only been turned for one second, and he was shaking himself free like a three-dollar newsstand umbrella in my hallway. There was water flying off his body all over my walls, and the linoleum was slippery. A melted skating rink. I almost broke my neck chasing the super soaker down the river running through my apartment. He rubbed his butt up against everything in his path like he was simonizing Cadillacs. He was way too fast for me. It was like trying to catch a seal without a net. Every time I tried to grab him, he whipped me with his otter tail and slipped out of my hands. When I eventually reeled him in, I carried him back to the bathroom, and I threw him back out to sea in my hairy tub. When I went to dry him off, he took off again. "No! Not the couch!"

Too late. He jumped up and down on the leather cushions like it was a trampoline. When he was through abusing the genuine cowhide, he gave it his turtle wax touch with his behind. He shined it up like Chachi Arcola shined the Fonz's motorcycle seat. Then he decided to give me a break. He stopped running from me. He curled up in a corner of the sofa, and let me dry him off. "That's a good puppy," I told him. Then he tucked his paws in under his chin—talk about cute—and fell asleep. I didn't. I couldn't even take a nap. I was on guard just in case he decided to get up and ambush my entertainment center. Or maybe I just didn't want him to get hurt, eat something that he could choke on. God forbid anything happened to him. I wouldn't have been able to live with myself. While I was listening to his gentle breathing, while I was putting my hand lightly on his chest feeling his heart beating, I heard the voices warning me again. "Bruce, you'll be sorry when he gets older. Let him get comfortable now and you'll never be able to pry away the hundred pound canine couch potato when he's kicking it back nibbling on a milk bone watching *Oprah*." Maybe so, but I wasn't about to wake him up. Who knew if this would ever happen again? Silence. This was the first time I actually got to sit down and catch my breath since the little varmint moved into my apartment. The last seventeen hours had been nonstop action. It was only around noon, and I had already walked him and I had already fed him and I had already gone shopping for him and I had already washed him. I finally understood what parents meant when they said their children were the cutest when they were sleeping. Especially later that night when he kept me up again. The puppy had slept so much during the day, between all his nap times, that he wasn't tired when it was my bedtime. He proved he wasn't stupid either when I tried using puppy psychology on him.

One of my friends had told me a way to make the puppy stop barking was to wrap an old tick-tock kind of clock in a cloth and then tuck it under his pillow. He was supposed to think it was his mother's heart beating, and he would feel safe and have nothing to cry about. When the tick-tock clock idea bombed, I tried putting one of my old T-shirts in his crate so he could smell my scent so he wouldn't feel alone. When the old underarm technique didn't work either, I didn't know how much more of this I could take. I prayed to the Lord above: "Let there be sleep."

God must have been snoring really loud—or the Almighty was teaching me some kind of lesson that I'd understand later in life, if I lived that long, because six o'clock Monday morning, when the sun shined in my apartment, the puppy was still barking his little head off.

"A-woo-woo-woo-woo-woo!"

"I give up. I give up."

23

POST-PUPPY DEPRESSION

I used to wonder what could possibly drive a woman to smack her child around on a city bus. I used to get furious when I saw a father hitting his son over snagging a couple of grapes in the supermarket. I used to wonder what in God's name could make a person hate their children so much that they could inflict pain on their own flesh and blood? I used to wish the worst on "bad" parents who chose primitive ways to express their love. Why couldn't they just throw kisses and give hugs instead of throwing punches? But who was I to judge? I never gave birth. I never had to take care of somebody else. I was never forced into a situation for which it was impossible to prepare. I knew nothing about being a pop-up parent overnight. I had no idea what it felt like to assume complete responsibility for another life. I never understood how mothers threw their babies in garbage Dumpsters until the day I didn't want mine.

I had been up for forty-eight hours. I was wired. Wide-eyed awake. Bloodshot. Invisible toothpicks held my eye lids open. Severe case of doggy-sleep deprivation. Everything was blurry and I couldn't concentrate. My body was aching. My head was vibrating. The veins on the side of my face were pulsating. My arms were shaking. My legs were tremoring. I was a manic-depressive mummy in a comatose state. The—puppy—was—killing—me. He had drained me of all my energy. I should have never mixed my lithium with this furry antidepressant. He was bad medicine. He didn't work fast enough. He didn't agree with me. A puppy a day was supposed to keep depression away. Not make me more insane. Everybody was so wrong about me getting a dog. I was allergic to responsibility.

Bringing a puppy into my world was the most stressful event in my life. Being responsible for a living breathing creature. It wasn't the easiest transition coming from the life I was used to: Me. When I first brought him home I didn't know what to expect. I suspected there might be some minor complications, not major life-altering situations. I never expected to compromise my lifestyle. I had never planned to sacrifice the basic things I had become so accustomed to in my daily routine. Like eating, sleeping, and going to the bathroom. From now on if my bladder felt like it was going to burst I had to take the puppy out first. In one night I went from being my mother and father's son to my son's mother and father. I wasn't used to having somebody being dependent on me. Despite all of the dog books I had read, there was no real preparation for my frustration. It was on-the-job training, 365 days a dog year. And I couldn't call in sick. Raising a puppy was like being drafted into the army. Except in the army they let you sleep. I was on call twenty-four hours a day. I had to always be in paws' reach if the little fella needed me. Feed me; walk me; talk to me; pay attention to me; love me; hug me; drop whatever you're doing and scratch my belly. Talk about needy. I had a whole new respect for my parents raising me. I was quite the handful, they told me. Like my puppy, they had to constantly keep on eye on me to see if I was eating something I wasn't supposed to be eating, like crayons, Play-Doh, or paste. I considered myself very lucky to have parents that took such great care of me. That put up with me. That loved me. Till this day they still worry about me. But my mother also said something one day when I was driving her crazy that I hadn't understood till now: "Bruce, I hope you have a child like you one day."

Never in a million years could I have seen what I was getting myself into. I had done everything possible to prepare myself for my newborn puppy. Only he wasn't a puppy. He was the roommate from hell. He was a monster. In only two days, my apartment wasn't my apartment anymore. It was a dog house. The whole place reeked of dog food and dog poop, and there was unidentified flying goop. There were huge clumps of black hair everywhere. And when it was breezy, it followed me around my wild, wild west ghost town apartment like Labrador retriever breed tumbleweed. There were so many dog food wrappers and empty milk bone boxes and plastic bags all over that I couldn't see the floor. I could barely see the dog. If I took my eyes off my problem child for one second, the furry-assed chameleon would be hiding out in a pile of my dirty laundry, but he didn't stay there for very long. He didn't have much of an attention span. But he sure had an appetite. The hungry, hairy hobbit taste-tested my whole apartment. He sampled my furniture like different flavored dumplings on a smorgasbord. Wood, plastic, vinyl, leather. Sniff, taste, and tear. He chewed on my Nikes. He chomped on my Calvin Klein sunglass case. There were chunks missing from my favorite chair. He had the habits of a beaver. The teeth of a piranha. He gnawed on my table legs like they were salami links from Oscar Mayer. Forget about my socks and underwear. The dog went *mad.* The whole place had been redesigned. The shedded, shredded, stained rug looked like a Jackson Pollack pee-and-poop painting. The stained Formica floor looked like a da Vinci, Mona Pissa portrait. Mona Pissa wasn't smiling. Neither was I. My nerves were shot. The battle had only just begun, and I already needed R & R from his "Rrrr! Rrrr! Rrrr!" I thought having a dog was supposed to be fun. Like they teach you in school: See Spot Run. If I taught the class, I'd tell the students how things really went down in the dog-eat-dog-eat-apartment world: See Spot give master midlife crisis in his midtwenties.

All I just wanted to do was pull out of the commitment. Return the damn puppy prescription. I just wanted to evaporate. Run, run away. But that little voice in my head kept interrupting me: "Bruce, stay. You have no other way. You have to give it more time. You just got him. Just go downstairs and let him out of his crate."

"Okay, okay." I took a deep breath.

My clock flashed 6:01 in red when I went to release the puppy from captivity. My face flushed red at 6:02 A.M. when he went to the bathroom on my rug again. His timing was too perfect. I felt like he was just fucking with me. This puppy wasn't from God. He was the son of Satan. "I give up. Do whatever you want puppy. You win," I said, collapsing into the mouth of my couch. "Now what do I do?" I bellowed. I curled up in a ball. I buried my face in the cushions. Tears sprayed out of my face like a fire hydrant. Sticky wet black leather.

"God!" I screamed. I didn't understand why God did this to me. Why did He send me hope when He was just going to take it away from me?

I thought I was done crying. I thought I was done suffering. I thought I wasn't going to be manic depressive anymore. The whole reason I quit advertising was because stress was aggravating my depression. Nobody ever told me raising a dog was going to be a full-time job—a prison sentence. It was the hardest I had ever worked in my life. Taking care of that dog was far more demanding of me than any boss I had ever had. Worst of all, I had signed a fifteen-year contract. I had made a deal with the devil dog himself. My so-called "friend" for life was ruining what little life I had left. I wanted to put an end to my misery by putting a stamp on my puppy's butt and mailing him back to Bohemia where he came from. Then I wanted someone to send me somewhere far away, with a sign that read: DO NOT OPEN TILL THERE'S A REAL CURE FOR MANIC DEPRESSION. I wanted to be put to sleep until that day. If that day would ever come.

I had to face the facts. I wasn't going to get better. This was how it was going to be from now on. I wanted to call Dorothy. Tell her that I made a huge mistake. I was going to be brutally honest with her. I wanted to tell her that I wasn't right for this dog. That this dog wasn't right for me. I wanted to pick up the phone and beg, "Take him back . . . please." My mental illness said I couldn't keep him. I couldn't handle him. She said that I could bring him back if the vet said there was something wrong with him. But she never said anything about bringing him back if there was something wrong with me. How could she not realize I was such a nutcase? How could she have put her baby's life in jeopardy by giving him to me? I wanted to call her so badly. But I couldn't. I just couldn't because I knew that if I returned that puppy, there was nowhere left to return me. I'd be throwing back my last chance of therapy. But it wasn't fair to Christopher. He deserved better. He had his whole life ahead of him. He belonged back in the country with the trees and the goats. So I couldn't be selfish. I had to stop thinking about me, *me, me*. I had to do the right thing. No matter how helpless I was, I had to call Dorothy and let her find a new home for him. Somebody who was capable of loving him. "I'm a self-indulgent manic depressive," I thought. "That's all I am. Now where the hell's the phone? Where is it?" The dog was probably eating it.

When I found it in the cushion, I called my mother instead. I wanted my mommy to tell me it was okay to send him away. I wanted her to help me not feel guilty about backing out of my responsibility. I woke her up before she went to work.

"Hello," she said.

I didn't say anything.

"Hello, hello, is anybody there? Bruce, is that you?"

"Yeah," was all I said. I gargled the rest of my syllables. My crying was so intense it sounded like I was drowning. I made the phone wet. The receiver was sticking to my ear from head sweat. The mouth speaker served as a sewer for my sorrow. I poured my heart out. I drained her.

"Ma, I'm sorry to bother you. I didn't want to bother you, I know you're not feeling well. But I didn't know who else to call."

"What's wrong, Bruce?"

"Ma, I can't. I just can't"

"You can't what?"

"I just can't do this anymore. You were right. I should've listened to you from the beginning. I don't know how to have a dog. I don't know who eats first or who pees first. He's taken over my life. I hate walking him. I haven't slept in two days. Two days. I'm so low. I think I'm having a nervous breakdown again. And my stomach is crazy again. And my apartment is a disaster. And, and, and, he goes to the bathroom everywhere. I'm gonna get rid . . ." Just when I was getting down to some real complaining my mother cut me off.

"Bruce, it'll be all right. Calm down. Calm down."

"I can't. My life sucks. And now I dragged this innocent crazy puppy into it."

"Bruce, lemme speak!" she commanded.

"All right, what?"

I waited in anticipation, hoping she had something soothing to say to me. Something that would make the puppy pain go away. I loved my mother to death, but when she asked, "Did you name him yet?" I wanted to kill her.

"Are you hearing anything I'm saying?" She wasn't taking me seriously. She didn't understand how much I needed her, how much I needed her to make me feel good about something. She had no idea how easy it was to lose her son. That I was completely undone. That I could just do myself in at any moment.

"Well, Bruce, did you, did you name him yet?" she asked again. "'Cause if you didn't, I have the perfect name. Why don't you call him Blackie. That's it. Blackie? It's perfect."

"Ma, I'm not calling him Blackie. Stop it."

"And why not?"

"Whaddayah mean why not? It's stupid."

"No it's not. He's black."

"Ma, stop stressing me out. You were so against me getting a dog. Now you wanna name him? C'mon. Not now."

"Well I'm just saying if he was my dog I'd call him—"

"For the last time I'm not calling him Blackie!"

"All right. So don't call him Blackie," she said. "But just get up. Bruce, get up and take the puppy out. C'mon Bruce, up, up, up."

"But I don't want to take the puppy out. I can't take him out."

"Why can't you?"

"Because I can't."

"Bruce, why can't you take him out? Talk to me."

"Because I'm scared. I'm not going out there."

When straight talking wasn't working, she pulled out all of that psychological motherly crap on me. "Bruce, but he's counting on you," she said. "Now you go take him out for a walk. Now. Bruce. Now. Go. I'm hanging up."

"But I don't wanna go," I cried.

"Go! Now!" she yelled.

"I cah-an't," I yelped.

"Bruce, I don't know what else to tell you. You wanted a dog. I told you not to do it, but you went ahead and did what you wanted anyway like you always do. And now you have a dog. And he's a beautiful dog. But now he needs you. And I have to go to work, so when I hang up the phone, I want you to put the puppy's leash on and take him outside. I'm hangin' up, Bruce, now go do it. I know you can do it."

"No, I can't."

"Bruce, just get up and take him out. Please get up. I love you. You have to really try. I know you're scared, but you have to do this. I don't know what else to tell you."

"Okay, okay. I'm gonna try. Promise me you'll call me later."

"I will Bruce, but get up now."

"I will."

About a half-an-hour later I put on the puppy's collar, I attached his leash, I shoved some plastic doggy bags in my pockets for his doody, but I froze at the front door. I couldn't go out there. "Yes I can," I told myself. "I can do this." I sniffled. I wiped my eyes with my arm. I looked up at God. I looked down at the dog. And I forced myself out the door. "God, I hope there's no people out there."

24

MY LITTLE BLACK MAGNET

It was one of those hazy, hot, and humid mornings. The air was thick and muggy. It smelled like curry. It was 6:23 A.M. on the island of Manhattan. Lexington Avenue was just waking up. The streets were deserted except for a few blue suit–wearing early birds trying to catch the corporate worm. *Wiggle, wiggle, wiggle,* they squirmed. I stood around waiting for the perfect moment when nobody was around so the puppy could poop, I could scoop, and we could both scoot the hell back upstairs. The puppy had different plans. As soon as I put him on the ground, he went smack on the red brick under my awning. "Oh shit." I panicked. My heart was ticking. Rivulets of sweat the size of jelly beans formed on my brow. My temperature was rising. My armpits were dripping. Balls of moisture slithered down my body like nervous serpents. I was hoping the few early risers who were out and about were too caught up in their own Monday morning mayhem to notice mine. I had to act fast. Fire in the hole. I dove down deep into my pocket to dig out my plastic bag glove. Then I dove down to the ground. I started the procedure. As I was squishing the puppy poop in my left hand, I kept sticking my neck up like a puppy periscope to make sure the coast was still clear. There weren't any people nearby, so I grabbed my pup by his scruff in my right hand. I tucked him under my arm like a sack of potatoes, and I got up in slow motion. As I was coming up for air, there was an intruder alert. I froze halfway at the height of a fire hydrant. My jaw dropped. She came out of nowhere. She was running across Lexington Avenue like a guided missile. Brunette. There was nowhere to run. I was frozen. I was under attack. She was dodging yellow traffic. She was waving her arms, jumping up and down, screaming something at me. "Ohmagah–Ohmagah–Ookatdapupeeeeeeee!" I couldn't make out what she was saying. "Ohmagah–Ohmagah–Ookatdapupeeeeeeee!"

What did I do? Did my dog shit in a no crap zone? Did I leave a stain on the sidewalk? My dog took a dump, and now I had to take the blame for a crime that I did not commit.

Whoever she was, she was coming right at me. *This is going to be the most humiliating moment of my life. God help me.* I just sat there crouched in midair, holding a puppy in one hand—a bag of crap in the other. Despite the stink emitting from my doggy baggy, there was no stopping this woman. She proceeded to close in on me. As she was hovering over me, she made it perfectly clear she wasn't interested in me.

"Ohmagah–Ohmagah–Ookatdapupeeeeeeee! Ookatdapp-eeeeeeee!"

Right before my very eyes her eyes blew up to the size of matzoh balls. Her voice went all giddy yap, yap, squeaky. She regressed back to early childhood. She acted like she was three. She acted as if I wasn't even there. Like the puppy in my arms was floating in the air. "Hi, pup-peeeeeeeeeee. Hi, pup-peeeee-upppee-uppeeeeeeeee," she said. She squeezed his cheeks like he was her grandchild. "Oh, you are just too cuuuu-uuuuute," she said. Then this grown working woman in a beige business suit got down on her hands and knees to rub my puppy's tummy. I had never felt more invisible.

When my eyes looked down, I almost fell down. I couldn't believe she let her guard down. Her nice white buttoned-down shirt wasn't completely buttoned. She was showing. I was blushing. She just didn't care. She didn't seem to care about the smell emitting from my puppy's rear end either or the bag of crap in my right hand. All she cared about was my puppy. And my submissive pampered puppy didn't care what she did. As long as she kept doing it. He was lying on his back, like a furry turtle loving life. She was just getting to know him better. "Are you a widdle boy or a widdle girl?" she asked.

After thorough investigation, she found out for herself.

"Uh-ohh, I see a liddle pee-pee. Look at your little puppy pee-pee. You're a liddle boy, all right. And what's your liddle widdle name?"

That was a tricky question. She wasn't talking to me. I felt like a broken-down goateed parking meter with a brown paper bag over my head that the dog's leash just happened to be tied to. Dead silence. I was scared to open my mouth, frightened of what words might come out. It felt like she had called me up in front of the class to make a speech in a foreign language, English. I was scared to make a mistake. Afraid I'd slur. Thanks to my lithium I had the worst case of cotton mouth. But she was waiting for an answer.

"Bruce, c'mon say it. Say it. Speak. Come on, you could do it," my subconscious kept nudging me. "Just speak to the nice woman. She won't bite. Just say something."

Considering that I didn't teach my puppy how to speak yet, considering I wasn't the greatest puppy ventriloquist yet either, I had no choice but to answer for him. The one who got me into this mess. Finally, after a *very* dramatic pause, I responded.

"Uh, he doesn'th have a nameth yeth."

Unfortunately, she had no idea what I said. "Excuse me." She asked the same question over again. I was anxious and jittery just looking at her. She was so pretty. When she asked me what his name was again, I answered the best that I could.

"Uh, he doesn'th have a nameth yeth."

"Ahhh, isn't that cuuuuuuute, the widdle puppy doesn't have a name yet. What are you gonna call him?"

"Uh, uh I don't knoweth yeth."

"Wha-da-yah-mean, you don't know yet? You godda give him a name. All puppies need a name. He looks like a little bear. You should call him *Bear*."

"I dunno, maybe. I haveth to think about eth."

"Don't take too long," she said. "How old is the little guy anyway?"

"He'th—thonly-sixth-andth-a-half-thweeks-tholdth."

"How old?"

"Sixth-andth-a-half-thweeks-tholdth."

"Aww, he's just a babeeeeey. I miss my dog when he was a puppy. He was so tiny too. You guys are going to have such a great life together. Just wait. You'll see. This is only the beginning."

The beginning of what? There was no chemistry between us. The puppy didn't even like me. I was just the guy that kidnapped him and yelled at him. I was his foster parent. He might have been cute and I might have been taking care of him, but at this point in time I had a better connection with my dead plant collection. I didn't understand what long-term puppy effect this lady was talking about. The only thing I knew for certain was that I couldn't believe this was really happening. Puppy pinch me. I was in shock that a woman this stunning was kneeling down next to me making casual puppy conversation instead of hailing a taxi. After a while, I felt comfortable enough with this woman to plop myself down on the ground. I stopped worrying about how I sounded. I wasn't worried what I looked like. The way she was looking at me reminded me of somebody I used to know. Somebody I used to be real close with.

As I crouched down by a dirty curb, I looked into this woman's eyes. I felt her breath. I felt something I hadn't felt in a long time. I missed looking deep into somebody's eyes. I realized how much I missed a woman's company. How much I missed affection. Female attention. I missed goose bumps and tingles. I missed being attracted to somebody. I missed communicating. Talking to this woman in the street made me realize that Paige wasn't the only one out there for me. Thanks to my puppy publicist for introducing me, I was able to see there would be other women in the four seasons of my future dreams. He lured her to me. She brought hope and understanding that there was somebody else out there for me. Someone who would correct my grammar and table manners. Who was the right one for me. Who would appear at the right time for me. When I was ready—I was far from ready. It was going to take a long time before I let my guard down and let another woman take my breath away.

At least fifteen minutes had gone by, and this woman wouldn't put my puppy down. But she had no idea how much her talking meant to me. I valued every word she said to me. She made my day. She made the puppy's day when she was rubbing his belly and hit his jackpot by accident. He started frantically shaking his little chubby leg, purring like a baby wookie.

"Warr-rr-uuu," said Chewie.

"I got the spot. I got the spot," she said. "My dog used to do that. I used to have an American Lab. He was tall and his nose was pointy. Is yours all Lab? He looks like he has a little Rottie in him."

"No. He's all Labth. He's an Englishth Labth."

"What a friendly face. He's a happy guy. He's so beautiful. He has so many expressions. Just look at the size of the head on that munchkin. He's gorgeous. Just look at those paws. He's gonna be huuuuuge, ya know. He's gonna be huuuuuge. I hope you have a big enough apartment."

"I hope I haveth a big enough apartmenth, too," I cringed, half smiling.

"You hear that pup-peeeeeeeeeee, you're gonna be a big boy someday."

Then if this woman wasn't excited enough, she raised her voice up an octave to the key of parakeet. "I love you pup-peeeeeeeeeeeeeeeeeeeeeeeeee!" she tweeted.

I could have lived with the bird calls all day. It was the embarrassment of holding that same bag of puppy crap that was getting to me. I had to get out of this stinky situation. Fast. But I had a little problem. The woman wouldn't stop playing with him. She looked like she was in some kind of a trance. Her blue eyes were hypnotized by my baby's blue eyes. I didn't know how to break the spell. Then I thought if I get up from my crouching position and started walking away the woman would get the hint and go to work. I thought wrong. When I started walking toward the trash can on the corner of Twenty-seventh Street to dispose of the damaged goods, the woman was still attached to my puppy like crazy glue. She was hot on my trail. As I kept walking and walking, she kept talking and stalking. Every time she got too close to my puppy, the farther I had to extend my right arm attached to the two brave fingers that dangled the swinging puppy poop pendulum pouch away from her face. It was hard to keep the bag still. God forbid some doody fell out on her. I had never seen anything like this in my life. Until thirty seconds later when history repeated itself.

Another obsessive com-puppy-pulsive person in a yellow sun dress screeching like a parakeet appeared on the scene. "Look at the pup-peeeeeeeeeeeeee! Look at the pup-peeeeeeeeeeeeee!" she screamed. Now I had two overly friendly ladies of the morning ganging up on me. They were goo-gooing and gah-gahhing and they were gawking. They played Brucie in the middle, poking and pulling, violating my puppy's privacy. They took turns tickling him like they were part of some puppy petting tag-team confederation. Just as I was getting the hang of juggling two women, a puppy, and a bag of puppy poop, a pretty lady in a navy blue business suit came running from across the street almost getting hit by a cabby to join in with the festivities. Now I had six arms in my face. Six exposed unguarded breasts bobbing up against me. I had lived in New York all my life and I'd seen some pretty strange activities take place, but this took the Twinkie.

"Aww, the liddle baby gave me kisses," one of them said.

I felt like I was the ring leader of a puppy kissing booth. I should have charged a dollar every time my puppy slobbered on one of them. And I mean *them*. Every time one of these woman said, "good-bye puppy" and stepped away, within seconds there was another woman to take her place. Suddenly, a black-haired woman with big green eyes, wearing a swanky swimsuit and flippity flop, flip-flops, came running out of my building screaming in a French accent, "Look at lé pup-péééééééééééééé! Look at lé pup-péééééééééééééé!"

Before I knew it they were everywhere. Before I could make it to the trash can they pinned me up against the tan brick wall of my building where they had their way with my puppy. There was tickling and tugging. Grabbing and rubbing. Poking and shoving. Elbows and boobs and hair in my face. There was squealing and squirming and squeaking and there was foul play. This one woman kept rubbing his furry purple puppy penis by accident. "Oops, sorry," she said. I felt so embarrassed for my barking little buddy.

It was invasion of the puppy petters. They flew in like a flock of seagulls on a sunny sidewalk. Every time one of them landed, they alerted another woman with their wild bird "pup-peee-up-peeeeeeee" call. Every time one of them landed, they asked him the same basic questions. "What's your name? How old are you? Are you a Lab?" Except for this one woman who paid special attention to details. She asked me, "If he's a boy, than why does he have nipples?" Oh, the puppy pirates of Lexington Avenue were a rare breed indeed. They had their own secret code. Their own hand signals. No matter what color or creed, black, Asian, Indian, or Caucasian, they communicated with one another like they knew each other from some distant puppy planet named Pluto.

"Give him to me. I'll take him. Just look at him. Puppeeeeeee. Did you ever see a face like dat? He's adorable. Scrumptiously, delumptious. Um, ummm good. And he has that fresh puppy scent. He smells better than my husband."

"I know. I know. I love him. I want to eat him too. Delicious. Deeeeee-licious. I'm not kidding. He's too cuuuuute." They didn't all want to eat him. They weren't all from outer space either. This one woman told me she commuted in from the Bronx. I could've sworn she was a reincarnated female version of Horshack from *Welcome Back, Kotter* when Horshackina raised her arm and said, "Ooooh! Ooooh! Would-chu-jus-look-at-dat-face! Ooooh, I just want to squeeeeeeze him!"

I used to think there was something psychologically wrong with Paige every time she saw a dog and turned into a five-year-old girl. But after this episode of *Wild Kingdom*, I was convinced that Paige was perfectly "normal." Talking about normal, I didn't want to jinx myself, but I felt Tony the Tiger *greeaattt!* I couldn't wait to call

Dr. C and all of my friends and family to tell them good news for a change. That this puppy medicine was actually working in some wacky-assed way. I felt amazing. I felt high. But not too high. Not manic, I-can-fly high. Happy-go-lucky high. Just right. I couldn't remember the last time I felt so alive. And I couldn't believe I was still holding that same bag of crap. It was time to make another run for the trash can. This time nobody was stopping me. Not even my puppy harem that was following me. Yes, following me.

As I dribbled my puppy all the way down center court sidewalk, weaving in and out, they stuck to me like the New York Knicks defense. By the time I got to the corner of Twenty-seventh Street to throw this dirty diaper out, there were so many women around me, I didn't know who I was talking to anymore. It didn't matter. The fact that I was walking and talking and smiling was all I could ask for. And now the moment I had been waiting for. In between all of the oohing and ahhing, the waving, the screeching, the tickling of my pup-pee-uppy's feeties, the *"Rrrr, rrrrr, rrrr,"* I took my foul smelling shot. I pulled a Michael Jordan on them. As I tossed the psychedelic smelling relic into the rusty waste receptacle in slow motion, as the crowd cheered, I had an epiphany of sociological and biological proportions. I had finally solved the puzzle man had been trying to figure out since the beginning of time: *all of these years the key to meeting beautiful women was picking up a bag of fresh puppy poop.*

I spun around in circles taking it all in. Thanks to my cute little crapper I was the luckiest man on Lexington Avenue. The hell with Wheaties. My puppy was the breakfast of champions. Talking about breakfast, I would have stayed out there all day chitchatting away but the little fella had to eat so I took the puppy's little paw in my hand and I waved *bye-bye* to the ladies. "We'll be right back," I told them. "I just have to feed him."

"Awww, you have to feed him. That's too cute. Too cuuuuute," they said. "Bye puppy. Go with your nice daddy. We'll miss you."

Daddy, I kinda liked the sound of that.

They chased us back to my building.

25

THE POOPER SCOOPER SUBCULTURE
OF NEW YORK

One cup of kibble coming up. I mixed in a cup of hot water. I mixed in baby rice powder. Then I told the puppy to hurry the hell up. We had to get back downstairs to meet the rest of the working women before they went to work. On the way down I thought that maybe all of that attention was a one-shot, freak occurrence. But the second I put him on the sidewalk like magic we were surrounded again. But this time it wasn't just women. Everybody was screaming, "Look at the pup-peeeeee! Look at the pup-peeeeee!" A business man in gray pinstripes came running toward us from Twenty-sixth Street. "Look at the pup-peeeee! Look at that pup-peeeeee! Holy shit! Holy shit! He looks like my Lab, Harley." A traffic cop came at us full speed from Twenty-seventh Street. "Look at the pup-peeeeee! Look at that pup-peeeeee! Wouldjah just look at the size of those feet. He's gonna be huge, you'll see." A homeless man with a shopping cart full of bottles and cans came rolling down the street. "Look at the pup-peeeeee! Look at the pup-peeeeee! Hey, I used to have a cocker spaniel when I was ten named Larry but Labs are the best, I tells yah. They're friendly as heck. Good with kids. Now take good care of him, yeh hear." Even the toughest, scruffiest-looking truck drivers were puppy groupies. This burly man covered in skull and snake tattoos just stopped his rig in the middle of Lexington Avenue in front of my building. He was holding up traffic. Pissed-off people were honking. And he's having a conversation with me.

"Hey, buddy, how old's yah puppy?"

"Sixth-andth-a-half-thweeks-tholdth."

"How old? I can't hear you," he asked again.

"Sixth-andth-a-half-thweeks-tholdth!" I shouted.

"Cool dude, cool. I got a yellow one named Bucky. Mine's three. He's dah cutest liddle thing. I love him even though he drives me crazy. Make sure you give him lots of love. And ice cubes. Bucky loves ice cubes."

"Thanks for the advice, manth."

Who said New Yorkers weren't friendly? Whoever it was must not have had a Labrador retriever. It was like I was living in a completely different city. It was like I had gone to sleep in Metropolis and woke up in the Magic Kingdom. It was a different movie. Rated R to Rated G. It went from *"Up yours, muthafucka"* to *"Gee whiz that's a cute puppy, Mister, can I see?"* I had to be dreaming. I was from a distant planet where people were rude and in a rush all the time. Including me. Before I entered this dog world, I was intimidating with my earrings and my goatee. More than one person in my life had said I looked like Satan. Even my own mother had said, "Bruce, I love you, but if I didn't know you I wouldn't want to run into you in a dark alley." Now everybody wanted to pet my puppy and talk to me. Everybody who crossed our path got this huge childlike grin on their face. It didn't matter how old they were or what they did for a living, everybody could relate to my furry little buddy. One minute I was shooting the shit with a bunch of construction workers, the next minute I was chilling out with a Rastafarian bike messenger. "Ya man, look at da puppy." Even the Thomas' English Muffins delivery man couldn't get enough of him. "Aww, you're so cute, aww you're so cute. A-booga-booga-boo." And then there were the hardcore dog people. Poodle Lady was just the beginning.

Once word got out on the street that there was a new puppy in the neighborhood, they were all over me. Literally. Suddenly a huge, muscular-necked pit bull with a head the size of a cinder block came lunging at me. "Whoa, whoa, easy boy, easy," I said, trying to stay calm, trying to protect my puppy by covering him with my arm. But what startled me even more was the dog's owner who appeared six feet later. She was a pretty, long-haired girl with the hottest ass I'd ever seen. Late twenties, wearing stringy jean shorts with plastic doody bags sticking out of her back pocket. "Oh my God! Oh my God!" Daisy Duke screamed. "Look at those feet! Your puppy is gonna be huge! Bigger than Rufus!" I gulped. Rufus was the size of a little truck. My stomach dropped. My puppy was nine and a half pounds and he was already too much for me to handle.

"Go on, Rufus, say hello."

"No, no. I'm sorry, but they can't play yet. He doesn't have his shots yet."

"Oh, that's too bad," she said. "Get down Rufus, you'll play with the baby at the dog run when he gets bigger. Now come here and give mommy kisses." French kisses. Lots of tongue.

"Thank you for understanding." I said "Nothing against your pitbull." I should've quit while I was ahead.

"Pit bull? Rufus isn't a pit bull," she said holding back her canine's jaw of death. "He's an American Staffordshire terrier."

"Oh, sorry. I didn't know."

"But even if he was a pit bull, not all pit bulls are bad," she explained. "It's the owners that make them that way."

"Oh, okay, okay," I said and the beauty and her toothy beast walked away.

Within a second, there were another five more dog people on the scene. One thing that was nice about the dog people was that they related to me. They seemed to know exactly what I was going through. A nice Jewish man with two little hot dog–size dogs looked at my eyes and said, "Don't vurry, don't vurry sonny, you'll start sleeping soon."

A brunette nibbling on pink cotton candy with a chocolate Labrador retriever asked me, "Is he eating up your shoes?"

"Yeah, he's eating up my whole apartment."

"Don't worry, he's just teething. He'll calm down."

"When?" I asked.

"About two years from now." She laughed.

The little guy was making some impression. Not counting the impressions he was making on the sidewalk. By the time lunch came around I had met so many people, my head was spinning. Everybody that was on their way to Curry in a Hurry on Lexington Avenue and Twenty-eighth Street had a slight detour—the front of my building. "Oh my God, that's the cutest puppy I've ever seen." I heard over and over and over again. It was like a drug. And I was getting addicted. I was craving more and more attention. This dog medicine was really working, but it wasn't unconditional love or anything. Not yet. We had just met. He was more of a good luck charm. A four paw-clover. A chick magnet. (Even though that wasn't why I had got him.) He was like a fancy black sports car. He was the ultimate conversation starter. And that was all right with me for now—the more the merrier. Because the more people I interacted with, the more I laughed and the more my slurring seemed to subside. The more I loosened up, the more people I talked to, the more my personality came back. The more people I talked to, the more my sense of humor came back. Every time I'd meet one of my "new" neighbors, I'd have to explain, "No, I didn't just move into the building. I've lived here for two years." Then they'd say to me, "What do you do all day? Don't you work?" After a while I developed a routine, like an amateur stand-up comedian. I said the same goofy things like: "My puppy's business is my only business," or "I quit my job for the summer to raise a puppy. I'm on maternity leave."

It turned out that one of my neighbors, Howie, was also on maternity leave, except he had a real baby. His son, Ethan, was born too weeks before my baby. His wife, Laurie, worked so he was home taking care of him. We had so many things in common. We both looked like shit. Red crusty eyes. Wearing the same dirty laundry. Layers of sweat. We were on the same schedule: "Please, God help me." Sleepwalk all day. Stay up all night. Never let him the hell out of your sight. We both had to teach them wrong from right. I couldn't think of a better prerequisite to having a baby than having a puppy first, especially if you were a single man in the city.

Who-ahh! Redhead in plaid miniskirt—twelve o'clock!

"Oh my God, look at the pup-peeeeeee! Look at the pup-peeeeeee!"

I spent the rest of the day out there just soaking it all in. God, this was better than working. This was better than anything. We were the greatest show on cement. Step right up, step right up and meet the world cutest pup. Please don't throw roses. Throw biscuits. Take a number, line forms to the left.

After the lunch crowd, we met the one o'clock shift and the two o'clock shift. After the two o'clock shift, we met the three o'clock shift. After the three o'clock shift, we met the four o'clock shift, which turned out to be a lot of the same people from the six o'clock in the morning shift. "God, you're still out here," one woman said. "I told everybody in my office about him. He's the cutest li'l thing." Not to mention the five o'clock shift were the same people I met on the seven o'clock in the morning shift.

"Hey, how's the little guy doing?" a man in a double-breasted business suit asked like we were old friends. I got this puzzled look on my face.

"We met this morning. I'm Larry, remember?"

"Oh yeah," I said. I had no idea.

"So did you give him a name yet?"

"Uhh, let me get back to you on that."

26

WHY DON'T YOU CALL HIM BLACKIE?

That question had been hounding me since I first brought him home. It had been three days, and I still didn't know. This was one of the biggest decisions I ever had to make in my life because the two of us would be stuck wearing it for the rest of our lives. This was going to take some time. I wasn't going to just name him the first thing that popped into my head. I wasn't calling him "Rover," "Spot," or "Jake." I mean how many more Maxes did this world need for heaven's sake? I wanted his name to mean something. I wanted his name to reflect his personality. I scribbled down name after name but nothing was good enough for him. Nothing fit. I tried naming him after everything. Animals. Beverages. My favorite gangsters.

I sampled "Sonny," from *The Godfather*. I called him "Carlito," after Al Pacino. When none of those made my day, I thought about calling him "Espresso" because I liked my coffee black like my canines. I thought about calling him "Cola" because he was dark and had a lot of energy. I thought about calling him "Caffeine." I thought about calling him "Lithium" but it was too soon to tell if he was really a mood stabilizer. I thought about calling him "Bear" because he looked and walked like a baby bear. I thought about calling him "Dumbo" because he had big floppy ears. Just for the hell of it I thought about "Mustafa" and "Midnight" and "King." *Boring*. I thought about calling him "Magnet." That worked. It made sense. But there was no emotion to it.

I was getting very discouraged that I'd never find the right name, one that had the right ring. A name that would sing. The only name that struck a chord with me was "Ozzy," after the singer, Ozzy Osbourne, from the rock band Black Sabbath. I'd been listening to his music, "Am I Going Insane?" "Diary of a Madman," and "Paranoid," since the sixth grade. "Ozzy" was the coolest name I could think of. But I was worried what other people would think about me naming my puppy after a guy who had bit the head off a live dove, blood splattering on everyone, so I passed on the Prince of Darkness. Next. There was no next. I had reached my wit's end. When I couldn't think of names anymore, I started running around my apartment calling my dog every name in the book. It came down to a toss-up between "No! Not my Nikes, you little bastard" or "No! Get the @##!*!!! off my couch you hairy little fucker!" I yelled at him so much that he must have thought his name was "No!" Why was this so difficult? Naming him was supposed to be the fun part of being a parent. I feared the worst. If I didn't name my boy fast, one day he'd have an identity crisis and have to see a doggy therapist. "I used to be called Christopher a long time ago," he'd say. "Until that day, that hurricane, when I was kidnapped by that goateed guy with the hoop earring who never called me anything."

When I think about it, maybe the reason it was so hard to name him was because I didn't want to make the same mistake my parents had made with me. I hated being called Bruce as a kid. I got made fun of for years. "Hey, *Brucie.*" The only thing that was worse than my mother naming me was my mother calling me a million times a day trying to name my puppy, trying to ruin his reputation. "Bruce, listen to me," she said. "What are you driving yourself crazy for? Just call him Blackie. He's a black dog. Why don't you just call him Blackie and get it over with? It's perfect. I like Blackie. Blackie. Blackie. Blackie." I hated the name "Blackie." It made me think about how little time she must have spent coming up with Bruce. I'm surprised my name wasn't Whitey.

What a day. What a crazy, amazing day. I had lived in my building for two years and only talked to two people. One of whom was Mr. Singh, my Hindu doorman who didn't speak English. Now I had this puppy for two and a half days, and I practically knew the whole building and the whole building next door to that. The whole friggin' neighborhood to be exact. Life was very strange. And I was *very* drained. All I could do was think about sleep. Unfortunately, thinking about sleep was all I was able to do. "A-woo-woo-woo-woo!" The puppy kept me up all night again. I was three for three.

27

IN PUPPY HELL

Seventy-two hours straight. Insomnia was an understatement. I was running on less than empty. I was running on responsibility. But I had to start the day. I was his personal chef. His nurse. His trainer. His secretary. I was his Guy Friday. My life revolved around the puppy. "Now what can I do for you today, your black midget majesty?" I was on constant dog duty. Twenty-four/ seven. I couldn't take my eyes off of him for a second or who knows, he might've stuck his paw or his tongue in an electrical outlet. I also had to make sure he didn't put anything in his mouth that he could choke on, a chicken bone, a nail, or a nickel, or I'd be performing the Heimlich maneuver on him. I also had to keep him away from spicy foods, like my shrimp fra diavlo, that might fall off the table or I'd have to deal with his upset stomach. Yuck, doggie diarrhea. "Bruce, you have to constantly watch him," my mother said. "He'll put anything in his mouth. He doesn't know any better. He's just like a baby." When she said *anything* in his mouth she wasn't kidding. If I didn't pick up his poop fast enough, the little *chaza* might eat it. I had read that some young pups had a feces fascination. Some species ate their young. Labs sometimes ate their own feces. But that wasn't as bad as eating certain house plants. My prized dieffenbachia. Dorothy warned me that one of her girls nearly died from eating one of the leaves. "Bruce, all of a sudden Cassie started gasping for air, she couldn't breathe," she said. "Her throat just closed up and I knew I had to get her to the vet immediately but when I called the vet he said there wasn't enough time to bring her to him so I had to carry her to the car in the pouring rain and bring her to another vet that was closer to the house. I was crying and praying all the way there. But thank God I got there without a second to spare. We made it just in time, the vet said. Any later, Cassiopeia, your puppy's mother would be . . ." Her voice got choked up.

"Dorothy, are you okay?" I asked.

"Yeah, yep . . . , I'm fine."

When Dorothy first told me about my plant being poisonous, I didn't throw it away. I couldn't. I loved that plant. I raised him myself. I had watched the plant grow over the years. It was my only plant that was still breathing. It was family. Dorothy said it was risky, very risky, but if I insisted on keeping it, she told me I should put it up on a high shelf, very high shelf, so there was no way the dog could get near it, or by spraying Bitter Apple, this horrible tasting liquid, on the leaves. Dogs hated it. Leave it to my furry food connoisseur—he acquired a taste for it. Fortunately, I tried it out on my sneaker first. Before he could try out my plants and die, I kissed my beloved dieffenbachia good-bye. "It's not worth it," I said as I stuffed it down the incinerator. While I was at it, I threw all of my dead plants down the incinerator just to be on the safe side. I was lucky I had Dorothy on my side.

God bless the Queen of Labrador Retrievers. I would've never made it had it not been for my puppy's surrogate mommy. She must have really loved her puppies to put up with a manic matzoh ball Jewish mother like me. I called her every day, many times a day, about every—little—thing.

"Dorothy, Dorothy, how come the puppy walks funny?"

"He's just getting used to his feet," she said. "Didn't you walk funny when you were a baby?"

"Dorothy, Dorothy, why are his eyes always bloodshot?"

"Bruce, calm down. Take it easy. That's normal. It happens to my girls too."

"Dorothy, Dorothy, he cries all night. I haven't slept in days. What can I do? I'm a zombie."

"Bruce, you might want to get on his schedule. Try taking naps when he does."

"Dorothy, Dorothy, why does he always have a little red erection?"

"Hah, hah, hah, God bless him. He's just very sensitive. Don't worry, he's too young to get anybody pregnant."

"Dorothy, Dorothy, what about his nose always being so wet and cold and what about his nails ripping up my couch and what about his—"

"Whoa, whoa, whoa, hold on Bruce. Hold on." I called Dorothy so often that she had no choice but to consolidate my worries. "Bruce, I don't mind you calling," she said. "I'd just appreciate if you write down all of your questions and call me when you have a big list instead of calling me every fifteen minutes. Unless, of course, it's an emergency." I had a few of those. Like the day he made diarrhea on my rug mixed with blood. "Oh

God, oh no. God please let Dorothy be home." I panicked. "Hello! Hello! Dorothy! Dorothy! The puppy's pooping blood! What should I do? What should I do?"

"Bruce, don't worry," she said. "It's probably nothing. He's probably just adjusting to his new food. Try feeding him a little Chinese white rice to bind him up," she said. "That should fix him up in a jiffy, and just keep an eye on his stool."

While I had Dorothy on the phone, I asked her, "By the way, how do I make him stop pooping and peeing all over my apartment?"

"Dogs always go to the bathroom in the same spot. They set up scent posts. It's very important that every time he makes in the house or the hallway, you clean it up really well with this special solvent called Nature's Miracle. It gets rid of the ammonia odor in his urine. Otherwise he'll keep going back there," she said.

"Thanks Dorothy. I don't know how I'd be doing this without you." Or without Nature's Miracle because as soon as I purchased Nature's Miracle it was a miracle. The puppy stopped pooping in those areas. Now all I had to do was prevent him from going in new ones. "Hello, Dorothy . . ."

"*Hello, Bruce.* Okay, this is what you're gonna do. As soon as you go to take him out of his crate in the morning, pick him up, don't put him down for a second, just be dressed already, have the leash in your hand, and carry him downstairs to the front of your building."

"What about him going to the bathroom on me?" I asked.

"Bruce, don't worry, he won't, trust me.

"Okay, Bruce, now when he goes to the bathroom outside it's really important you give him lots of praise. Scream, 'good pu-peeee! That's a good boy!' and immediately follow it up with a treat. My girls love Bilford's liver treats. They come in a little white container with red writing on it. Bruce, the trick is to catch the puppy before he makes, and since you're home with him all day you have the advantage. Take him out immediately after he eats, immediately after he drinks, and immediately when he wakes from a nap. And Bruce, if he does happen to have an accident inside your apartment, and he will, for a little while, make sure you say, 'No puppy! Bad! Make outside!' It's important you be firm with him. It's all about the tone of your voice. And you have to catch him in the act, otherwise he won't know why you're yelling at him. The best way for him to learn is if you see him making, yell at him, and pick him up and bring him outside as fast as you can so he can finish making in the proper area, then praise him. Got it?"

"Got it. Thanks Dorothy."

"Hey, it'll be rough on you for a little while, but don't worry, he'll get the hang of it. Labs are really fast learners. They want to please you."

"Dorothy, one more thing."

"Yes, Bruce."

"How much longer am I restricted to the front of my building? When can I bring him around the city?"

"When he gets the next two sets of shots he'll be okay, a couple of weeks. Just be really careful, like you've been doing. Keep him away from other dogs."

"What about all of the people we're meeting, is that okay?"

"Yeah, that's great. Keep socializing him. The more he's exposed now, to sounds and smells, the easier it will be for him to adapt later. He won't be scared of anything. And Bruce, try and stay calm, you're doing great."

"Really?"

"Yeah, really. Now, I have to go take care of my girls. Bye, Brucie." *Mommy's coming,* she yelled in the background. It was great to have Dear Dorothy give me advice, but every time she hung up the phone I was all alone again. A single parent in New York.

The toughest part about being a puppy papa bear was that once I started I couldn't stop. It was like a marathon that would last for years. Dog years. There were *so* many things to do. If I wasn't picking up poop, or feeding him, or reading a bunch of books on how the hell I was gonna train him, I was on the telephone trying to track down a good veterinarian. Not a quack. Somebody who really loved animals. Somebody who came by recommendation. Somebody I trusted. And considering that raising a growing puppy was so expensive and required a trust fund, and I didn't have one, I had to look into getting pet health insurance to ease the unexpected expense, and I had to get a dog license to make my father happy. And since he was a purebred, I had to register him with the American Kennel Club, which meant I had to fill out all of this puppy paperwork so they could provide him with all of the proper ID, and then I had to get him a name tag just in case he decided to run away. Not just any name tag. I didn't want a boring one or a corny, fluorescent yellow bone-shaped one like Allen bought for his hairy son. Me, I had a vision. I was going to art direct it myself. I wanted a customized silver one. I wanted his name to be engraved. His name was going to be huge. It was going to make a statement. It was going to be in big block letters. Futura Extra Bold. The world was going to know my dog's name. My puppy was going to strut around town feeling proud of his name. There was just one problem. He didn't have one yet.

Over the last few days I had written down pages and pages of possible puppy names but when it came down to it, Ozzy was still the coolest name I could think of. I tried it out around the house in a variety of real-life situations. "Ozzy, no." "Ozzy, stay." "Ozzy, good boy." *Sounds good to me.* The only thing stopping me from naming him was that I was still worried about what other people might think about my puppy being named after a heavy metal "Prince of Darkness," so I took my name game to the street. I took Ozzy out for a test drive. "Let's hear what the average New Yorker has to say."

So there I was picking up puppy crap (squish, yuck, it hadn't got any easier), and these two girls smiled and giggled to each other as they walked passed me. Then one of them with wild blond curly hair and a pink tank top smiled at me as the magical puppy power lured her back to me. She knelt down and asked me the usual stuff. Except this time when she asked me, "What's his name?" I responded, "I'm thinking about naming him "Ozzy." What do you think?"

"Awww Ozzy, I think it's cute," she said.

Cute? Yeah, I guess it was pretty cute. I could call him fazzy, wazzy, Ozzy, and scratch his little belly. But what made the name so great was that it also worked on a cool level when he got older and bolder. It also said, "Hello, my name is Ozzy. Don't fuck with me."

I tried the name out on a few more people before I made it official. "Fucking cool man," my friend George Chambers said, and he had a six-inch scar going down the side of his big bald head. On the lighter side, I asked one of my best friends, Gina. "Ozzy's awesome, Bruce, it's so you," she said. "It's perfect for the little munchkin. Oh, he's so cute." So Ozzy it was. Settled. I just had to make it official. When I finally got around to registering Ozzy with the American Kennel Club, they told me he needed a last name too. That wasn't too difficult to think up. He earned it. His full name was now Ozzy Black Magnet. Nobody had a problem with his name accept for this pink curler–wearing old lady. "He's adorable. What's his name?" she asked me.

"His name is Ozzy."

"Hah, hah, hah," she almost laughed herself out of her girdle. "So where's Harriet?"

"Oh no, no. Not that Ozzy."

I tried explaining to this woman for like ten minutes that I named my puppy after the man who sang "Crazy Train" and

"Diary of a Madman," not after an ancient 1950s TV show that my parents used to watch eating Jiffy popcorn. But she just wouldn't quit. "You should get another dog and name her Harriet. Like *Ozzie and Harriet*. Get it. Don't you get it?" I got it all right. *Now get the hell out of here Grandma Dynamite and go watch Nick at Nite. Come back when you know the words to "Iron Man."*

"Where's Harriet" was only half of my problem when I named my dog Ozzy. From now on nobody would ever ask me my name again. I was known around town as Ozzy's daddy. I had lost my personal identity.

One day I went to throw some garbage away at my incinerator. I ran into one of my neighbors. I smiled and said, "Hey, what's happening?" She looked at me puzzled for a second, and a little frightened like I was gonna mug her or something. Then I said one word that would set the record straight: "Ozzy."

"Oh, I'm sorry," she said. "I hardly recognized you without your puppy."

28

SEPARATION ANXIETY

I wouldn't have recognized me without my puppy either. I hardly left him alone, especially since he had pooped all over himself a few days earlier when I went to the pet store. As far as I was concerned, this was my life now. Going with the flow. This was my new "normal." I was a dog person. My friends had a different take on the situation. As much as they were happy for me that I had found something to keep me busy, they didn't think spending every hour of my day with a dog was too healthy for me, so that evening when they got off of work, David and Isabella stopped by my dog house and decided they were going to take me out for sushi. They practically had to drag me. "C'mon,

Bruce, it'll be good for you," they begged. "You've been trapped in here with him for days. Just put Ozzy in the crate and he'll be fine. He'll go to sleep. That's what dogs do."

"I don't know. He doesn't like to be alone."

"How do you know? You never leave him," David said. "What are you never gonna go back to work again? You have to learn to be away from each other."

"But suppose he gets hurt or something? Or goes to the bathroom on himself?"

"Bruce, suppose he's okay? He'll be fine, I promise."

"Oh okay, okay, I'll go out for dinner, but can we stay close to the apartment?"

"Sure, we'll go to East on Third Avenue. We'll get Japanese. Now c'mon, go throw your Birkenstocks on."

Before I left, I fed Ozzy his dinner. I walked him again. I couldn't handle any more accidents. Then I tucked him in his crate and fluffed his pillow. "Don't worry puppy. I'll be back," I whispered. "I'm only going out for a half-an-hour."

By the way he responded I didn't think he believed me. He screamed his head off like I had abandoned him forever. "A-woo-woo-woo-woo-woo!"

My neighbors and I could hear him crying all the way to the elevator. I felt terrible leaving him alone. "Maybe I shouldn't go? Maybe I shouldn't go. Let's just order something in— Chinese. He's freaking out. He's having friggin' separation anxiety," I pleaded with them.

"No, Bruce, you're going. C'mon you have to go," Izzie insisted. "Don't worry. He'll be all right."

He wasn't the one I had to worry about. From the moment I took my shredded Birks off and climbed down into the sushi pit, I didn't feel right. I didn't have an appetite. It wasn't the food. It was my mood. I was the one with the separation anxiety. It was me. I couldn't be away from my puppy. I couldn't believe it either. In only a few days I had gotten so dependent on the little guy's company. And now I was gonna learn the hard way. When it came time to order I couldn't concentrate. Maguru and ebi or Spanish mackerel and Dragon Rolls with avocado, and there were so many different colors—greens and reds and yellows. The menu was just too complicated. No matter how hard I tried, I couldn't make a decision. I felt myself slipping back into that dark place I had thought I was done visiting. I felt that all too familiar wave of sadness coming over me, taking over me. I felt stupid. I couldn't smile. I felt flat yet scattered. My mind was all over the place. If I wasn't missing the puppy or worrying over the puppy, I was worrying about me feeling out of place. I felt like everybody was watching me, including my friends. As close as I was to them, I felt so distant.

"Hey Bruce, want something to drink?" David tried to break the ice.

"I dunno."

"C'mon, have a beer and relax."

"All right, sure. Gemme a Sapporo."

What the hell was I thinking? I wasn't. Beer was a depressant. It intensified all negativity. Not to mention it was an absolute *no-no* while taking my medication. Suddenly I was anxious and scared. My heart was beating like a war drum. Less than half a beer in my bloodstream and I was *depressed*. Over everything. Over nothing. I felt my head fill up with liquid emotion. I felt like I was going to burst into tears right there. I wanted to just climb out of that damn sushi pit that our legs were crossed in and run the hell out of there. But I fought it. "Calm down, calm down," I told myself. "It'll pass. It'll pass, deep breaths."

When it didn't pass I tried opening up to my friends. I told them what was going on. "Hey guys, I feel a little off," I said. But they didn't understand. They were drunk on sake, feeding each other edamame. Making goo-goo eyes at each other.

"Bruce, have another beer," Izzie suggested. "Relax."

"No, no thanks, I can't." My heartbeat seconded that notion. I was sweating. I was jittery. I was biting the inside of my mouth, the excess skin. I was twisting my toes around each other trying to take my mind off my biggest fear—the puppy. But I wasn't scared about being away from the puppy anymore and I wasn't scared for the puppy being alone anymore—I was terrified of being alone with the puppy. It was too much for me to handle. I dreaded the inevitable. That when I got home I would have to walk him, which meant I would have to talk to people. A lot of people. "No, no, no," I thought. "I can't do it. I just can't." But I couldn't stay in the restaurant any longer either. *I'm outta here.*

"Dave, Iz, thanks for dinner but, but, but I have to go," I told them.

"Bruce, whadayah doin'? Stay out a little longer."

"No, I'm sorry, I really have to go. The puppy needs me." I lied to them.

"Bruce, are you gonna be okay? You don't look that great. You look pale. "

"No, no, I'm fine. Really, I'm just tired. I need sleep."

"Okay, let me at least walk you home."

"Nah, I'm okay."

"Okay, take care of yourself. I'll talk to you tomorrow."

David got up and out of the pit to give me a hug. I almost lost it in his arms. Then I put my shoes back on and ran home, jumping curbs, in and out of cars.

"C'mon, c'mon where the hell's my key?" I fumbled in my hallway. I didn't want any of my neighbors to see me. "Finally." I locked the door behind me, chain and all, and started bawling on the imitation wood floor. The dog was barking his head off in the background. "A-woo-woo-woo!" But I couldn't go near him. "I'm sorry puppy, Christopher, Ozzy, whatever your name is. I can't. I just can't. Fuck, fuck, fuck, why is this still happening?" I put my hands over my face. "Fucking bipolar. I'm a chemically imbalanced freak. I can't do this anymore. This was supposed to stop! This was supposed to stop! I don't want to live like this anymore!" I sat there for over an hour until I realized that nobody else was coming by to walk him. So I wiped my eyes, I pulled myself together, and I took the dog outside.

Thank God there were hardly any people around. After the puppy did what he had to do, I ran back upstairs where I finished where I had left off—losing it in the privacy of my own apartment. It was just like old times. I blamed my mood swing on lithium. I blamed God. I blamed Dr. Williams. I blamed Dr. C. I blamed the puppy. I blamed everybody and everything until I had nobody left to blame but me.

"I'm a fucking manic depressive and I'm never gonna get better. I'll never be normal again!"

I couldn't find a place for myself so I locked the puppy back in his crate and climbed up to my loft bed. I prayed that I'd be able to drown my pain by going to sleep. But the puppy wasn't being too cooperative. "A-woo-woo-woo!" Here we go again. I begged and pleaded to the beast. "Shut up! Shut the hell up! Please! It's three o'clock in the fuckin' morning!" I screamed. I was huffing and puffing. I was hyperventilating. "A-woo-woo-woo!" Then I gave up. I didn't have the strength to yell anymore. "A-woo-woo-woo! A-woo-woo-woo!" He kept going and going. There was only one thing left for me to do. I went downstairs, knelt down in front of his crate, and spoke to him like a human being:

"Ozzy, puppy, please, please give me a break and stop barking, stop crying, I have to sleep. I've been up for days. I really have to sleep, or I'm never gonna get better so I'm asking you as a friend to please help me. I'm begging you. I'm begging."

And that's when it happened, that's when it happened.

Absolute silence.

It was a miracle. I couldn't believe it. Ozzy understood me. He really understood me. And he wanted to help me. I could tell by the way he was looking at me through his barred window, with those beautiful blue eyes, smiling all innocently, contently, not making a peep. He looked like a little Buddha. He looked so good. So pure. I was overwhelmed with emotion. I couldn't believe I had actually communicated with a dog. "Good boy," I said. "Good boy. Ozzy's a good boy. Now you go night, night. I'll see you in the morning."

As I tiptoed backward, I watched him make himself comfortable. He curled up in a ball in the middle of his pillow, he let out a little yawn, and in a matter of seconds he closed his eyes and went to sleep. Before I went back upstairs, I just stared at him, longer than I had ever done before. Wondering where this beauty came from. Wondering who this little soul was. He was more than a dog. He was a messenger from God.

Under the covers a few last tears ran down my cheeks. I closed my eyes with a smile on my face. I could actually feel my blocked-up chemicals release. "Pleasant dreams, puppy," I whispered what my mother had always said to me. Then I drifted off into a deep, deep sleep.

I awoke to the sweet sounds of "A-woo-woo-woo!" one hour later but that was okay. The fact that Ozzy listened to me, that Ozzy and I had begun communicating, was good enough reason to start my day, so I jumped up while it was still dark outside and took him out to pee. When the sun came up, I told all of my neighbors, my fellow dog people, the good news:

"Ozzy let me sleep! Ozzy let me sleep!"

They were so happy for me. "Good for you, that's just great. Ozzy let you sleep. It'll keep getting better. You'll see."

They were right. The puppy must've been getting more comfortable with his living arrangements *and me* because the next night I slept for two whole hours and the night after that, three and a half. It was amazing. Every day he was sleeping one more hour than the last. Then one night the cutest little thing happened. After a long day of being a puppy, Ozzy had fallen asleep under the kitchen table. He looked so peaceful that I didn't want to wake him up to put him in his crate and I didn't have to. Around 2 A.M. he woke up on his own. He had the same look on his face as a grown man who had passed out on the couch watching Jay Leno. And just like a person, Ozzy yawned, he stretched. He got up from under the table and proceeded to his bedroom. *Five steps straight. Make a left. In through my little gate to my soft pillow. Awwww, that's better.* And after days of homesick hysteria, it seemed that Ozzy had long forgotten all about Dorothy and the farm in Bohemia, Long Island. This was his home now.

"Thank you, God." I wasn't alone anymore.

29

TEACHER'S PET

From now on I always had someone to do things with. Ozzy was my best friend. And it didn't matter what we were doing either because it wasn't about what I was doing. It was about who I was doing it with. Ozzy was good company. Whether we were playing tug-o-war with an old, chewed-up Black Sabbath T-shirt, or just kicking it back watching a video, *The Godfather*, *Jaws*, or *Raiders of the Lost Ark*, it didn't matter. He wasn't picky like Paige, that friggin' foreign *Babett's Feast* with the subtitles, throw it out the window with her lemony artichokes please. Ozzy was just happy to be with me. He was happy to just *be*. He was happy about everything. Just give him his yellow latex cat toy, and he was a happy little stinkpot. He lived in the moment. God bless him. I had a lot to learn from him. But you know, even though Ozzy didn't care, I occasionally popped *Benji* or *Lassie* in the VCR just to be fair. He was just so good. *So* good. No matter what I wanted to do, his response was always the same: "Cool, Bruce. Cool."

Thanks to Ozzy I never had to worry about making plans for the weekend, plans for anything. From now on I always had somebody to eat with: breakfast, lunch, and dinner. And he loved the crust of my cheeseless pizza. Most important I always had somebody to talk to. I told Ozzy all of my problems, and what I didn't tell him about me, he witnessed firsthand. He knew all about my stinky bathroom, my mental outbursts, he saw me pick my nose. He saw me naked. Every now and then I'd catch him staring at me. Thinking about things. "What are you looking at Mr. Ozzy?" "Uh, nuttin'." He was more than a dog. I knew it. He was a higher being. He was a mystical mongrel from another dimension. But I couldn't tell anybody else that. Then they'd surely commit me. They'd call me crazy. The last Jewish guy to talk to his black dog was Berkowitz, the Son of Sam. His black Labrador told him to kill people. But my dog worked for the other guy. He had wings. Ozzy was here on special assignment. To show me how to love. People. Myself. Some days I'd just watch him, watching the world. His puppy point of view. Like he knew the answers to everything already and he was just here to show me the way. But my yelping Yoda wasn't about to make it easy on me. That's not how you learn things. So I played along with my mushy master. I pretended he was just a dog. "Come here, boy."

When it came time to training Ozzy, I thought about calling in a professional or sending him to obedience school. I thought about it, that's it. After reading a bunch of books on the subject, I decided that I would be Ozzy's teacher. "I can do this, I think." I wanted to be the one that Ozzy listened to. I wanted to be Ozzy's master. The truth of the matter was that I think I was scared to share him. I didn't want Ozzy to be influenced by an-other person. I didn't want him to run away. To leave me. Like Paige did. I didn't want Ozzy to like somebody more than me.

When I called up Dorothy to tell her I was going to train Ozzy by myself, she said, "Whoa city slicker, not so fast. Bruce, before you can train a dog, you have to first train yourself, mentally. You have to have plenty of patience because puppies don't have a lot of patience. They're like children. They can't focus for too long without getting bored. So remember, only train him ten minutes at a time. Also, Bruce, it's very important to look him his eyes when you're talking to him. You need to make sure you have his undivided attention. Otherwise you're wasting your time. But don't worry, you'll be all right. And if you do something wrong, don't worry because Ozzy will tell you. Labs are really smart and he wants to learn. Ozzy wants to please you. Just give him plenty of praise and plenty of treats when he does something right, and you'll have a perfect little companion. Okay, Bruce, I gotta go. Call me if you need me and make sure you give Ozzy a big hug and a kiss for me and send me pictures, I love pictures."

"I will, Dorothy, thanks again for everything."

Over the next week I prepared a whole canine curriculum for him. I looked at a billion books. Class was in session. Lesson One: "Ozzy, sit." I held a liver treat in my hand over his head, and while he was paying attention to the treat, I took my finger and gently pushed the back of his tushy to a seated position, then I said, "Ozzy *sit,* " and let him eat the treat. While he was sitting, I screamed like a lunatic, "Good boy, Ozzy. Good boy!" After a couple days of this, he got the hang of it, and I didn't have to touch him at all. All I had to do was hold the treat over his head and say, "Ozzy, *sit,* Ozzy, *sit,* " and he would sit. It was amazing, watching his beautiful brain work. I felt so proud of him. And myself. I couldn't believe he lis-tened to me. We had such a connection. Dorothy said that after a while I wouldn't even need the treats anymore. Ozzy would obey my commands for the praise that I gave him.

The next thing I taught Ozzy was how to be quiet. That was pretty easy. Instead of telling him to shut the hell up when he was barking his head off, I encouraged it. While he was screaming, I said, "Ozzy, speak! Ozzy, speak! Good boy!" and I rewarded him with doggy Cheez-its. Then when he got the hang of it, I taught him, "No speak." I was lucky that he had already picked up the word, "No," since I had used it in every other sentence from the first moment he came home. So when I said, "No speak," he understood me pretty quickly. "Good boy, Ozzy! Good boy! No speak! No speak!" Once Ozzy learned how to speak, I taught him how to say, "Please." Since it sounded like "speak" it was an easy word for him to learn, but Ozzy was smarter than I had thought. He actually developed a different bark for "Ozzy, speak" than for "Ozzy, say please." His "Please" was a much nicer, calmer yelp, almost human sounding in comparison to his rough ruff for "Speak." Ozzy figured out that if he was polite he would get treats. "Good boy, Ozzy. Good boy." I couldn't believe the dog was developing a vocabulary.

Some days I expanded my classroom from my apartment into the hallway. It was like Ozzy's schoolyard. It was out there where I taught him how to "come," and how to "stay," until my neighbors opened up their door. "Ozzy, no! Get back here!" Class dismissed. He'd run away due to curiosity. "Close the door! Close the door! Watch out for the dog!" I screamed. Too late. He was fast. Really fast. He ran right into my neighbors' apartments, just about all of them, and I ran right in after him. He'd run into people's living rooms and bedrooms whether they were dressed or not. Ozzy didn't care. He was sniffing and licking, and of course he had a few accidents. As he was knocking things down and chasing screaming children into the bathroom, I would be running all around my neighbors' apartments chasing after him, with a bottle of Nature's Miracle and a roll of paper towels in my hands, picking up after him, while introducing myself. "Hi, I'm Bruce and that's Ozzy in your kitchen making a turkey sandwich."

I made a lot of good friends this way. It was how I met Mike, a photographer, and his stunning wife Ann Marie, a Victoria's Secret model. They had lived a couple of doors away from me for over a year, and I hardly ever said hello. It took a dog to bring people closer. And further. There was a curly-haired girl who was terrified of dogs down the hall too. She was already pissed off at me because one time I took her polka-dotted granny panties out of the washing machine early. "Get that beast away from me." We didn't become good friends.

Aside from Ozzy's curiosity and his obsessive, compulsive puppy need to invade other people's privacy, Ozzy was a quick learner. I was proud of myself that I trained him so well. One "expert" in front of my building didn't think so. He claimed that he used to be a professional dog trainer back in Rio de Janeiro. This tan man in seven-hundred-dollar silver sunglasses saw me trying to train my little puppy and stuck his accent in my face: "In my country, you *con't* train a puppy until he is at least six *monts* of age."

Oh yeah?

"Ozzy, sit," I said and Ozzy sat.

"Good boy, Ozzy." I gave him a treat and pet him on his head.

"Oh, but he'll *foget* everything," Mr. South America said.

It was at that moment when Ozzy looked up at me, with the biggest grin on his face, and I knew we were both thinking the same thing: "Daddy, somebody should train that guy to not be such an asshole."

"You got that right, little guy. You got that right. Now who's my special little guy? Speak! Speak!"

"A-woof! Woof!"

30

BRUCE, SPEAK

Just because Ozzy started listening to me and I was sleeping didn't mean I was cured by any means. I mean some mornings were still tough. No matter how good of a mood I was in when I went to bed, I still woke up in a funk. I still had to force myself out of bed. I still needed to call my mother or my sister and go through the whole, "You can do it, Bruce. C'mon you have to do it, the puppy is counting on you." Then once I eventually got up to take the puppy out the hardest part had just begun. Dealing with the public. With my *slithium* slurring and my arm and head shaking, it was so *embarrasthin*. And forget about it if somebody asked me a question, and I went blank on them, talk about pressure, especially if it was in the elevator. I felt retarded, like I would never be normal again, and I'd start sweating. Really sweating. Dangling salt water down my nose into my mouth off my chin. But thank God for Ozzy. I could always talk to him. He understood me completely. If I wanted to avoid somebody, the quickest way to do it was to jump down to the ground and play with him. He was my doggie diversion. "Oh you're such a good boy. You're such a good boy, Ozzy," I'd mumble, rubbing his belly. Nobody would suspect a thing.

As for Ozzy, he didn't care that I was depressed, that I was a sweaty mental case, an emotional train wreck. He didn't judge me. He was the only one who knew what went on behind closed doors. Beware of bipolar. He knew that I wasn't "normal." He accepted my mood swings. He accepted me for me. I think this was what they meant about dogs loving unconditionally.

The only good things about my morning misery was that it was temporary and that it was right on schedule—I discovered a pattern to my manic-depression chemistry. No matter how low I was when I woke up, as long as I got outside with Ozzy, somewhere along the line, talking to somebody I'd feel all right. Out of nowhere, I'd be happy, carefree, enjoying life. I would feel good for hours at a time, sometimes really good: talking to a million people at once, being funny, laughing like a hyena, "Well aren't we happy today?" they'd say. Sometimes I'd feel so good I'd start singing (my original material), "My friend Ozzy is the liddlest, liddlest, liddlest guy in town, cha, cha," or when he was on his back, I'd grab his legs like he was a little piggy we were having for dinner and I'd sing, "We're gonna have roast Ozzy! Oh, we're gonna have roast Ozzy!" But the mood wouldn't last. What goes up will come down. I would always crash. No matter where I was or who I was talking to, all of a sudden, smack, I'd feel slow and scared and I'd have to get the hell outta there. But then I'd eventually feel amazing again, and when I felt great again, I blamed my depression on the medicine. It couldn't be that I was still fucked up, nah, not my chemicals, not genetics. I just wanted to flush all of my pills down the toilet. Again. But before I did anything stupid the phone rang. It was Dr. C. She always sixth-sensed when I wasn't okay.

"Hello Bruce . . ."

She wanted to see me. And the puppy.

I had a little problem. Since Ozzy didn't have all of his shots yet, I couldn't just walk him up to Fifty-seventh Street. Then I had an idea. My black Paragon duffel bag was staring at me in the corner.

31

THE ULTIMATE DOGGY BAG

I hadn't been to the gym since I got Ozzy, so I dumped my sweaty gym shorts onto the floor and replaced it with thirteen pounds of Labrador. I made it all comfy in there for him. I gave him a little blanky. I threw a few treats in. Then I zipped him up real good like my mother used to do to me. "Enough, enough already. I can't breathe in here," I used to say. But Ozzy seemed okay. My pup was snug as a humungous bug in a rug. You could hardly tell he was in there unless you were looking for him. He was black and so was the bag. Only his little head, his eyes and teeth were showing. Ozzy was ready for his first road trip.

I wasn't. I was a nervous wreck. I had a lot of packing to do. I converted my green Kipling backpack, with the dangling furry green monkey, the one that Paige gave me, into Ozzy's official doggy diaper bag. I packed it with the necessary yet neurotic puppy essentials: Water was number one on the list. It was ninety-something degrees out there and I didn't want him to get dehydrated, so I picked up a Poland Spring water bottle, the one with the green sport nipple. And just in case Ozzy got too hot and I needed to hose him down I brought along a spray bottle (that I used to water my plants with). After all, he had a fur coat on. Next came the food. I didn't want him to starve, so I packed an extra-large Ziploc bag full of puppy chow for his lunch and an early supper just in case we were still mobile. And since Ozzy wasn't an animal—okay, he was an animal, but I didn't want him to eat off the ground like one—I ran out and bought two tiny tin bowls— one for eating, one for drinking—to serve his meals in. It was like we were going camping. *"Puppy, isn't this fun?"* The tins were just big enough to hold Ozzy's cute mug. *Look at those jowls. So cute. You're adorable. Adorable.* I couldn't believe I was turning into one of those obsessive com-puppy-pulsive women in front of my building. But so what. I was proud of my son. And since he was only going to be a mush ball once, and I didn't want to miss anything cute that he did, I brought along my point and shoot James Bond–looking *zoom-zoom-zooma*-zoom camera to capture his canine Kodak moments. *Smile. Say liver treats. Did somebody say treats?* Ozzy couldn't get enough Old Mother Hubbard Bacon and Cheese biscuits, so I filled a mini-Tupperware container to the brim with them, then I zipped it up in one of the outside compartments of my backpack for easy access. What's next? Did I forget something? Oh yeah, toys. I didn't want Ozzy to get bored when I was talking to Dr. C so I brought along his orange basketball and his squeaky one-earred yellow cat. And while I was at it I threw in his brush-and-comb kit and a couple of dog books just in case I needed to learn something on the spot. And last but not least, since I didn't know exactly how long we'd be out, I didn't take any chances. I packed at least ten D'Agostino doggy doody bags. And since I didn't know exactly how long *I'd* be out for, I didn't take any chances—I packed plenty of Imodiums. "Well, that about does it. Wait, my journal. Okay that's it." I'd started documenting our wiggedy-waggedy whacked experiences.

I popped my green backpack on, then I lifted my doggie duffel bag off the ground very carefully. "C'mon, puppy, you ready to go for a ride?" Ozzy was smiling so I played around with him. I made car sounds. *V'rooom.* Prepare for take-off. Puppy, buckle your seat belts. Three. Two. One. Blast off! Ozzy has left the building. Hello, New York City.

As we made a left onto Twenty-seventh Street, Ozzy's soft, floppy, velvet rabbit ears hung over the edges of my duffel bag like expensive drapery from Laura Ashley—flapping elegantly and free like they were leaves on a palm tree blowing to the beat of a gentle breeze in Miami. Occasionally he came up for air like a pop-up puppy submarine. He'd pull his neck out like a periscope. He didn't want to miss a thing. Everything was so new and exciting. The smell of a pizza parlor, the honking of a horn, the scent of other dogs. When a truck backfired, he ducked for cover. There was so much for him to take in. He was my curious little monkey. I should've renamed him Georgie.

Ozzy had boarded a magical hovercraft of the future. I was his own personal tour guide to the Big Apple amusement center. I had to be really careful not to stumble or trip even though I occasionally spun him around like the Astro Tower in Coney Island to spice it up a bit. *Don't worry, little buddy, you're not going anywhere. I got you covered.* I tucked Ozzy in tidier than the Hebrew midwife tucked baby Moses in a papyrus basket before she sent him on a one-way ticket down the Nile River. I took Ozzy on my own dangerous mission. I snuck him on the R train trying to avoid a hundred-dollar ticket. I prayed he didn't bark.

It was dark and loud down there but I held onto my kid like he was a top secret briefcase. *He goes anywhere. So do I.* I was a little shook up since it was my first time in the subway since that day with Satan. But I took a few deep breaths and I was all right. I stayed five feet away from the platform until the train came. So far, so good. The train rocked back and forth, and nobody spotted my camouflaged canine chameleon. People were too caught up in themselves and the whole rat race to notice a cute puppy's face. Not everybody. On the other end of the car I noticed a little boy staring at my feet, smiling. But he wasn't staring at my feet. He was playing peek-a-boo with my puppy. "Ma, ma. Look. Look," he said to his mother, tugging her blouse, trying to get her attention as he pointed down in the distance at my gym equipment. "Mommy. Mommy. Look at the puppy," he insisted. She finally looked. "What are you talking about? I don't see anything. Behave yourself Tommy."

"But Ma, I saw him. I really saw him," he pleaded with her.

"Saw who?"

"Never mind."

When the boy had to get off at his stop, he blew a little kiss and mouthed the words to Ozzy: "Good-bye, boy."

"Next stop: Fifty-seventh Street," the conductor said.

"C'mon, Ozzy, that's us." I petted him on his soft furry head. And up the stairs we went. "Just a little longer, baby boy, we just have to walk a couple blocks and we're there."

It felt weird going to see Dr. C feeling . . . I was scared to say it too loud but "happy." The last time Dr. C saw me I wasn't exactly jolly.

"C'mon Ozzy, this is the place."

32

WALKING OZZY OVER THE BRIDGE

When we got out of the elevator, we waited patiently in the reception area with the other mental patients. *What's his story?*
What's her story? I would've never guessed in a million years
that I'd be coming to a place like this. Then again, I would've
never guessed in a million years I'd have a dog either. I
thought about all of the times I came to this office running for
my life. And today because of Ozzy I was beginning a new life.
I felt so lucky. "Thanks, Ozzy, you're the reason I'm getting
better," I whispered under his silky ear flap. "I should've
started taking you a lot earlier. You're my furry antidepressant." I made myself laugh. "Now I want you to be on your
best behavior when you meet Dr. C, okay?" He grunted. "Now

fix your ear, Ozzy, fix your ear. It's sticking up. I think she's coming."

"Where is he? Where's the little guy?" Dr. C screamed from down the hallway. So I dumped Ozzy out of the bag onto the floor of the reception area and he took the hell off. He ran right toward her. "Oh my God! He's the cutest thing I've ever seen!" she screamed. "Come here, puppy!"

"In a minute," Ozzy said. He stopped in the middle of the corridor, sniffed, and got into a squatting position.

"Uh oh."

"No Ozzy, make outside."

Too late. He pooped on the carpet. Ozzy christened the halls of psychopharmacology.

"I'm so sorry," I said. I grabbed some cleaning supplies out of my bag and I proceeded to clean it up. "He doesn't usually do this. He's just excited."

While I was cleaning up shop, the little psychopathic puppy ran around in circles like a manic chicken, as all the therapists and psychiatrists of the clinic were running around giggling like schoolchildren trying to catch him.

"I gotcha, little one." Dr. C kidnapped my puppy and brought him into her office.

When I walked in on the lovebirds, Dr. C was sitting in her green shrink chair, and Ozzy was jumping all over her. "So you're the guy who's been taking care of my patient. You're doing such a great job. You deserve a treat." She pulled out pig ears and cow hoofs like she was a dentist giving a little kid red lollipops. All he can eat.

"A-woo-woo-woo!"

"Oh you're very welcome. A-woo-woo-woo-to you too. Oh, you're so cute. You're such a cuuuttieee, patuteee, oh I've never met a puppy as cute as you, Ozzy. Ozzy baby," she squeaked. I didn't want to disturb them so I just took a load off, and I let my eyes wander around the room. There were acrylic moons and pastel blue and yellow butterflies and there were rainbows and then there was that scraggly little sketch of a bridge with paper-torn edges, starring me as a little stick figure. He was all the way to the left. He had a long way to go to get across it. It was dated January 24, 1996. I got overwhelmed with emotion. I couldn't hold it in.

"Are you okay, Bruce?" Dr. C asked, handing me a tissue.

"Yeah, I guess. It's just my bridge. Something's missing." I got up. I took a black marker off of her desk.

"Bruce, what are you doing?"

"Relax, I'm not crazy." I got close to the wall. I crossed out the little stick figure man all the way in the left corner. Then I started sketching a new man toward the other end. But that's not all I did. I sketched a little black puppy dog next to him. "Now, that's better."

"Aw, Bruce, that's so true. Ozzy is saving you."

"Yeah. Well, I guess I'm feeling better. A lot better. I mean I'm having good times again, I really am, thanks to the little guy, and I'm meeting all of these people, but I guess, I guess, I'm still getting depressed. I'm still a little off. The mornings are still bad. And I flipped out in a sushi restaurant with my friends. I couldn't breathe. Freakin' anxiety. I mean is this ever going to end? Will I ever be normal again?"

"No. Bruce, you, you'll never be *normal.*"

"What?"

"You'll be Bruce. You'll be better than *normal.* You'll be balanced. Now, come on, smile. You're doing so well. You're almost over the bridge. First you walked, then you took a hel-icopter, and now Ozzy's walking you to the end."

"Yeah, I guess."

She got all serious. "Bruce, do you know how lucky you are?"

"Yeah."

"No, you don't."

"Whadayah mean?"

"I mean, Bruce, do you know how lucky you are? That you're alive. It's a miracle quite frankly. That you haven't been institutionalized, at least once. That you haven't attempted suicide. It's practically unheard of in my profession. I mean you're a rare one. A real rare one. And it's because of him. He's your guardian angel. Ozzy's been sent here to help you. He's a miracle. You're a miracle. Do you understand?"

"Yeah, I guess."

"You guess. Bruce, you don't see yourself. I do. That's my job, and you've made so much progress in the past few months. It's night and day. It took a little while for you to come around to taking the medicine and everything, but you did come around. And I'm so proud of you. And I'm so proud of you too. . . ." She looked at Ozzy. "I am, I am, I am . . . Getting a dog was the best idea. I'm so glad I told you to get one. What Ozzy is doing for you is incredible," She said. "I mean he's getting you up and running everyday. He's got you doing things. You're on a schedule. You're not wrapped up in yourself. You're not just sitting around, thinking, wallowing in your self-pity. You're getting a life again. A life, do you see what's going on here?"

"Yeah, but it's still rough sometimes. I'll be in the middle of a conversation and just like that I fade out. My subconscious interrupts me. I feel so far away. Like I'm never gonna come back."

"But you do come back. Bruce, maybe you just have to adjust your medicine, get the right dosage."

"Yeah more side effects."

"Bruce, don't start. You have to keep taking those blood tests. When are you seeing Dr. Williams?"

"I dunno."

"Well I'll make an appointment for you. Maybe she can put you on some other meds. I heard Depakote is helping a lot of manic-depressives."

"Yeah."

"Listen, Bruce, you've come too far. Just give it some more time. Keep enjoying Ozzy and you'll be fine."

"Well, Dr. C, if I'm doing so good then why do I have to stay on all of these pills? Sometimes I feel they're messing me up more . . ."

"Bruce, don't even think about it. Don't you dare stop taking them, then you're really crazy. Bruce, if it wasn't for that lithium, you wouldn't have made it to this point. Trust me. You'd be dead or in Bellevue. You certainly wouldn't be well enough to be taking care of a puppy. Listen, you have to trust me. Give it time. I've dealt with many patients like you. If you go off your medicine, it's going to get worse, and then it will be harder to stop it. Remember this is manic depression. It's a real thing. A real disease. It's like diabetes. If a diabetic doesn't take their insulin, what happens, they die. That's what happens. And you're not going to die on me. You've come too far, kid. You know I love you."

"Ah stop it." I blushed. "You're embarrassing me in front of my dog. Besides, you can't say you love me, that's illegal. I'm your patient."

"But Bruce, I do love you. You're one of my babies. So you have to keep taking your lithium. Trust me, you don't want to go back there. You're sane now. Don't ruin a good thing, You're doing great. Just continue taking the lithium, seeing me, seeing Dr. Williams and of course loving Ozzy. 'Cause it all works together. Do you hear me? *It all works together.* Ozzy and the therapy and the medication. It's not all or nothing anymore. That's the old Bruce way."

"Okay, okay. Hey, Dr. C . . ."

"Yes, Bruce."

"I just want to say . . ."

"Stop, you don't have to thank me. Just don't disappear on me or I'll hunt you down. I want to see you every two weeks. I want to see the two of you. You got that, Ozzy? Make sure you bring him." Then she whispered something in his floppy ear. Something like: "Keep up the good work. This is just the beginning to

Bruce's recovery. You're my partner now, little puppy. My cotherapist. You take care of him because I can't always be there, okay? And don't be afraid to be tough on him. Now gimme kisses if you understand me."

Ozzy licked her face.

"Oh, he's the cutest little thing. Dr. Ozzy. My little love puppy. I hope Marvin doesn't get jealous. He's gonna smell you all over me. Ehh, I'll explain it to him. All right, enough, now gimme a big hug. Group hug. The three of us. Now, I'll see you in two weeks. Time's up."

"Bye, Doc."

"Hey, Bruce, one more thing." She looked me in my soul and said, "Remember, remember this, the more love you give Ozzy the more love he'll give back to you. All you gotta do is love him, really love him like you've been doing, and it'll all be good. Now get outta here. I have another patient."

"Okay, thanks, Doc. See ya in two weeks."

I didn't think shrinks were supposed to show their feelings, but Dr. C wasn't a shrink to me anymore. She was my friend. And she was right. I wouldn't have made it this far without the medicine. Lithium, the magic mineral salt, had kept my head stationed in reality, from getting mentally decapitated. It protected me from me. But more important, I would've never made it this far (Point A: insanity to Point B: stability) without Dr. C's supervision, her love. She never gave up on me, even after all the times I gave up on me. Now it was time to put all my attention on Ozzy. I wanted more out of life than survival. So bring in the furry little buns. Full force. It was time for operation puppy.

"C'mon, Bruce, let's go," Ozzy said. "We got a lot of work to do on you, crazy boy."

"Who you calling crazy, just one second. Get over here, Stinky," I said gently grabbing his head. "You got eye boogers." I bent down and wiped the crust out of his baby blue pupils.

Hey, who's taking care of who?

PART THREE

BRUCE, HEAL

33

THE TRUTH ABOUT WOMEN AND DOGS

By the end of July, Dr. Giangola at Animal Health Center gave Ozzy his next set of shots, and we were no longer restricted to the front of my building. We were off to meet the other 5 million puppy people in the city while we were getting to know each other. We were the Bruce & Ozzy Show coming to a street corner near you.

"Hi, you've reached Bruce and Ozzy and we're not here right now, so please leave your name and phone number and we'll get back to you as soon as we can, thank you very much. Ozzy, speak." "A-woof!" "Good boy." *Beep.*

Thanks to Ozzy, every day was a beautiful day in the neighborhood, and I mean every neighborhood. Since I had nothing really to do but get better, every day we visited a different part of Manhattan like we were on an unauthorized puppy petting tour. I threw out my watch. No time schedule. No pressure. I just packed my baby bag, food, water, camera, treats, etc., and we were off wherever the day would take us. And it didn't matter where it took us, where we walked, because for the first time of my life, I wasn't in a rush to get anywhere. I wasn't searching for anything. I was just walking my puppy. Well, he was walking me. Every now and then Ozzy would look up at me, and give me the cutest smile. He had to make sure I was still by his side. God, he made me smile. The journey really was the destination. It was nonstop puppy pit stops all the way.

"Hey, Oz, let's check that out."

"Cool, Dad." He'd pull across the street.

"Hey wait for me! Gimme back my arm!"

No matter where the day took us we always seemed to wind up at Union Square Park. My old emotional stomping grounds. Where I first kissed Paige, where I first went crazy, and now it was where Ozzy taught me that it was okay for a grown man to play, to just lose myself in the moment. To be happy. And he was making me so happy. And I really loved making him happy. I used to teach Ozzy how to play fetch with his tiny basketball in the empty lot where they held the Green Market on the weekend, right across the street from that big-assed Barnes & Noble on Seventeenth Street. There was a fence, but I had him attached to a retractable leash anyway, so there was absolutely no way he was running out into the street. God, he was the cutest little thing. Sometimes when I threw the ball, he got into his little hunting stance and instead of coming back with the ball, he fetched pigeons instead. He ran after them like a little kid. He couldn't control himself. He was a bird dog. Women couldn't control themselves either. "Oh my God! Oh my God! Puppeeeeeeeeeeeeee!" Here they come.

Instead of rushing home during rush hour, woman after woman would stop to watch me, dear old doggy daddy spending quality time with his boy. And what started out as an innocent game of fetch turned into an innocent, very addictive sporting event. It was kind of like fly-fishing. Except I was using a really cute puppy for bait. It took worms and patience to catch a fish. All it took was Ozzy attached to his twelve-foot retractable leash to catch the interest of a female. The game went like this: As soon as I tossed Ozzy's ball and snapped the release button on his leash, I yelled "Go get it!" Ozzy got it all right. Ozzy always lured somebody back to me. This one redheaded woman in a power suit broke down and said, "I know, I know it's a chick magnet, but he's so cuuuuuute. U'mmmm. So cuuuuuute. I couldn't resist. Look at dat face."

"Yeah, he's my baby. He gets his good looks from his mother's side of the family."

And if for some reason a woman tried going on her merry way, Ozzy made sure she wasn't going anywhere. His incredible force of cuteness lured them back to me. And if Ozzy's kisser didn't work, Ozzy's scent would. Chanel had nothing on New Puppy Smell No.5.

"Oooh, puppy, you smell so new."

After Ozzy got a woman's attention, he really got their attention by jumping all over them and then nuzzling his way up their skirt. The women always thought he was so cute and innocent. "Hee, hee, hee, getta outta there pup-peee." That's when I'd cut in.

"Bad boy, Ozzy," I said. "I didn't teach you that."

"I bet you did."

"I didn't, honest. I swear."

"Good boy, Ozzy, keep it up," I whispered when she wasn't looking. "Wanna treat?"

Puppy love was a drug. I watched many a woman just drop whatever it was that they were doing to sit down and have a conversation with me and my dog. Anywhere. Anytime. One day this girl sat down with me in the middle of the sidewalk on Park Avenue during rush hour (people literally climbing over us) to tell me how Ozzy reminded her of her puppy, the one she had when she was five. "Ooh he's so adorable. He's just like Bandit. God, I miss him so much. You are a lucky man. I see you all the time. Is this all you do, play with your puppy all day when the rest of us are working?"

"Well kinda, but it's not that simple . . ."

I got so comfortable around women that I started sharing my story (the unsatanic edition) with them. "Yeah I got depressed and then I lost my job, and then my girlfriend split and then there were all the shrinks and I still wasn't getting better but then Ozzy came along. He was a miracle. He's the reason I'm sitting here with you. I'm still a little off, hey life's tough. But I owe the little guy my life."

"Is that true?" they'd ask Ozzy. "Did you really save your master's life? You're such a good boy, ooh I wanna eat cha."

No woman could resist Ozzy. It was a law of nature. It was like waving a carrot in front of a rabbit. Or a shrimp cocktail in front of me. Ozzy bridged the gap between two genders, boldly going where few New Yorkers had gone before. He actually approached strangers on the street and made eye contact. A picture may have said a thousand words but my puppy's eyes said, "Hey ladies. . . . Hi my name is Ozzy and this is my best friend Bruce. He's too shy to talk to you, he's actually bipolar and takes lithium, so it's my duty to introduce the two of you. Since you and a million other young women won't give him the time a day in a bar or when he used to commute on the Staten Island Ferry, I'm here to show you that he's all right. He's a good guy. You can trust him. I should know. He takes great care of me. Bruce gives me treats. He plays with me. I love the big lug even though he gets on my nerves sometimes. He's so moody in the morning. He drives me crazy. He's a neurotic baby. But hey, nobody's perfect. You should give him a chance. Go on a date with him. He'll buy you candy and make you laugh. He's not only interested in getting in your pants.

But what do I know, I'm just a dog. Come here sweetheart and rub my belly. Yeah that's the spot, yeah, yeah, yeah . . ."

Ozzy was right. I wasn't trying to sleep with them. That wasn't my motive. I was just having fun. I was having such a great time meeting all of them, and I mean all of them. I never knew there were so many kinds. I met blond ones. Brunette ones. Redhead ones. Purple with yellow streak-haired ones. Skinny ones. Chubby ones. White ones. Black ones. Asian Ones. Haitian ones. Puerto Rican ones. I met young ones. Old ones. Really old ones. Heterosexual ones. Bisexual ones. Lesbian ones. I met smart ones. Dumb ones. I met face-lifted ones. Breast-implanted ones. I met tattooed ones. Pierced-tongue ones. Pierced-belly-button-ringed ones and God-knows-what-else-was-pierced ones. I met some women that were so beautiful I couldn't even look them in their eyes to talk to them ones. But I wasn't just attracted to the looks of these women that were attracted to the looks of my puppy. I was attracted to the look in their eyes. What went on backstage in their minds. I was interested in their *lives*. Their style. Their intellect. I loved hearing other people's stories and I loved telling them mine. After a while I noticed that some of the women weren't just interested in my puppy. They were interested in me.

One day I came home after a long day with Ozzy, and Mr. Singh, my little Hindu doorman, said, "Mr. Broose. I got something for *yew*." He handed me a letter. I was hoping it wasn't an eviction letter because of all the barking and urine stains in the hallway. I couldn't believe somebody ratted me out and told the management company. Then I noticed it wasn't even addressed to me. On the outside envelope it read "To Ozzy:" in red curly penmanship. Inside, there was a letter. *Dear Ozzy & Bruce, It was really nice meeting you guys the other day. And Ozzy, if you ever need someone to walk you, I'd love to. (I suppose Bruce can come along too.) Please call, Allie.* She enclosed a business card. She worked at an advertising agency. My first reaction after I blushed was, "Who the hell is Allie?" My second reaction was, "Good boy! This is fucking amazing!" I couldn't believe it. This woman actually wanted to go out with me because I had a dog. I tried playing back all of my dog conversations in my head. I had absolutely no idea who she was. I thought it might be that Fran Drescher woman I met the first night I brought Ozzy home. *"Hayy look at the puppay."* God, I hoped not. I waited two days to see if the secret puppy admirer came forward. Then I called her.

"Hi, Allie, it's Ozzy. I was wondering if you'd like to take me and Bruce for a walk one day?" Allie started laughing and said, "Sure, Ozzy." She made plans with my dog to take me to Central Park the following Saturday. I had no idea what she looked like. She told me, "Hey I don't usually do this but it's hard to meet nice guys in New York, and you seemed like a nice guy with your dog so I figured what the hell."

Wow. This was the first time a woman didn't use me to get to my puppy. She used the puppy to get to me. I was flattered. I—was—a—nervous—wreck. As far back as I could remember, I had never been much of a ladies' man. I could have sure used a puppy back in the awkward pimply, McDonald's-arched hair-doo days of adolescence. I was so unattractive that the first girl I ever made out with *had* to make out with me. Her friends dared her to in a game of Truth or Dare. Now, thanks to Ozzy, my furry aphrodisiac, I wasn't just a guy anymore. I was a guy with a cute puppy. I was sensitive by association. I was a candidate for fatherhood. If I could pick up puppy poop, I could change smelly diapers. I was a provider. I was somebody they could trust. I was a guy that wasn't scared to commit. And women smelled that a mile away.

Saturday was the big day. My big date. My blind doggy date. I still had no idea what she looked like. I had Allie meet me at my apartment. The moment I opened my door I remembered what she looked like. "Oh, now I remember you," I said. She was five-seven or so. Wavy blond hair. She was cute. There was no immediate, "Ooh, la, la, let's dance," but I gave it a chance. She seemed funny. She laughed. Besides, I had to hop back on the dating bandwagon sooner or later. I had to become romantic again. I was going to have to familiarize myself with the words "compromise" and "sacrifice." Petty fights like Paige and I used to have. "Bruce, I don't wanna watch *Beavis and Butt-Head.* I wanna watch Newt Gingrich." God, I still missed Paige. But I knew I had to move on. I was just so nervous. I felt like a virgin. Globs of sweat were forming on my forehead. Just watching a new woman mush her tush in my leather couch was bizarre.

While Allie was telling me one of her dog stories, I drifted back in time. I saw Paige on the same couch smiling at me. It seemed like another lifetime. I was going to have to get used to being around the opposite sex again. Perfume and pocketbooks and periods, oh, my. But Allie was going to have to get used to being treated like a movie star.

We took a cab up to Central Park. When we got out across the street from the old Plaza by the smelly horse and carriages, I felt like John F. Kennedy Jr. It's an ambush! Holy puppy-paparazzi! We were surrounded. We were surround sounded. "Oh my God, it's a pupeeeee! A pupeeee! A pupeeee!" They came from all di- rections. They came in all nationalities. They were pointing and shooting at us. Standing there with all the noise and the flashes, it occurred to me that we weren't just standing in one of New York City's largest tourist traps, we had also become one. It was puppy pandemonium.

One by one, they would crouch down in front of Ozzy. Like he was the puppy pope. But I was even more amazed that Allie was such a good sport, considering I was paying a lot more attention to the women paying attention to my puppy than her. Families were the worst. They made a day out of it—like Ozzy was Epcot. They'd bring over strollers and all kinds of baby crap and yeah, there were balloons. It was like I was wearing an invisible sign that read, "Step right up and stick pretzels in my dog's face." They would just park little Joey next to Ozzy's body and say stuff like, "It's okay, baby. Go on touch little Ozzy, wazzy, on his wet nose." Ozzy took a lot too. I prayed he didn't eat little Joey's fingers, and I wouldn't get smacked with a lawsuit in front of the pink-ass baboon cage at the zoo.

After this episode of Get Your Kid's Paws Off My Doggy, we spent the rest of the day riding Ozzy's magic black carpet all around the park while greeting his adoring fans. He was waving his left paw and his right paw. "Thank you. Thank you," Ozzy said as people gave him free milk bones that these dog freaks just happened to be carrying in their pocketbooks.

Suddenly Ozzy stopped. He got really hot. He didn't want to walk anymore. He kept stopping. I kept having to go back to peel him off the pavement like he was twelve-pound burnt pancake stuck to a frying pan. Then I sprayed his feet with water. "Is that better, Ozzy, is that better?" Better for a second. He walked two more baby steps to the right, and then he dropped and gave me twenty—twenty minutes of agony. He was an official fat black welcome mat. It didn't take long before we were under another attack. Rollerbladers. Mountain bikers. A guy on a unicycle. Dog people from the five boroughs. There were even sailors from the navy. Long-haired rock band members. So many sweaty hands grabbing his silky, shiny black fur. Who knows where their paws had been? At first it was fun, a lot of fun, but enough was enough, I was getting a little overwhelmed. I wished I had a spray to keep people from petting Ozzy. I had had enough of this for one day. I just wanted to enjoy my date. Just the three of us. Not three thousand of us. Finally I picked up Ozzy and hid him under my arms. "Allie, look! Over there!" I grabbed Allie's hand and smuggled the smelly celebrity to the far corner on the big green lawn, Sheep's Meadow, where nobody could find us. We staked

Photo: Bruce Goldstein

out under a big oak tree. Not too far from where Satan came to get me that dark day back in May. But that part of my life was over, I prayed. Thanks to Ozzy.

It was so quiet. So peaceful. For approximately twenty-three seconds. The true puppy lovers sniffed him out. People started coming over in private groups to see The Prince of Labrador Retrievers. "Hi, it's our turn to play with your puppy," they said.

It was?

What was I to say? I enjoyed watching Ozzy make other people's day.

It was organized canine at it's best. It was an event. Step right up and see the "Greatest Puppy on Earth." This young couple were on an all-points puppy bulletin.

"Hi, we've been thinking about getting a puppy before we have a baby. Then we spotted your little cutie pie. Is it okay if we play with him, please, please, please."

"He's all yours. Take him away."

Seconds later, a group of four approached us to pet Ozzy's fur.

"We couldn't help but notice your puppy. Is it all right if we pet him?"

"Why, sure."

For the next two hours we did back to back performances of "Shakespaw-in-the-park." I should have charged a fee. Allie and I just laughed as Ozzy ate grass, shook paws, bit toes, and took naps. I got to know Allie a little better when she told me all about her dog that she had growing up, Freddy. She said, "When I used to watch TV, Big Freddy would sneak up on me and lay the biggest farts in my face. Dog farts are the worst." How appetizing.

That night I treated Ozzy and Allie to an outside early dinner downtown at slick and trendy Luna Park, where I had taken Paige on one of our first dates. The hostess, Fiona, escorted the three of us down the cement staircase to show us to our table where our very exotic looking waitress, Martina, gave him the royal puppy treatment. She served him a big tin foil bowl of water. Ozzy wasn't interested. So he pawed it out of his way. Then I explained to Martina that Ozzy liked his water on the rocks. "Oh, sorry," she said jokingly. And she brought out a tray of ice cubes. Ozzy said *grazie* and he chomped away. Dinner was great but it had nothing to do with the food. It had nothing to do with Allie. It was all about Ozzy. Attention à la mode. Every time one of the waitresses or customers came over to tickle Ozzy's belly, I felt euphoric. I felt endorphins being released. I was so happy for him. For me. I was laughing. I felt like singing. But there was something wrong with this picture—Allie. She was a nice girl. But I would have preferred to be alone with Ozzy, just the two of us. Me and my furry mini-me. I had a nice day with Allie. But I wasn't ready for another relationship—with a woman anyway. So I said, "Good night, I had a good time," and I didn't call her again. I called Ozzy instead.

And when Ozzy listened, I mean when he learned his name the first time and he came running when I called him, with those big blue eyes, and all that slobbery slobber, and his velvety ears flapping in the wind, and he was tripping all over himself with his big goofy feet, I was ecstatic. "Come here boy! Come here, Ozzy! Good boy!" Words can't describe how proud I was of him. How happy I was that I was alive. I was never more happy in my life. And it was only August. We had the rest of the summer to be together. We had the rest of our lives.

34

THE SUMMER OF PUPPY LOVE

What little I knew about relationships—I knew that if you spent enough time with somebody there was compromise, give and take. Well, my puppy was big on generosity. Without saying a word of gibberish, every day he was teaching me more and more not to be selfish. To not just think about myself. To be nice to everybody, and by doing that, it was having a boomerang effect on me. Basically, Ozzy taught me if I was going to chew Chiclets to make sure I brought enough for everybody. Go on, give the Bangladeshi cab driver a twenty-dollar tip for taking you and your puppy down Broadway. Put a smile on his face. I was amazed at how canine karma worked in the galaxy. Under Ozzy's hot black fur jacket lay a heart as cool as a white-uniformed Good Humor ice cream man whose only purpose in life was putting people in good moods all across the land. Ozzy's master plan to plugging me back into the master outlet of humanity was to set me free from my prehistoric ways of thinking. Jealousy was a biggie. I never wanted to share Paige with anybody. Now I wanted to share Ozzy with everybody. We pretended we were living back in the sixties. It was the summer of free puppy love in New York City. By sharing his love with everybody, by rubbing off on thousands of people in a positive way, the love was rubbing back off on Ozzy, back off on me. Tenfold. A millionfold. Quadrillionfold. My puppy was rubber. I was glue. The good energy he threw out to the iffy universe came back positive. His love was unstoppable.

Whenever I walked my puppy around the city, I felt like I was walking a magnetic angel on a retractable leash. I used to imagine that there was this soft purple glow around me, continuing all the way down the lead attached to my spunky pet power source of positivity. It was a beautiful array of colorful cosmic energy. I felt like a boy in a bubble with my hop-a-long trusty sidekick, Barney Rubble. It was the only way all of this mental magnificence made sense to me. Spiritual electricity. Why else would God's cement creatures all come up to me? Anybody who crossed his path was in for a mood swing. Turn that frown upside down. Chill out, child. Smile. It was love at first sight of Ozzy's aura. "Hey, lady, cheer up. Don't look so glum." Ozzy said. "Come here and pet my tushy. Now don't be shy." Like a doctor hitting somebody with a rubber reflex hammer on their knee, Ozzy was just making sure people got their daily supplies of Good and Plenty. People would often say to me, "Looks like he's taking *you* for a walk" They weren't kidding. Ozzy weaved me in and out of all kinds of wacky situations. Whether I wanted to go down that block or not, Ozzy knew what was best for me. He took off. "Get back here," I'd shout, as I was being dragged down the street. And I'd always wind up running into who I was supposed to meet—whether it was a job opportunity, a girl, or a homeless person that really needed to talk to somebody. Ozzy was my personal seeing-eye dog. Every day he pulled me more and more out of darkness and the depths of despair. He just so happened to be the same guy who chewed up my underwear.

I took Ozzy everywhere with me. I mean everywhere. From outside cafés, Diva in Soho for a plate of spaghetti marinara, to Duane Reade to buy toilet paper. I took him to buy CDs at Virgin Megastore. I pointed at the posters of his namesake. "That's your uncle Ozzy Osbourne," I'd say. "Did you know he ate a dove's head off, he did, Ozzy, he really did." I took him to buy gourmet coffee and Imodium A-D. I put him in a shopping cart and wheeled him around Bed Bath & Beyond to look for a new can opener. Nobody told me that they had just waxed the floors. "Puppy coming through! Watch out! Wild puppy coming through!" I even took him to buy a new pair of black pants at the Gap, like I really needed them. Boy, they loved him over there, especially in the ladies' dressing room. "Puppeeee!" And if there was a place in the city that wouldn't let me bring Ozzy, then I just didn't go there. Anybody who didn't take to my dog was *suspect*. It just wasn't the same without him. People just weren't the same. Before Ozzy, I used to *just* pick up my lithium prescriptions at Hampton Chemists, a sterile pharmacy on Twenty-eighth Street. Now, I joked around with Ricky, the manager. "Hey, get that vicious dog away from me. Ah, I'm just kidding, Brucie. God, I love that puppy." Before Ozzy, I used to just pick up my laundry at my dry cleaner. Now, I had twenty-minute conversations with Jun, the owner. "Hey, how's the family?" And whenever I took Ozzy to pick up Chinese food at Noodles on 28th, they'd say, "Make him do tricks." I'd get Ozzy to speak, then they'd give him a fortune cookie. One read: *You are in love with a special somebody.*

It didn't matter where we went, Ozzy always made it fun for me. More than fun. Profitable. He made getting a little loan a lot easier. I didn't need a cosigner. Ozzy was interest-bearing enough to loan officer Linda Cooper. "Hello, Mr. Goldstein, how are you two today?"

Twenty-five thousand dollars richer, why thank you.

"Bye, cutie. You too, Brucie."

Ozzy's cuteness sure went a long way. One day a crowd of people were around a baby stroller. When Ozzy showed up, they left the baby to come say, "Look at the puppy." But nothing was cuter than when we went to the Greenmarket every week and the same guy with the white beard and the white sheep dog always gave Ozzy free vegetables. Ozzy loved munching out on monster-size carrots. Loved 'em. He held onto them with his big paws like he was eating an orange lollipop. People formed circles around us to watch him. Some guy said, "Hey, your dog's a vegetarian. He eats like a rabbit."

"Just don't stick your hand near his mouth." I said. "He eats people fingers for dessert."

The only thing that ever got more attention than Ozzy was this guy over on Seventy-sixth Street walking his pet monkey or these nine-year-old skateboarders dressed in bright red clown's costumes. But then one evening the dream team gave Ozzy his first skateboard ride. One of the kids hugged my kid and said, "We love you, Ozzy. You can hang with us anytime." I took a picture and had it framed.

All of this attention started going to my puppy's big head. Especially when King Ozzy defeated the knights of the round table on jousting night in Union Square. There were all of these guys running around in tights and suits of armor stabbing each other with swords. There was a pretty big crowd. But as soon as we arrived, Ozzy stole the show. All I had to do was get him to speak, and the ladies went gaa-gaa.

One day Ozzy realized how to make this cute puppy thing really work for him. Whenever I told him, "Ozzy, down," this would make crowds of women form circles around us all over town. His big block head would drop to the floor, flush flat with the rest of his body. His legs would go straight back. His chubby puppy pawed arms would go straight forward. He looked like a baby bear rug. His eyes were the only things that moved. He looked up and down. Left and right. Over and out. Then he wiggled his eyelids like he had a twitch. If there was a fly on his nose, he'd go cross-eyed and he'd wiggle his nostrils like *Bewitched*. This drove women wild. "Awww. He's so sweet. That's the cutest pup-peeeee I have ever seen." If he tried to lift his head off the ground in the slightest way I'd point my finger to the ground.

"Ozzy, all the way down."

His head dropped back down flat to the ground. What Ozzy figured out was that he didn't need me to give him an order. All that he had to do was plop down anywhere, assume the bear rug position, and he would be in the spotlight.

"Awwww, pick him up. He's tired. He's just a baby. Awwww, carry him. He's schleeeeepy." Ozzy would savor the moment. My dog had groupies. One time, while walking back from my therapy appointment, this woman came running out of an office building on Fifty-seventh Street screaming at me. "Oh my God I can't believe it's him. Make him do the thing! Make him do the thing!" She was a regular Ozzy fan so I knew exactly what "thing" she was talking about. So did Ozzy. He was already doing it. The bear rug. Occasionally he'd throw in a little wookie whimper for effect.

"A-roo-roo-roo." He was a ham, I tell ya.

Some of my best days with Ozzy were when we had no plans at all. We played it by dog ears. Sometimes I would just let him lead. We would leave our apartment early in the morning and not return until eleven o'clock at night. I used to come home filthy. My white T-shirt was no longer white. My toes would be black. My khaki shorts were no laughing matter, they were coated with eye boogers, poop spots, and doggie slobber. My friends used to say give the poor dog a break. Ozzy took his own breaks. It would've been nice if he warned me.

One day he decided to take a nap in the middle of the side-walk—the heart of the diamond district. I couldn't believe how many diamond dealers came running out of their stores, leaving jewels unguarded just to see my sleeping beauty. This Israeli woman said, "Now he's got the right idea. He's tired. Let him sleep, ehh." So I let him sleep. Sometimes when he was sleeping, I loved to just look at him. The way I used to watch Paige. So peaceful. So at ease. There was something so soothing about watching somebody you love breathe. Sometimes I'd catch him dreaming. He'd be kicking his chubby little arms, and making all kinds of weird sounds like he was romping around chasing cats in a doggie Disney World. But if he looked frightened, if it was a nightmare, I'd gently touch his shoulder to wake him up, and then I'd give him a hug and tell him I loved him. "It's okay, puppy. It's okay, baby. Daddy's here now." When Ozzy eventually awoke from his nap on Forty-seventh Street, twenty-five min-utes later, the very nice owner of a jewelry store gave me her card. She said, "My name's Rachel Schlussel. When you're in the mar-ket for a *vrock* give me a call. I'll give you good deal. Now you be a good *mensch* and take care of my liddle *mamashaina*."

"Shalom, lady. We'll be seeing ya."

Another time I was caught in a storm in the band shell in Cen-tral Park. A semi-selfish riot broke out. Everybody was knocking into me and my puppy trying to stay dry. "Whoa, whoa, watch out for the baby," I said. But nobody seemed to hear me except for this guy in a red bandanna with a tattoo of a scorpion on his neck. "Yo! listen up! Everybody, step the hell back. Nobody betta' fuck with dat puppy. He's wit me."

Ozzy was my get-in-free pass around the city. One night my black beauty introduced me to the owner of the Park Avenue Country Club. He said Ozzy reminded him of his yellow Lab, Sheila, when she was a puppy. So he invited the two of us to come by the club to meet the Yankees. He said the whole team was going to be there signing autographs. "Bring Ozzy by for a beer, just ask for Bobby at the door."

"Thanks, man."

Ozzy even got my socks free from a vendor on Twenty-first Street who remembered me from previous purchases. "You're that guy with the puppy, right? Hey, how's he doin'?"

"He's okay."

"Good, good. Here take an extra pair on me. Lemme know how they feel, okay? And say hi to the little guy."

My Ozzy, he was becoming a li'l celebrity all right. He rubbed paws with the rich and famous. He nibbled on Al Roker on Twentieth Street. He got trampled by tourists outside of Planet Hollywood. People came from thousands of miles away to look at Bruce Willis's boxer shorts but one look at Ozzy and then, "Oh look at the puppeeee! Ain't he the cutest little thing." And since he couldn't get his paws on the wall of celebrity hand prints, he took a dump underneath it. "I'll be back," he barked at Schwarzenegger. Ask Ferris Bueller. Matthew Broderick waved his cigar Ozzy's way in Gramercy Park. And the cast of *Grease* couldn't get enough of his furry little butt either. Because Ozzy was the word around town. And there was so much more to come. *So much more* cause everybody had a soft spot in their heart for my little dog. Even the hookers on my corner.

One Saturday night at around 2:30 in the morning, I got a craving for a pint of Ben & Jerry's Chunky Monkey ice cream, so I took my chunky little monkey for a walk across the street to the Korean deli. I saw some neighbors Ozzy and I hadn't met yet. There were around four Sassy Susannas congregating out front. They were all gussied up in their big-butted fishnet stockings, and one of them had cleavage. *Cleavage.* They smiled at us when we came out of the store. A really cute dirty blond one, wearing not much at all, said, "Look how cute. Is he a Lab? I used to have a Lab."

"Oh yeah." I made some small talk even though it made me feel kind of sad. That this woman used to be a little girl from Indiana or Philadelphia. She had a mother and a father. *How the hell did she end up here?* Anyway I told her to take care of herself out there, and I started walking away. Except Ozzy didn't. I tugged his leash. "C'mon, Oz. Let's go." He just sat there. He was enjoying himself. And then I couldn't believe my eyes. He had a hard-on. "Ozzy, put that thing away. Put that thing away," I commanded. But he just sat there smiling with his little red rocket. Then this other big mama jama, wearing leopard spotted panties inside-out and pink stilettos, walked over and said, "Hah, hah, hah, Ozzy knows where the pussy's be'n at. Ain't that right Ozzy?"

Ozzy was smiling. I was blushing. "C'mon, Ozzy, let's go get you a bitch," I told my kid. Some foxy poodle. "You don't have to pay for it."

"Das right, Ozzy, listen to your daddy."

I met so many *amazing* people that summer. People were just so much more approachable around my furry little fella. I didn't know what it was, that human/animal magnetism, but Ozzy was a strong force—sometimes a little too strong. Occasionally the little magnet backfired on me and attracted the wrong characters. But hey, even the best medicine had side effects.

One day Ozzy and I ventured off our usual path. We ended up on Eighth Avenue in Chelsea. We were just minding our own business, as my boy took care of his business, when suddenly, this leather vest–wearing, bare chest, motorcycle guy look-alike appeared out of nowhere. There was nothing unusual about this, other than he was wearing mascara. But hey, this was New York.

So he got down on the ground and did the usual pet-my-puppy-thing.

"Oh you are so cute, you are so cute," he said.

Only when I looked down he wasn't looking at Ozzy, he was looking directly at me. "And so are you, puppy. And so are you," he said.

He got up slowly, and got very close to me, *very close*, and looked me in my eyes. He winked.

I looked down at Ozzy. Ozzy looked up at me. And we both looked at the Road Warrior with the eye shadow.

"Sorry buddy, but you're barking up the wrong tree."

35

A GUY WITH A PUPPY ISN'T AN AX MURDERER

With all the day-to-day craziness in New York City, I guess I became what you call an overprotective parent. From now on when we crossed a street, I walked first. I held Ozzy behind me a few feet, so if a car came rushing down the street I would go down and my puppy would be safe. He was young. He had his whole life to live. Besides if something happened to him, what good was I without him?

One day Ozzy started limping in the middle of this street fair. "Ozzy, what's wrong, pup?" I asked him. "What's wrong?" He stopped walking, he gave me this look, so helpless, then he handed me his paw. "Oh no, Ozzy, oh no." There was a little blood leaking out. When I got a closer look, I found a piece of glass in his pad. "Hold still, pup, this will only take a second . . . . , got it. All better, daddy made it all better now." There were so many dangerous things in Manhattan to worry about. Like antifreeze—toxic. "Ozzy get away from that green pee," I screamed. But bike messengers were the craziest. One of them got off his bike and came running after us because he thought I said something to him. "You said, 'Yesssssssssss!'" he hissed at me. "Oh no I didn't. Don't come near us." It was broad daylight. It was just me and Ozzy and his new silver chain link leash. I got so frightened for Ozzy when the nose-pierced, green-haired freak was about to get up in my face. So I let him have it. I waved the chain that was still attached to Ozzy, and I released my bipolar beast: "Get the hell away from my puppy," I screamed louder than the city. "Or I'll kill you! I'll kill you! You don't want to fuck with me and my puppy!" He backed up. Jumped on his bike. Never heard from him again. I was so frightened for my child's safety that I was still shaking. But then people started clapping like it was a Crocodile Dundee movie. An old woman said, "Right on, young man. I'd a done the same thing."

"C'mon, Oz, let's get outta here. It's safe now."

Crazy people were only half the trouble a dog owner had to worry about. There were the stupid telephone poles, the broken ones with all the stupid wires sticking out. If I wasn't careful watching Ozzy, one lift of his little leg and he'd get electrocuted, he'd fry in a couple of seconds. And then there were those chicken bones all over the sidewalk, K.F.C. Killing Fucking Canines. There were hundreds of them. And only a dog could find him. "Ozzy, what are you eating? No!" I couldn't tell you how many times I stuck my arm down his gooey throat to fetch a drumstick so he didn't choke. Not to mention the 101 piranha marks on my hand from his razors.

But the most dangerous position I ever put him and myself in was the night I almost hung him.

I had been bullshitting with my doorman and the elevator came. I let Ozzy go in first. I said, "You don't need me Ozzy. You know where you live, boy." I don't know what the hell I was thinking because when the door closed, Ozzy was in the elevator and I wasn't. But the worst part was that the end of his leash was still on the first floor with me, sticking out of the silver door. I had the worst images. I pictured Ozzy hanging from the ceiling like a chandelier. When the elevator light stopped at the second floor I ran up the stairs, praying every step of the way. I almost went to the bathroom in my pants in the stairwell. But thank God when I arrived at the scene of my crime, he was well. Somehow the leash was mysteriously with him, and my puppy was in one piece. My little buddy. "I'm so sorry. I promise to be more careful in the future." And I was. I *really* was.

I did whatever it took to make his life better. The little things. I hate to be cheesy, but I was cheesy. Like if Ozzy was thirsty, I must've stolen ice cubes from every Korean deli around the city. Or if the smoky black pavement was too hot for Ozzy, I pulled out my trusty spray bottle and cooled off his feet. Each little piggy individually. "Now this little piggy got a little bath, splash, splash, splash, there, now that's better." One day I was doing the feeties thing in front of the Chrysler Building and a hot dog vendor came running over; he left his stand unattended. "Oh my God, you very good man. Very good man. That's the nicest thing I've ever seen. Cooling off your dog's feet. He reminds me of my Mimi back in my country."

"Nah, get outta here."

"No, you good man," he insisted. Then he gave us free hot dogs and Ozzy complimentary diarrhea. Now that was a doozy. Some people think it's funny, but it's not when you're chasing your dog down the street with a baggie and the evening edition of the *New York Times*, leaving streaks on the sidewalk in front of outdoor cafés while all these beautiful women are giggling. It was humiliating. It was stinky.

After a month or two of being a doggy daddy, there was nothing that I couldn't do. One day I was on my hands and dirty kneecaps taking the boogers out of Ozzy's eyes, "Now sit still, sit still, Ozzy," when this old lady with pink curlers and a lime green jacket came up to me and my satanic goatee and earring. Instead of running away from me like I was the boogie man, she said, "Excuse me, sonny, which way is Nineteenth Street? I'm looking for the movie theater. The matinee."

I pointed her in the right direction. Then I said, "By the way, what made you ask me?"

"Because you look like somebody I could trust."

"But lady, I'm an ax murderer and I kill people." I raised my arms like the boogie man.

"No you're not. Don't be silly. Anybody who can take care of a cute little puppy like that isn't any ax murderer."

As she walked away I thought that if I ever decided to become a professional hit man for a living, or a bank robber, I now had the perfect disguise. *But it wasn't a disguise.*

Something had happened to me ever since Ozzy came into my life. I wasn't the same selfish, self-absorbed guy. All I cared about was Ozzy. Making sure he was all right. He was my full-time love. And for the first time in my life, I actually loved what I was doing for a living. I was actually living. My day didn't revolve around making money anymore, or tooting my own horn in advertising. Screw all that. Creativity was all about designing your time. My life revolved around Ozzy. He had become the center to my universe. He was my hub. My heart. He grounded me. He kept it real. He was the best part about me. He was my higher self. He was better than a person could ever be. Nonjudgmental. Not a jealous bone in his body. He was the best thing that had ever happened to me. And he taught me something new every-day. Pill after pill after pill, my puppy gave me what no medicine could ever give me. He wasn't milligrams. He didn't come in a bottle. He was 100 percent unconditional love. He was my furry antidepressant. I mean if the slightest bad mood started to seep in, if something scared me, all I had to do was look him. Because it was the way he looked at me, with those eyes, those more than human, those humane, facial expressions, that told me how much he loved me, and that tore down my mood swings. Like a sledgehammer. And that made my demons pack their bags and move back to Transylvania. The fact that he was so concerned about me just made me start crying, but in a good way. He would follow me all over my apartment just to be near me. He would sit by me when I was doing the dishes in the sink just in case the knives were up to their old thing. He would sit next to me when I was on the bowl, and if I was sick and depressed over my irrita-ble bowel syndrome that would never go away, he would give me this look, and I knew it would pass, that I was just having a bad day. He was always there making sure I was okay. He would sit on my feet. He would even lick my feet. Oh, that killed me. The fact that he loved me, that he really cared about what happened to me, was just too much for me. That this little mush ball had so much love in him. God, he was a mush. My only hope was that I could learn in one lifetime to love him back enough. Then one night I *really* got my chance.

36

OZZY, PLAY DEAD

As time moved on, I had good days and bad days and every now and then I had some really bad days, but one day something happened, something horrible happened, the worst thing I could've ever imagined happened because it didn't happen to me—it happened to Ozzy.

I had been out with my friends watching *Braveheart* for the ninth time, and I just didn't feel right. I had a lot on my mind. I felt depressed. Ozzy was home alone in his crate. And I really wanted my own bathroom—it was a Crohn's day. So I left.

When I got to my building, I was so looking forward to spending a quiet night with my dog, but from the moment I got out of the elevator onto my floor, I knew something was very wrong. It smelled *so* awful in the hallway. Foul. Like an old hospital. When I ran into my apartment, I was immediately informed that there was a change of plans in my evening.

"Ozzy, Ozzy, oh my God." I ran to his crate. "What happened? What happened, little buddy? What did you do?"

There was diarrhea all over the place. Oh Jesus. And it was bloody, bloody, and not just a little bloody, a lot of bloody. But then I saw the saddest thing. Ozzy was all the way in the corner of his crate. He had this look on his face like he had screwed up, that I would be mad at him or something. His eyes were so watery. "No Ozzy, oh Ozzy, it's my fault for not being here for you. I'm sorry. I'll clean this up in a second. Everything's gonna be okay." I tried to convince myself anyway. I wanted to close my eyes so badly and see that this wasn't really happening because before anything was gonna get better, things were getting a lot worse. A lot faster.

When I let him out of the crate he didn't even try to run. He just sat there like he was stuffed. Then he started coughing. He was heaving and hooing. He looked so helpless and I didn't know how to help him. And then he started hacking up his lungs and then he started throwing up and not just throw up. There was more blood. More blood. Little droplets. It was really bad. I panicked. What am I gonna do? I thought. *What am I gonna do? Stop it, Bruce, stop, calm the hell down and help him. He could die. Oh shit. He really could die.* My baby was going to die. It was the dreaded Parvo puppy killer disease, I knew it. I knew it. What luck? I must've put him on the ground one too many times. I let him get too close to one too many dogs butts. I took him for one too many walks. There were so many warnings. *How could I have been so friggin' careless? Why?* I had to pull myself together. *Myself.* The hell with myself. I had to do something. So I called Ozzy's vet, and he was gone for the evening. I tried Information to get poison control, and they told me to go to the Animal Medical Center and they told me nothing. They had a friggin' answering machine: "If your dog is dying, press 3. If he's not dead yet, please bring him in for a visit, our hours are, click—" Shit, shit, shit. I threw *another* phone against the wall, crushed in a million pieces. "I'm sorry, Ozzy, but I'm not good at this." Ozzy wasn't doing too good either; he was still throwing up all over the place, so I grabbed his leash and said, "Come on, boy, let's get the hell outta here." Before I could put his leash on, there was more diarrhea on the floor, on my rug, and since I had left the front door open, he took off down the hallway. Thank God they were going to be changing the carpet. And he wasn't done yet. He had diarrhea in the elevator, in the lobby, and whatever he had left he excreted in the front of my building. It wouldn't stop. Where the hell is it all coming from? He made trails up and down the block, and when I ran out of paper, I told myself I'd pick it up later, but then I ran into one of my neighbors. "Hey, clean that up," he said. "This isn't a garbage dump."

"What?" I wanted to rip the guy's head off, but I couldn't even go there, all I cared about was my puppy's health. "It's not his fault, you asshole," I yelled. "He's sick."

He was sick. I thought Ozzy might've gotten better with the fresh air, but the truth was that I was really scared to take him to the emergency room. I couldn't comprehend the concept of losing him, so I told myself he would be okay, but he wasn't okay. Oh God, I hoped he was going to be okay so I ran into the middle of street, almost getting trampled by a herd of wild Lincoln Continentals. I had one arm clutching Ozzy and the other was hailing a taxi.

"Taxi, taxi!" I screamed. And nobody was stopping.

"Taxi, taxi." And nobody was stopping. Because they didn't want to dirty their immaculate driving machines. "Well screw them," I told my little man. "You're cleaner than most people. You know that, you know that, booga-boo?" I tried to make him laugh.

"Ozzy, it's gonna be okay, it's gonna be okay, baby bear. Somebody help him, please. Oh God, please don't let him die. Please don't let him die. Please, please, stop somebody, Help me. Help me. Hold on Ozzy, hold on." A cab pulled up. "The Animal Emergency Center, on sixty-something and York, hurry, hurry, please, he's really sick."

We sped down the avenues, blowing lights. "Keep going, keep going!" I held Ozzy in my arms so tight. "Please God, let us get there in time."

"Stop the car!" I threw a twenty at the guy, you're a really good person, thank you, and I jumped out and took Ozzy up the ramp through the emergency room. "Sick puppy coming through. Sick puppy," I screamed. I saw dogs with those lamp shade things over their heads, and there was a crippled rabbit and plenty of cats too. Then a bunch of nurses came and took him and I followed. They let me in the room. While the nurse was sticking a tube up Ozzy's butt and hooking him to an IV setup, she asked me what happened. "I don't know. I don't know. I just came home and found him covered in bloody dog doo and then he started throwing up." Then the nurse asked me to leave the room so they could do something else to him. Like what? "It's okay," she said. "He'll be okay."

I didn't know what they were doing in there, but I know it hurt. I heard little yelps from behind the door. The suspense was killing me. "What the hell are they doing in there for so long? What are they doing to my dog? Don't hurt him. Please God, be in there with him. Be in there."

I paced back and forth for what seemed like hours, and then the nurse came out and said, "Mr. Goldstein?"

"Yeah, is he okay, is he okay, please tell me he's okay." I was shaking.

"He's gonna be okay."

"Thank you, thank you. Well, what the hell happened then? What about all the blood?"

"We found this."

She put her hand out in front of me. It was this black thing in a plastic bag. It was a Combat bait station. "And it is poisonous, but it's not the bait," the nurse told me. "It was the plastic part. The black part is very, very toxic, Mr. Goldstein, and luckily Ozzy is a healthy plump puppy and he didn't eat enough of it to have any serious damage. It just cut him up a little bit but he'll be okay. It's nothing to worry about, really. A little medicine and he'll be fine. He has a mild case of colitis. A little inflammation of his intestines."

I started laughing. "Like father like son."

"What do you mean?" the nurse asked.

"Forget about that, can I see him?"

"Of course you can, you're his daddy."

When I saw Ozzy on that bed, when I saw his eyes, when I saw that smile, I just started crying. For the first time in my life, I had absolutely nothing else on my mind.

"Daddy, I'm all right," he said. "I'm all right."

"I know you are. Now, get the hell over here, you little munchkin. Combat bait station, I'll give you a bait station, what's a matter, I don't feed you? Just wait till I get you home. I'm gonna eat your nose. You're grounded."

Walking out of the hospital, I carried out my dog like he was my blood. My family. I breathed in the city: the red glittering lights, the purple-speckled noise, the rotten vegetable garbage. Everything was the same, but something had changed. I felt it deep inside. For a moment that night, the world had stopped for my boy. *Something had changed.* Yeah, something had changed. I looked down at the twinkling stars, in the mirror of my puppy's eyes. I was the luckiest man alive. But luck had nothing to do with it.

37

PUPPIES ARE BETTER THAN PROZAC

Just because I was feeling better (and thank God, Ozzy was feeling much better), I didn't stop going to therapy. Ozzy looked forward to going even more. As soon as we got in the cab to go there, Ozzy knew exactly where we were going. He knew the routine. The second the taxi stopped, Ozzy bolted out of the cab and dragged me across Fifty-seventh Street. Then he pulled me into the building, into the elevator, and right into the reception area where he waited very impatiently, barking and trying to squirm his way out of my arms and into Dr. C's office before it was our turn.

"Okay, let him go!" Dr. C screamed from down the long corridor. "C'mon, Ozzy!"

I released the hound. He took off like a bolt of furry lightning, stopped to pee on the rug, and then proceeded to topple over Dr. C in the hallway. I didn't know who was more excited to see whom. As much as Dr. C was therapy for me, Ozzy was therapy for her. She would put Ozzy's leash in his mouth and let him walk himself to her office. He knew where to go because every time we showed up, Dr. C spoiled Ozzy rotten with rawhide, pig's ears, and cow hooves. And she let him jump all over her and her couch.

I gave Dr C a quick breakdown about everything that had been happening. "I mean Dr. C, it's crazy out there. We meet hundreds of people a day. It takes us an hour to walk one block. I should put a mustache and baseball cap on Ozzy to disguise him. I mean it's nuts. We're constantly getting stopped. I mean, it's fun, for the most part. Everyday I meet so many interesting people. But I still have some bad days. The mornings are still the most difficult for me. I'm like a cold shaky car that needs a jump start. After Ozzy forces me to talk to about four or five people, my head stops shaking, I stop slurring, and like magic I'm talking a mile a minute. I'm ready to start our day. Do you think I'm manic?"

"Well, Bruce, you are manic depressive. There is always going to be a little touch of *mania*. But I think you're doing a lot better, and as long as you keep getting your blood checked you'll be fine. I mean hey, you're light years away from when you first stormed in here back in January. Remember? 'I'M NOT BIPOLAR! I'M NOT BIPOLAR! NO! NO! NO!' Don't you think? I mean come on, Bruce."

I smiled. "Yeah, life's pretty good thanks to Ozzy."

"I'm so happy you found each other. I mean this dog really loves you. Just look at the way he looks at you. He just adores you. Oh wait, Bruce, I almost forgot to tell you, you're going to love this. There's this patient of mine that has been very depressed lately. She's been on all kinds of medication, and it still wasn't helping. But then yesterday, she came to her appointment all excited. She told me she saw the cutest black puppy she had ever seen in her life playing fetch with the littlest basketball in Union Square Park so she approached the owner about where he got him. And she told me all about how nice the owner was and how she spent like an hour hanging out with him and his puppy, answering a million dog questions, and how he gave her his puppy breeder's phone number so she could get one too, so I said, 'Let me guess, were their names Bruce and Ozzy?'" She gave me chills.

"It's a small dog world, Dr. C."

"Yes it is, Bruce."

I wasn't sure who the patient was that she was talking about. I had given Dorothy's number out like hotcakes. But whoever she was, I was really happy for her. Her life was going to be so much better. I knew mine was.

"Bruce, I'll see you in two weeks," Dr. C said. "And keep up the good work, Ozzy. You're doing amazing things with him. You really are a miracle. You walked Bruce over the bridge. You did it! Yay Ozzy, you did it!"

"Yeah, I guess he did."

When we left Dr. C's office, and started walking down the street, Ozzy looked hot so we made a little puppy pit stop. We parked our butts in the shade. "One second little guy, Poland Spring coming right up." As I was on my knees, bottle-feeding my puppy—Ozzy flopping his pink little tongue, drooling all over the place—I felt a presence. When I looked up, there was this blond woman just standing there, staring at us. She was wearing a red dress and she wouldn't stop smiling.

"Now that looks like a man who's in love."

You got me.

38

MY GOLDSTEIN RETRIEVER

I hadn't seen my friends in a long time. It was more like they
hadn't seen me. The real me. Ozzy and I met them up at the Great
Lawn in Central Park for a picnic. The whole Martha's Vineyard
gang was there. There was David and Isabella, Liam McNulty
and his friend Spencer, Allen and Barney, and there was Ricky.
And there was me. But this time I wasn't alone.

"Ozzy," they screamed. "How you guys doin'?"

"Woof! Woof!"

"Great, can't complain. Right, Oz? Speak! Speak!"

"Woof! Woof!"

It was a beautiful day. Everything was perfect. The blue. The green. Under the trees away from the Frisbee throwing, I found a nice place in the shade with a breeze to lay out a blanket. I took out Ozzy's little tin cup bowl to give him some water to wash down his twigs. While I was wining and dining my prince charming, one by one my friends took turns playing with Ozzy. I felt weird around my friends. I felt weird being—*happy*. I couldn't believe I was the same person that used be scared to be around them. I couldn't believe I was the same person that my friends used to worry about doing himself in. I couldn't believe I was the same guy that hit Ricky. What the hell was I thinking back then? Who was I? Whatever it was, I was feeling better now, and that's all that mattered. That horror story was over and done with. The End. Bruce Lived. So I stopped questioning. I didn't want to jinx myself. My friends didn't bring it up either. They were just happy to have me back in the present. I was happy to have them back too. I loved my friends. They helped get me through some rough stuff. But there was only one guy who had the healing touch. Ozzy was the only one who really knew who I was. He was my true love. Now where is he? Where's my special little guy? "Come here, Ozzy, don't be shy. Everybody wants to meet you, you're my hero. You're the puppy who saved my life."

Lying under the sun, lying on my back I raised Ozzy above my head high above the grass, the trees, way up beyond the clouds. "Upsy daisy, upsy daisy," I said.

"A-woo-woo-woo!"

"You can say that again."

I used to say how the hell can I get a dog in New York when I can hardly take care of myself. Well, that day I said, how did I ever survive this world without one. I was so grounded now that I had sticks poking me in my ass. I was a new man. A born-again puppy person. I had a whole new appreciation for life. I felt blessed to have come so close to death. Thanks to Ozzy, I had a whole new list of priorities. If there was a fire in my apartment, save the dog. Let everything else burn. Everything else was just everything else. It was stuff. It didn't breathe. It didn't know how to love. They say every dog has his day, and today was the day of me and my dog. Every day was. And nobody was taking that away from us. I had a new leash on life. Ozzy had given new meaning to my life. And I never felt more alive. He taught me so many things that I'd never forget. How to laugh. He taught me self-respect. Responsibility. Commitment. Ozzy taught me if I did something wrong to get it off my chest. He taught me to confess. He taught me to talk about what was bothering me instead of keeping it all buried it like a bone inside. He taught me to say, screw foolish pride. He tore down my ego like a gorilla peels a banana. He taught me to free myself from self-destructive negative thinking. He abolished me from subconscious slavery. He educated the two sides of me about stopping the insanity. He preached to my double-edged-sword manic-depressive demons living and breathing deep inside of me to listen up, class is in session. I'd like to start off today's lesson with "Can't we all just get along?" He showed me how much fun I could have chasing pigeons. Not to be afraid of getting my new sneakers muddy. My puppy personally removed the word "worry" from my vocabulary.

Before Ozzy came along, my spirit had been on empty. Now he was my everyday energy attendant. He filled up my soul with unleaded love and prosperity. My once temperamental tank now overflowed with pride and joy. There wasn't a day that went by that I didn't spend with my boy. We were inseparable. Attached by co-dependency. He was an extension of me. He was my American Pet Express. Don't leave home without him 'cause when you're with Ozzy you never know who you might meet. I never felt such a sense of family and loyalty than when walking my puppy on dark, empty streets. Getting soaked and wet in the rain, stomping my feet in the puddles was exhilarating. Rejuvenating. The Fountain of Youth.

When I was alone with Ozzy, I was with the whole world at once. I felt things. I was complete. We were one. When I was with Ozzy, I was living in the moment—the present. And like Deepak Chopra said, "The present is a gift." Oh, what it was to laugh again. I never wanted my days to end. I was having the best time on The Great Lawn with my friends.

Everything was great. My friends were having fun. Ozzy was eating sticks and getting tons and tons of tickles and attention. I hadn't a care in the world until I started thinking about Paige. I started traveling down my manic-depressive memory lane.

39

TURN THE PAIGE

It would have been our one-year anniversary. It was about a year ago that we lay out in Central Park in the great green grass holding hands, kissing lips. Cherry ice pops and honey bees. When I fell in love, I had absolutely no idea what I was falling into. I was blind. Everything was so new and exciting. It was the first time I ever made love. It wasn't just sex. It was the first time I caressed a woman's neck. It was the first time I told a woman, "I love you." Until things changed. When I got hurt. And I never thought I could love somebody again. I never thought I could love myself. Well, I was wrong. It just took a special furry somebody to show me how.

From time to time I wondered what Paige was doing. How she was doing. As much as I didn't want to, I thought that I might run into her. It was a small city. I also thought that if she was going to run into me, I hoped she ran into me when Ozzy and I were talking to all of these people. Not to get her jealous. All right, a little jealous. To just let her see that I was doing all right. To see that I was done seeing faces and talking to knives. For the first time, I could look back at everything that had happened to me and honestly not be angry at Paige for leaving me. I mean, somebody was bound to break my heart in life sooner or later. Somebody had to be my first love, and I'm glad it was her. Paige was loving, caring, and would always have a place in my heart. And only now did I know that she left me because she had to protect herself. And I had to get better. This was a journey I had to take alone, well, not alone. Sorry, Oz. So Paige had to leave and I loved her for it. I loved her for letting me love her. "God, we had so many good times together, Ozzy. You would've liked her. And she sure loved dogs."

Reminiscing about her made me *really* miss her. But it wasn't just her that I was missing. I missed a female. I had to face the fact that Ozzy was a dog and couldn't fulfill all of my needs. The human kind. And I wasn't just talking about being horny. I never thought I'd say this in a million years, but I missed watching Paige read, having a nice candlelight dinner together, snuggling. Yeah, I wanted to love a woman again. And this time I wanted to do it right. I wanted to let myself go completely, but when the time was right. That summer I must have met thousands of women. There were sparks, sure, just not the continuous current of electricity that went through me like that first night I met Paige in that downtown divey bar. Her big brown eyes. She was radiant. She made me tingle. She was the first woman who let me touch her heart. And the first woman who touched mine. I started remembering all the good times. Vermont, the Bronx Zoo, and Pete's Clam Bar, camping and cooking sausages in Lake

George, toasting marshmallows under the stars. God, I missed her, the smell of her hair. Well, it was the end of August. The heat was really getting to me. I thought about that air conditioner that I carried up six flights of stairs for her. Somehow I managed to convince myself that it was all right to call her. That I was strong enough now. So I hung up Ozzy's leash, and picked up the phone. I made the call from the wild.

"Hello," she said.

One word was all I needed to hear, and I was transported back in time. I heard in that "hello" the sweet innocent voice that helped create and destroy me. I got all choked up. I felt sad. I felt like I was talking to somebody who had come back from the dead. I felt familiar stored-up emotions that I had forgot I even had come tumbling down from my overhead compartment. I forgot how much stronger love was than me.

"Hi, Paige. It's Bruce. Remember me?"

"No," she paused. "Of course I do, Brucie. Hi, how are you?"

"Great. Great, I quit my job and I got a puppy."

"You got a puppy, a liddle puppy, that's so great."

"Yeah, I'm not depressed anymore. Well, sometimes, I still take my pills, but my chemicals are pretty much under control. How about you, how are you doin'?"

"I'm good. I'm still working at the same ad agency."

"What are you working on?"

"Some feminine hygiene stuff. I'm not proud, but it pays the bills. Anyway enough about me, I'm so happy for you. You sound like the old belly-laughing Bruce. You really sound great. It's so good to hear from you."

The conversation was going well until I got hit on the head hard with a dose of reality. While I was getting my life together, while I was growing stronger, I never considered that Paige had also moved on. "Bruce, Bruce, Brucie, I can't believe you got a liddle Lab pup-peeeeee. Awwww, he sounds so cute. My friend

Bradley (*Bradley*, my stomach dropped) at my Hamptons house (*Hamptons house?*) has two Labs. A yellow one and a chocolate one. They're so much fun. They're always running around and swimming in the pool." The more she talked about him, his Labs, their fun, the more I imagined the woman I had once loved loving another. And who knew how many others. I felt weak. I couldn't believe that after all of these months I was right back where I started. Somebody shoot me. I wished I never made the call. But I called her for a reason. I had nothing to lose, just all the self-respect that Ozzy had worked so hard at helping me get back. So what the hell? I had no plans for the holiday weekend. So I blurted out, "Hey Paige, do you remember Lake George where we went camping last year? Well, this is gonna sound crazy but if you don't have any plans, I was wondering if you'd like to go up there again this Labor Day Weekend with me and you and Ozzy? You can meet Ozzy."

"Oh, Bruce, Oh Bruce, that's so nice."

"Yeah, yeah." I was getting all excited.

"Yeah, I'd love to meet Ozzy. He sounds so great, but . . ."

"But . . ."

"But I can't. I'm sorry. I just can't. One of the guys, Barry, at the beach house is giving me a one-on-one sailing lesson next weekend and I'm so psyched. Hey, maybe we can have lunch the week after that?"

"Oh, okay, yeah, all right. Great. Have a great weekend. Bye."

"Bye."

When I hung up the phone, I hung my head in shame. What the hell was I thinking? I shriveled up in the corner like a self-respectless raisin. I couldn't remember the last time I felt this miserable, but I sure remembered how it felt. Why did I do this to myself? Why couldn't I just accept that Paige was not a part of my life anymore? I should've never made that call. But I let my memory and my heart go soft. I was a loser. Now I had to pay for my stupidity. That night I felt really low. I didn't feel like talking to anybody. I walked Ozzy really fast and locked the door behind me. I just wanted to be left alone. But I wasn't alone. *I wasn't alone.* At around midnight I heard a voice: *"Bruce, Bruce, you thought we forgot about you . . ."* It was coming from the kitchen.

"Oh God. Not again."

40

"OZZY, SAVE MY LIFE . . . GOOD BOY"

My heart was pounding, pounding like it wanted to get out. "This isn't happening," I thought. "This isn't happening. This really isn't happening." Suddenly, I felt my body temperature heat up. Sweat was oozing down my skull like candle wax. This overwhelming evil presence surrounded me. The fearful follicles stood up on the back of my neck. Then my mind started racing down that all too familiar road to malevolence. I put my hands over my face, ten fingers spread like webs, trying to escape the madness.

Haunting images flooded my brain. The harsh return of my dark reality. I was strapped down, plugged in. My past was sent to get me. One minute I saw Paige dumping me in that coffee shop. I could feel her sweetness, ripping my heart out all over again. I saw that evil face with the sideburns tattooed on my brain. I saw myself tearing through the thorn bushes of Martha's Vineyard, running away from Ricky. I saw myself trapped in that evil advertising agency. Those bricks, the thick gray mortar. I felt like I couldn't breathe. The anxiety. *The anxiety.* I could feel the electric current, that bzzzz go through my veins. It was all happening again. Like it never left me. And now my demons were swirling around inside of me. They had awakened. I fell to my knees. My head leaned back. Palms up. My arms spread out like wings.

"I thought this was over!" I cried out "Why is this happening again! I'm taking my medication. Lithium doesn't do anything!" I tried to regain control for a moment. "Maybe I'm just stressed out? Maybe this is a bad dream? Or maybe it's just an anxiety attack?" It wasn't an anxiety attack.

I tried thinking of something else—anything—but I couldn't change the channel. I couldn't shut me off. Something much larger than me had stolen the remote control to my soul. "Get out of my head!" I pleaded. "Get out of my head!" But I felt there was no escape. I feared I couldn't win. I started trembling. I knew this was just the beginning. I had been here before. Possessed. I knew what happened next. It was all happening as planned. I was a marked man. The number of the Beast, 666, was in the middle of my social security number. And now the dark side had come to get me. That ladybug had saved me in Central Park. But not this time. Lucifer, the venomous vulture, waited patiently, till I was weak—easy prey—ripe for transformation—to join him—to become him—Brucifer.

"Get outta here! Get out of me!" I begged for mercy but I couldn't stop rubbing my fingers feverishly through my goatee. And then on the mirror of my mind I saw a demonic face. *His* face. Then I saw my face. Then I saw our face. A masochistic metamorphosis was taking place. The demons were inside of me. Taking possession of me. I felt like a little boy and this red monster had devoured me.

"Oh Bruce, oh Brucie, it's time to kill yourself. To kill yourself." Their voices were calling from the kitchen sink. *"Kill yourself. Kill yourself."* The "real" prince of darkness was coming through my cutlery.

I was frozen. Too scared to run. Nowhere to hide. I felt the wickedness all around me. Inside of me. I sat there trembling for an eternity in the palm of an evil presence. I felt so minuscule, trapped in this demented dimension. I was sprawling in hell. Crawling. I had a death sentence. I thought of the headline in tomorrow's newspaper: DEAD ADMAN SLASHED AND GASHED ON LEXINGTON AVENUE.

"Come here Brucie, come here," the sink called me near. *"Closer, closer, just kill yourself already. Kill yourself. We're waiting. We're waiting. Now don't make us angry. Do it. C'mon, do it."*

My heart pounded like a war drum. Like a madman banging on your door at three in the morning."Leave me alone. Just leave me alone. You're not real. The doctors say you're not real. I can't touch you. I can't even touch you." But I could *feel* it. It was everywhere. I thought of people to call to help me but nobody could.

"Maybe Ricky?" He always knew the right thing to say. Even though it was really late, I called him. I spoke to his answering machine.

"Hi, Ricky Rick, are you there? Are you there? Pick up, c'mon man, pick up. I'm freaking the fuck out man, I'm really fucked up. . . ."

"Hello, hel-lo," Ricky answered. "Bruce, just slow down."

"I can't. I can't. I mean I'm really fucked up man. You know all that devil stuff, the evil face I used to see and the knives, the talking ones in the sink, well it's happening, it's happening right now and I'm not crazy either, it's really happening, I gotta talk low or they'll hear me."

"Who'll hear you?"

"The knives in the sink. The Farberware from Bed Bath & Beyond. The black and silver set, there's six. *SIX. SIX. SIX.* You get it. That's not a coincidence. You gotta help me, man, please. Help me."

"Bruce, go back to sleep."

"What? What? Rick don't you hear me? They'll get me in my sleep. He's the fucking devil. The ring leader. He orchestrates the whole thing. The knives are an extension of him. There's nowhere to run. I'm doomed. I'm *so* doomed."

"Well, what do you want me to do? Take more medicine."

"This isn't about medicine. That's what *they* want you to think."

"Bruce, I'm sorry. I don't know what to tell you. Go to the emergency room. Call your shrink."

"She can't help me. Nobody can. The voices and the face are real."

"Bruce, again with that face. I thought we got past that."

"Yeah, well so did I. So did I!"

I put my hands over my skull and squeezed my sweaty brain.

"Oh God, I'm going crazy again."

"Bruce, stop it. Now stop it. You're going to be okay. I want you to hang up and call Dr C."

"Why? Why? Why? She can't help me. She can't help me. Nobody can. Nobody can. This is evil we're talking about. Pure evil. Maybe if you just stay on the phone with me he'll go away?"

"Well, okay. So Bruce, you know Allen is in the hospital, right?"

"What do you mean?"

"He got hurt really bad last night. He got jumped, Alphabet City. Got hit with a bat. He's pretty messed up. Where were you?"

"Whoa, whoa, what do you mean? I didn't put him there, do you think I put him there, 'cause I didn't. I was here all night. Yes I was. Ask Ozzy. I didn't fucking do it."

"Bruce, calm down. I know you didn't do it. Why would you think I would think you did it? Relax, don't get all crazy."

"What do you mean? Crazy. Don't you call me crazy."

"Bruce, I didn't call you crazy."

"Stop it. I'm not crazy. Why do you think I'm crazy?"

"Bruce, I didn't say you were crazy, but what kind of medicine are you taking anyway?"

"What do you mean what kind of medicine am I taking? Who is this? Who are you?"

"It's Rick, your friend."

"No. No you're not. You're one of *them*. One of the psychiatrists. You're the guy with the beard and you think I'm crazy. We'll I'm not crazy. I am not crazy! I'm not cuckoo for Cocoa Puffs. You're not taking me to any gymnasium insane asylum." I threw another phone across the room. "I'm not crazy! I'm not crazy!" I fell to the floor. I lay flat on my back, my arms and legs extended out like I was making snow angels, shaking.

"Now Bruce, where were we?" the satanic stainless steel hissed at me.

"No, no, no. I'm not listening. You're not real. You're not real. You're not real. You are not real."

"Yes Bruce, we are very real."

Trembling. I wanted to call my mother so badly, but she wouldn't understand. This psychotic stuff was out of her mental jurisdiction. My shrinks, forget about it, they would've surely had me committed. Nobody would understand that this was really happening. Again. Again and again. Is this ever going to end? Nobody would understand that there really was evil in this world, that the devil does creep into people's souls. That people are possessed. That *The Exorcist* wasn't just a movie. That people do appear dead in their apartment for no reason at all.

"Oh, Bruce was doing so well, we were so proud of him," they'd say over their morning coffee. "But he must've been really sad underneath it all."

"Yeah right," I'd shout from the afterlife. "Hello! Hello! The devil made me do it. The devil made me slash my throat with a knife. I didn't. . . . God, God, when is this going to stop? God, please release me. Send me back to my dog. Good is stronger than evil. Good is stronger than evil. . . ."

I sat on the ground by the couch until I felt my intestines about to rupture. They were on fire. I had to go to the bathroom so badly. Crohn's disease was a demon in itself. But there was no way I was going near that kitchen, no way. "Somebody will eventually save me. Yeah, right." My stomach was rumbling. Nobody was saving me. I had to make a decision. Have a serious accident or make a run for it.

"Oh God help me."

Suddenly my mind went into hyperspeed. It was racing all over the place. I started thinking about every horror movie I had ever seen. "When people are up against demons, how did they escape?"

Then it hit me, that they all had one thing in common. "Love. Love conquers evil. Love conquers all."

And there was my furry ticket curled up in a ball. I didn't even realize it. What's he doing sleeping through this? I needed his unconditional love more than ever. I needed him to hold my hand so I could go to the bathroom. But something was wrong. Something was really, really wrong.

"Ozzy come here, come here boy," I whispered. And he just wouldn't come. He wouldn't move a muscle. So I crawled to him. I curled up beside him, I put my head on his heart. He was breathing but he wouldn't wake up. "C'mon Ozzy, get up, get up." It was no use. The dark side had gotten to him first.

"What did you do to him?" I stood up. I yelled through my ceiling. "Damn you! Damn you!" They had captured his soul. He had my puppy in his clutches, the dark depths of hell. I wrapped my arms around Ozzy, and I prayed. But it wasn't working. It was like he was dead. He was in puppy purgatory. "C'mon, boy, get up, *up, up, up.*" Nothing. He was sinking, deeper and deeper.

My stomach was growling louder and louder. I couldn't hold it in much longer. "What the hell am I going to do? What am I going to do?" My eyes scanned the room.

Just then, I spotted a box of Kellogg's Corn Pops on the table a few feet from where I was sitting. I had an idea. God, how I prayed this worked. I knew I was definitely a little crazy doing this but there was no other way.

I emptied out a bunch of Corn Pops on the floor next to Ozzy's nose. I made a little pile, and then like magic, his nostrils started twitching like he was waking up from satanic smelling salts, from his devil-dog-induced coma.

"Yes, yes, it's working." His eyes opened. Ozzy stretched. He— was—alive.

"Come, Ozzy. Come, come," I whispered on my hands and knees, spider-walking backward, leaving a trail of Corn Pops to the other end of my apartment, and it was working. Ozzy was sleepwalking toward me. Eating every single beautiful sunny-day yellow Corn Pop in his way. "Good boy, Ozzy. Good boy."

"Nice try Bruce, nice try, but now you're going to kill yourself. Kill yourself," the knives said with a sharpness in their voice as we neared the kitchen. They glistened from the distance, but I wasn't listening. And Ozzy wasn't listening. I just kept dropping those Corn Pops and looking at Ozzy's face. That crunchy, drooling, adorable face.

I made it to the bathroom. But the evil presence was still there, swirling and swirling. "Stop it. Get outta my head! What do you want from me?" I cried.

Wicked walls closed in. Why the fuck did I buy a black shower curtain? I dropped to the floor and sat on the cold tiles. I put Ozzy in my lap, and I just hugged him and hugged him, kissing his head. "Love, love, love, love, love," I said. "Ozzy make it go away. Make it go away." I held onto him so tight, like he was a life preserver trying to save my soul from drowning in such a tormented reality.

And that's when it happened. As mysteriously as my demons appeared, everything grew quiet enough to hear—my baby's gentle heartbeat. He was vibrating. A soft buzz. I could feel his good energy. His pure, untarnished soul. He was my force field against evil.

The tighter I squeezed him, Ozzy embraced me. My little puppy had drowned out all negativity. And I felt safe again. He was so warm and so soft and so furry that I had nothing else on my mind. I got so lost in his love. His warm Labradorious breath. His puppy dog scent. And his paws—black velvet. He was perfect. He was the most beautiful thing on this planet. And he was glowing.

There was a soft yellow light, this wonderful aura radiating around him. Around his whole body. It was like a halo.

"This isn't happening. This isn't happening."

But it was happening. And when I looked into his baby blues, I saw the whole universe. I saw the stars. I saw all that was good in the world. I saw a reflection of myself—that was myself. I wasn't possessed. Maybe I never really was?

Maybe this was my illness? My manic depression? Just the psychotic symptom revisited. Maybe Dr. C was right when she told me that I had created my devil out of fear. And maybe this was just a relapse, a manic episode triggered by stress. Well there was one thing I did know. I never wanted this to happen again.

Not with Ozzy in my life. I had to take care of him. I couldn't end up dead or in a mental hospital.

Lying there on the bathroom tiles, I told Ozzy, the first thing I was going to do the following morning was call Dr. Williams and Dr. C to tell them what happened to us. I think we definitely had to adjust my lithium and try some other options. Maybe that Depakote I had read about?

Twenty minutes or so had passed. I listened quietly to see if the voices were still there. But all that I heard was the tiny pitter patter of a puppy's tongue licking my beard. We sat there till Ozzy felt it was safe. Then he took me by my mind, back to the real world—outside. Even if I did take more medication, I knew this might not be my last encounter with talking knives, with my dark side. As long as I had Ozzy in my life there was nothing to worry about. Because that night, when I was praying to God, begging him to show up, he had been there all along.

Nibbling on my toes.

41

OZZY, STAY

Paige or no Paige, I wasn't about to let the past ruin my Labor Day weekend. So I packed up Ozzy and Ricky, and we drove up to Lake George. It was a great weekend. We rented a cottage. I took Ozzy swimming for the first time. What a blast. My Lab was a natural retriever. I just couldn't accept that summer was just about over. That it was time to get serious about my life again. I wanted to make every last day count.

So while all the kids were getting ready to go back to school, putting away their white pants, I went to play in the park with my black Lab. There were still so many more people to meet before they went into hibernation. I was going to do everything in my power to stall my so-called advertising career. I didn't want to go back. But things were different now. I wasn't just supporting me anymore. I had to put dog food on the table. I was a single parent. As far as I knew, there was no such thing as puppy welfare. I didn't know what I was going to do. In the meantime I took Ozzy with me to get a haircut from my barber Don Fifi at Astor Place. I was always in the greatest moods when I got a haircut. And now so was Ozzy. While I got buzzed, Ozzy chilled out on the hairy floor, and everybody fed him ice cubes.

The first thing I did when I got outside after I picked up after Ozzy was check my voice mail: You have one new message.

"Hi. Bruce, it's Paige . . ." I froze listening to it in the middle of the street. " . . . Well, I was just calling to see if you wanted to get together and have that lunch we had talked about before Labor Day. Call me." She left me her number in case I forgot.

Call her. She had said she was going to call me the week after Labor Day. That was three weeks ago. I waited for that call. I sat and stared at the phone on my couch more than I wanted to admit. "No way, I'm not going back. I've come too far." I knew seeing her would be a big mistake. "That's it. I'm not calling her. Maybe I'll call her. Bruce, don't do it. You'll regret it. All right, that's it. I'm not calling her."

I called Ozzy instead. I said, "Ozzy, let's go," and we walked all the way home. But my mind wouldn't stop playing. "Should I call Paige or shouldn't I call Paige? Should I call Paige or shouldn't I call Paige? Should I call Paige or shouldn't I call Paige?" As much as I didn't want to call Paige, I felt bad for her. I heard the loneliness in her voice. The same loneliness that I heard in my voice when I had called her a few weeks earlier.

No matter how hard I tried to ignore her voice in my head, Paige's message was playing back to me over and over and over again. *What do I do? What do I do? No. I'm not going back there. She's not going to meet Ozzy. I'll become weak again. Don't do it, Bruce. Don't do it.* But I kept doing it. All night long, I kept thinking about Paige. She was haunting me. But I had made up my mind. I wasn't going back there. To her world. I wasn't going to lose myself again. Just thinking about it was driving me mad. I needed to go on with my life, but it wasn't fair to Paige to just leave her hanging. I wanted to give her closure. I needed closure. I wanted to tell her that it was still too soon to be friends. But I didn't want to talk to her. Talking to her would've been like touching my emotional third rail. Still I knew I had to communicate with her somehow. So that night at about three o'clock in the morning I climbed out of my bed, and with Ozzy Osbourne's "Good-bye to Romance" playing softly in the background and Ozzy passed out in my arms, against my chest, I called Paige's answering machine at work, knowing she wouldn't be there, and I left my message. My words felt very spiritual leaving my body like I was speaking to a ghost or something. I felt like she was listening to me. I felt her presence surrounding me. I spoke slowly.

"Hi Paige, it's Bruce. How are you? I got your message and I hope you're doing well. I don't think it's fair for either of us to see each other. Paige, I miss you a lot, but my life is going really well now. I love Ozzy to death and I'm going to be going back to work soon. I'm actually thinking about writing a book about my whole experience. So Paige, take care of yourself, and I'll call you when the time is right. I'll call *you* when the time is right. Good-bye."

And I never did.

I never did.

When I hung up the phone I felt like a part of me had died. I knew that I couldn't take back what I said. I had just cut off communication with the woman I once couldn't live without. I had cut her out of my life for good. I couldn't believe that all that was left of me and Paige was a twelve-second recording. I'd never forget Paige for as long as I lived. She was my first love. As

Photo: Joe Fornabaio

I sat there crying my eyes out, Ozzy got real close to me and started licking my tears. "I'll be okay, puppy," I told him. "I'll be okay." And by the way my boy looked at me, I knew I would be okay. Because no matter how many women passed in and out of my life, Ozzy would always stay. "You're a good boy, oh you're such a good boy. C'mon Oz, let's go out."

As I was wiping away the last few tears on Lexington Avenue, a curly-haired brunette woman in a red shirt came running up to us. It was Fran Drescher's voice double. Here we go again. "Oh my God, Look at the puppay. Is that Ozzay? Is that the little puppay from the beginning of the summa? He got so big. I can't believe it, oh he grew so much."

I looked down at Ozzy. And Ozzy looked up to me. *If she only knew how much the owner grew.*

I had no idea where I was going from here. But I had no fear. I had faith that my seeing-eye dog, my mood-swing messiah, would continue to show me the way. Thanks to Ozzy, I was really looking forward to my future—the place I thought I'd never get to see.

"Ozzy, save my life. Good boy!"

I thank God this book was written by Bruce Goldstein.

Not in memory of.

EPILOGUE:
BIPOLAREALITY
11 YEARS LATER

WRITER WITH BIG BLACK DOG. That was my profile on Yahoo Per-
sonals. It had a picture of me in the East Village, crouched down
next to my eight-year-old, 110-pound Labrador retriever. After
all Ozzy and I had been through, I made it very clear that you
didn't just go out with me. We were a package deal.

I started dating Brooke three years ago. But then, to cut to
the chase, so there'd be no surprises, no mentally insane
skeletons in my closet, I gave her an early copy of the manuscript to read at her beach house in Fire Island. "Brooke, if
you're still interested, if I'm not too crazy for you, call me
Monday."

Dating Brooke was a hard adjustment for Ozzy. For years, it had been the Bruce and Ozzy show, so when I first brought her around, Ozzy was very territorial. He would always bark at her. He would nudge his way in between us when we were making out on the couch. It took a while for him to trust her, for her to prove to him that she wasn't going anywhere, because my boy wasn't going to watch me get hurt anymore.

Then one night when I was taking a shower and Brooke was lying in bed reading a book, Ozzy decided to show her who was really the boss. He moved in and rested his black, furry anvil of a head on the edge of the bed. He growled at her. Then he put one of his bear paws on the mattress. She got nervous. Then he jumped up on the bed and started barking like a mad dog in Brooke's face to get the hell out of his side of the bed. Brooke later told me she was frightened at first, but then she took control of the situation.

"Ozzy, no! Get down! Now!" She barked back.

And that was it. He backed off. She had earned the title Mrs. Alpha Dog. Today they are the best of friends. Brooke calls Ozzy her furry little stepson. She gives him treats when he's good. And bad. Lucky dog. We're a happy family.

As far as my mental health is concerned, overall I feel great. My life is going perfect. Brooke. My writing career is taking off. Good times ahead. We see children in the near future. I try and enjoy life as much as I can. Because about two years ago (before we were married) I did have a relapse. The kind that the big red, mental textbooks warn manic depressives and their loved ones about.

Although there were no hallucinations, no knives in the sink, it was pretty bad. And there's no one way to say what caused it. Maybe it was stress. Maybe I needed an adjustment in my meds. But whatever it was, the mania monster had reared its head. I couldn't sit still. I didn't sleep for three months. Nonstop anxiety. Once again, everything had become overwhelming, even walking Ozzy. Thank God Brooke was there to take care of him and me.

So I started seeing this "well-respected" psychiatrist, who immediately wanted to commit me to a mental hospital. As terrified as I was, I wouldn't go, so the Upper East Sider (Mrs. Ratchet) in her white coat drugged me so much that I couldn't even keep my eyes open. I actually fell asleep at a restaurant on Brooke's birthday. I can still see her worried eyes across the table, wondering what happened to the easygoing, funny guy I had used to be.

Aside for me feeling horrible for me, I felt so bad, so guilty for what I was doing to Brooke. I loved her so much. I wished I never dragged her into this. But despite her tears and the fact that her friends had been advising her to consider moving on, Brooke hung on. Only God knows how she was so strong. Every morning when I was too depressed to get out of bed, too scared, she would give me a great big hug, a big squeeze, before I went to work. "Stop the stinking thinking," she'd say. "Work is easy. You've been doing it for years."

Brooke meant well, but I wasn't getting any better. I had a bad panic attack at work and ran out of the building during a meeting.

Then one day in Madison Square Park, as if things couldn't get worse, Brooke told me she didn't know how much more she could take. It was hurting her too much to see me like this. I was draining her. She had nothing left to give. One night she left me alone. She went out with her friends to clear her head.

"Make sure you walk Ozzy," she said.

"But, but, I can't . . ."

"Bruce, you have to. He's your dog."

I panicked. I dreaded going out and walking him. Dealing with the public, the whole damn thing. All over again. And as I was lying on the floor, tears pouring down my face, Ozzy was just watching me.

"What? I'm sorry, boy, but I can't."

But it didn't matter what I said to him, he wouldn't turn away. He didn't flinch.

He just looked me in my eyes. And he spoke to me in the most gentle way.

"It's gonna be okay, Bruce. We've been through this before. And now we have Brooke. Don't worry, she's not going anywhere. She loves you. She really loves you. Trust me, I know. We're all in this together. Now, we're gonna take one step at a time. You're going to get a new doctor, she's going to adjust your medication till we get it right again, and we're going to start spending more time together. It's not easy. I know it's not. But we'll do it. We've been through this before. Now, get up slowly, when you're ready put my leash on, and let's go out for a walk."

The little guy was right. *We had been through this before.* Ozzy and I have been through everything together, and everyday since then he continues to help me while I help him.

Since then I've been feeling good for over two years. But if my monster does creep up on me again, and it might, I am blessed to have Brooke and Ozzy in my corner.

But what gets me scared these days is when Ozzy and I go for a walk, and he walks really slow. People still look at Ozzy and smile. But they often ask me, "How old is he?" And I gulp. It kills me every time, because unlike me, everybody who has ever loved a dog knows, they don't live forever. And to be honest with you, it's hard to write this without the tears that are trickling down my face. I just can't think of life without him. But there's one thing I do know. When it's Ozzy's turn to move on, he'll always be with me in my heart.

For now, so what if he's slowed down? He's seventy-seven years old, for God's sake. And you know what? He still has his great days. He still loves to swim. And if he falls in spontaneous love and he spots a dog he wants to hump—man, I can't hold the little horn dog back. Ironically, sometimes when people ask how old he is and I say eleven, they don't believe me. They say, "Ahhh, look at him. He's just a puppy."

And I smile. And I think, "Yeah, he's just a puppy."

Till this day, one of my favorite things to do is when I stay up real late to write, I take Ozzy out for a walk at three in the morning when the world is asleep. It's our time. Just me and my boy. Sometimes I let him off the leash to give him some freedom, but he always turns around to make sure I'm just a few feet behind him. The best part of it all, I mean the greatest feeling in the world, is when I look down at Ozzy, and he looks up at me with those beautiful puppy eyes, and he's smiling. *He's smiling.*